Global Trade Liberalization

WORK – TECHNOLOGY – ORGANIZATION – SOCIETY

Edited by Wiking Ehlert, György Széll and Heinz Sünker

ARBEIT – TECHNIK – ORGANISATION – SOZIALES

Herausgegeben von Wiking Ehlert, György Széll und Heinz Sünker

Band 26

PETER LANG

Frankfurt am Main · Berlin · Bern · Bruxelles · New York · Oxford · Wien

Serajul Hoque

Global Trade Liberalization

Impact on the Readymade Garments Industry in Bangladesh

PETER LANG
Europäischer Verlag der Wissenschaften

Bibliographic Information published by Die Deutsche Bibliothek
Die Deutsche Bibliothek lists this publication in the Deutsche Nationalbibliografie; detailed bibliographic data is available in the internet at <http://dnb.ddb.de>.

Zugl.: Osnabrück, Univ., Diss., 2003

"Gratefully acknowledging the support of
DAAD – Deutscher Akademischer Austauschdienst and
V.A.U.S.T. e.V. – Verein Arbeit – Umwelt – Soziales – Technik"

D 700
ISSN 0946-8811
ISBN 3-631-52278-9
US-ISBN 0-8204-6579-8

www.peterlang.de

Dedicated to
My Parents
Alhaj Master Nurul Kabir
and
Rasheda Khanam

Acknowledgements

I begin this note of acknowledgements by expressing my profound sense of gratitude and thanks to my supervisor Prof. Dr. György Széll, for his valuable guidance and encouragement at every stage, which has enabled me to complete this work. I am extremely grateful to him for spending a lot of precious time out of his busy schedule, for continuous advices and for illuminating points which were greatest help to me while preparing this thesis. Without his kind supervision this dissertation would not have taken its present shape. I am equally grateful to Prof. Dr. Wiking Ehlert for his valuable comments on my work.

I am thankful to the German Academic Exchange Service (DAAD) for their financing and supporting my study in Germany, and especially grateful to my DAAD contact perosn Mr. Benedikt Romberg for his all types of support and cooperation.

I express my gratitude and regards to Prof. Dr. Albrecht Weber and Prof. Dr. Lothar Knüppel, for their spontaneous encouragement and adivce in need during the course of my work. I also like to thank Prof. Dr. Peter Lange and Dr. Johannes Jaenicke for their valuable comments and suggestions.

I am particularly grateful and indebted to my former supervisor Prof. Syed Abul Kalam Azad, Treasurer of National University, Dhaka, Bangladesh, for his every help and assistance to me in completion of this work in Germany.

I pay my humble thanks and regards to some of my colleagues of the Department of Marketing, University of Dhaka, particularly, Prof. M.A. Quddus, Prof. Dr. Syed Rashidul Hasan, Prof. Dr. A.K. Fazlul Haque Shah, Prof. Abu Syed Talukder, Prof. Dr. Haripada Bhattacharjee and Prof. Dr. Zakir Hossain Bhuiyan for their moral support and kind cooperation.

I am thankful to the staff of Export Promotion Bureau (EPB), Bangladesh Garments Manufacturers and Exporters Association (BGMEA), Centre for Policy Dialogue (CPD), Bangladesh Institute of Development Studies (BIDS) for providing me various necessary information and data relating to my work.

I owe a debt of gratitude of the various authors whose works have enlightened me and enriched my thesis writing. Also my deepest gratitude to workers and management authority who patiently replied all sorts of questions related to my field research.

I wish to express my heartfelt gratitude and thanks to my wife and daughter Mrs. Atia Parveen Koly and Maliha Bushra Hoque, without their constant support and love, my study and research could never been completed. Special thanks to my younger brother Mohammad Hamidul Hoque and brother-in-law Gaziul Hassan Mahmood Opu, for their assistance for various materials from Bangladesh, relating to my study. I also thanks to Ms. Kathrin Woltering for her computer support in preparing final draft of the dissertation.

I also wish to express my thanks and regards to uncle Prof. Abdul Halim for his valuable suggestions regarding final manuscript preparation for publication of this thesis from Germany. Thanks also to Mr. Shahjahan Babu for computer support in this aspect.

Finally, my profound regards I owe a great debt of gratitude my parents, other family members and to my in laws family, whose moral support and affection stimulated me to complete this study.

September, 2003 Serajul Hoque
Germany

CONTENT

LIST OF TABLES

LIST OF FIGURES

ACRONYMS

ASEAN	Association of South East Asian Nations
ATC	Agreement on Textiles and Clothing
BBS	Bangladesh Bureau of Statistics
BGMEA	Bangladesh Garments Manufacturers and Exporters Association
BIDS	Bangladesh Institute of Development Studies
BIGWUF	Bangladesh Independent Garments Workers Union Federation
BMRE	Balancing, Mordernisation, Replacement and Expansion
BRAC	Bangladesh Rural Advancement Committee
BTMA	Bangladesh Textile Mills Association
CAD	Computer Aided Design
CBI	Caribbean Basin Initiatives
CCG	Country Commercial Guide
C & F	Cost and Freight
CIP	Commercial Important Person
CM	Cut and Make
CPD	Centre for Policy Dialogue
DCCI	Dhaka Chamber of Commerce and Industry
DEDO	Duty Exemption Drawback Organization
DOT	Department of Textiles
EPB	Export Promotion Bureau
EPZ	Export Processing Zone
EU	European Union
FDI	Foreign Direct Investment
FTAA	Free Trade Area for the Americas
FY	Financial Year
GATT	General Agreement on Tariffs and Trade
GDP	Gross Domestic Product
GOB	Government of Bangladesh
GSP	Generalised System of Preferences
GTAP	Global Trade Analysis Project
HPCT	High Tech Park for China's Textile Industry
HS	Harmonised System
IFC	International Finance Corporation
ILO	International Labour Organisation
ISI	Import Similarity Index
ISO	International Standard Organisation
ITC	International Trade Centre
L/C	Letter of Credit
LDC	Least Developed Countries
LTA	Long Term Arrangements
MFA	Multi Fibre Arrangement

MFN	Most Favoured Nations
MOU	Memorandum of Understanding
MVA	Manufacturing Value Added
NAFTA	North American Free Trade Agreement
NGO	Non-Government Organisation
NIEs	Newly Industrialised Economics
NIFT	National Institute of Fashion Technology
NIPP	New Industrial Incentive Package
NTR	Normal Trade Relation
OECD	Organisation of Economic Cooperation and Development
OEEC	Organisation for European Economic Cooperation
OPT	Onward Processing Trade
RMG	Readymade Garment
SAARC	South Asian Association for Regional Cooperation
SITC	Standard International Trade Classification
SOEs	State Owned Enterprises
SSA	Sub-Saharan Africa
STA	Short Term Arrangement
TMB	Textile Monitoring Body
TPLs	Tariffs Preferencial Levels
TSB	Textile Survillence Body
UK	United Kingdom
UNCTAD	United Nations Conference on Trade and Development
UNDP	United Nations Development Programme
UNICEF	United Nations International Childrens Emergency Fund
UR	Uruguay Round
US	United States
USITC	United States Internaltional Trade Commission
USTDA	United States Trade and Development Act
UTPS	Unity Through Population Service
VAT	Value Added Tax
VERs	Voluntary Export Restraints
WTO	World Trade Organization

CHAPTER ONE
INTRODUCTION

1.1 The Background of the Study

Bangladesh the country of world famous Moslin fabric and the Great Royal Bengal Tiger has now emerged an apparel giant in the world textile and apparel market. The country exports its garments products worth about $5.50 billion per year to the EU, USA, Canada and most of the Scandinavian and middle eastern countries. At present the country is the 6th largest garments supplier to the USA and EU countries.

The history of garments industry in the area now comprising Bangladesh dates back to seventeenth century and probably much earlier. In seventeenth century this industry attained a high degree of efficiency and world reputation. It produced many specialised products (e.g.Moslin) which were exported to Persian and European countries. (Islam, 1996). Since late sixteenth or early seventeenth century, the spinning and weaving activities of cotton had been continuing in Great Britain. As the domestic manufacturers of Great Britain could not produce, at that time, "the soft moslins" and beautiful "printed calicoes", England had been importing these fine clothes from India since 1631 that were popular with the"fine ladies" including even the Queen herself (Hammond,1897). Before 1947, today's India, Pakistan and Bangladesh were integrated in the one colony called Indian sub-continent ruled by the British. The chronological development of textiles and clothing industries naturally originates from Indian history. Historically, cotton industries, made most of the textiles in the sub-continent. Moslin, Jamdani, and various cotton and silk fabrics were produced. After the industrial revolution in Britain in the eighteenth century, the fabric manufactured and dyed in British factories satured the Indian markets. But, after 1947, most of the capital and resources of Pakistan came under the hegemony of West Pakistan. After the independence of Bangladesh in 1971, the government of Bangladesh nationalised the textile industry and Bangladesh Textile Mills Corporation (BTMC) was formed to cater the textile industries. Bureaucratic obstacles combined with other problems such as low productivity in the labour force, lack of planning, indiscipline, lack of accountability and poor machine maintenance and operation resulted in a lack of profits (Hasan, 2000). The government, therefore, incrementally denationalised the production of textiles. But this industry suffered a setback with the appearance of cotton textile mills (henceforth to be called textile/garments industry/apparel) with the advent of the Industrial Revolution in England.

By 1978, it was like an infant industry with a very few export potential, but the pace of Readymade Garments (RMG) industry gathered in between a very short period of time was simply incredible[1] (Hasan, 2000). Bangladesh garments sector has been able to sustain a momentum of robust growth for over a decade and half (1985-2000). Real growth rate of exports of the readymade garments, at 12%, was about three times higher than that of GDP over the matched period (Bhattacharya & Rahman, 2000). By any reckoning, this should be recognized as quite a remarkable record.

There can be no question that Bangladesh has truly put in a stellar performance in tapping its comparative advantages and exporting labour-intensive clothing products over the last twenty years. Presently, the industry occupies the enviable position of being the largest manufacturing and export business in the country, employing about 1.8 million workers, 90 percent of whom who have migrated from the rural Bangladesh in search of better economic future.[2] Among the top two dozen major exporters of clothing products in 1998 none has grown faster than Bangladesh since 1980. And even since 1990 no major Asian exporter of garment products has exhibited higher growth rates than Bangladesh (Spinanger, 2000).

About 1.8 million workers are presently employed in over the 3500 RMG factories, which are now free of child labour [3]attendent positive externalities in the form of increased economic activities in such as banking, insurance, transportation, real estate, hotels and tourism, packing and recycling, consumer goods and utility services. A rough estimate shows the sector, through linkage effects, currently generates about $2.5 billion worth of domestic economic activities. For example, 80% of garments accessories, accounting for about $0.7 billion, are now locally produced (Bhattacharya & Rahman, 1999).

A commodity wise export earnings of Bangladesh for the financial year 1998-99 shows that export of clothing (readymade garments and knitwear) accounts for 75.67% of the total export earnings of the country making the sector the most important for the economy of Bangladesh. Again, readymade garments industry in Bangladesh, being labour intensive, has its competitive advantage over other manufacturing sectors in the country which exploits the cheap labour, mostly women. Inspite of this advantage, the clothing products of Bangladesh, at present, have restricted and reserved access (quota) to the readymade garment markets of the developed countries, particularly, the United States and the European Union. From 01 January 2005, as per the provisions of the WTO Agree-

1 "Bangladesh Apparel and Textile Exposition" BATEXPO, 2002, available at www.nation-online.com/200210/21/n2102103htm. downloaded on October 22, 2002.

2 "The History of Bangladesh Garments Industry" available at www.bangladesh-review.co.uk/garments.htm

3 "A Partnership Approach to Improving Labour Relations and Working Condition in Bangladesh Garments Industry" Signing Ceremony of an Expanded Project between BGMEA and ILO, The New Nation, Business and Finance Page, Volume 2, Number 706, Available at www.nation-online.com/200210/02/n2100203.htm downloaded on October 3, 2002.

ment on Textiles and Clothing, garments and textile manufacturers of Bangladesh will have to cope with steep competition from such countries as India, Pakistan, China and Thailand from which Bangladesh now imports raw materials to satisfy the demands of its textile and clothing sector. All these countries will be able to inflate their RMG exports, now limited by quotas, when the WTO establishes its free market in 2005. As a result, Bangladesh's RMG sector will have to face tough competition from the countries like China, India, Vietnam, Cambodia, Mexico, CBI and Sub-Saharan countries. The process has already been started. Some factories are getting closed every month and the workers are becoming jobless.[4] Factories are generally closed with out issuing any prior notice to workers. Even no step is taken to pay the dues of workers before closing down a factory. About 1.3 million garments workers out of 1.8 million may lose their jobs following implementation of the new laws and regulations of the WTO in 2005.[5] It contributes substantially to our foreign exchange earning and also create huge employment, particularly for the economically backward women. It also help women's empowerment and energies other sectors of the economy.[6] The growth of industry resulted from globalisation and trade liberalisation, the role catalyst as well as the conducive government policies. This study, therefore, attempts to analyse the RMG sector of Bangladesh in the viewpoint of social and economic aspects vis-a-vis the possible impact in the context of trade liberalization.

1.2 Evolution of Readymade Garments Industry in Bangladesh

During the 1970s, the main export products of the country were raw jute and jute goods, tea and shrimps etc. But during the 1980s, increasing use of synthetic products and container transport reduced the international market for jute resulting in a decline of this sector of the economy. However, this decline in jute export was offset by a relocation of RMG in Bangladesh due to rising wage costs in the "tiger" economics and the very low wages in Bangladesh. The RMG industry that flourished in Bangladesh operates principally on the basis of "CM" (cut and make) orders from the overseas buyers. CM is a labour-intensive activity that is well placed to exploit an unlimited reservoir of cheap labour in the country.

Reaz Garments was one of the first firms to engage in export in 1977. A few other firms were struggling to export at the same time. In 1978, a retired

4 "Garment Industry and future of Bangladesh" (In Bengali version), available at www.prothom-alo.net/2002-09-15/15cat4.html

5 "Impact of international trade regime on female garment workers in Bangladesh" by Mashuda Khatun Shefali, available at www.nation-online.com/200211/14/n2111409.htm

6 "MFA Phase-out after 2004: Critical Challenges Await for the Economy's Thrust Sector" – available at www.independent-bangladesh.com/news/may15/15052003 pd.htm, downloaded on May, 15, 2003.

civil servant in collaboration with a South Korean company Daewoo set up a garment factory named Desh.

Table 1.1
Number of Garment Industry Over Time

Year	Number of Industry	Growth Rate of Number of Industry
1977-78	9	-
1978-79	22	144.00
1979-80	47	114.00
1980-81	69	47.00
1981-82	83	20.00
1982-83	90	8.00
1983-84	308	242.00
1984-85	632	105.00
1985-86	744	18.00
1986-87	749	0.70
1987-88	751	0.26
1988-89	754	0.40
1989-90	804	7.00
1990-91	935	16.00
1991-92	1300	39.00
1992-93	1695	30.00
1993-94	1839	8.00
1994-95	2190	19.00
1995-96	2353	7.00
1996-97	2503	6.00
1997-98	2726	9.00
1998-99	2963	9.00
1999-00	3200	8.00
2000-01	3500	14.00

Source: Research, Development, Trade and Information Cell, Bangladesh Garments Manufacturers and Exporters Association (BGMEA)

At that same time, trained workers and supervisors were not available in the country. Daewoo gave free training to 130 Desh supervisors and managers at its ultra-modern Pusan garment plant, the biggest in the world at that time (Quddus and Rashid, 1998). The Daewoo trained employees of Desh were soon enticed away at multiples of their salaries by new garments firms that were being set up in large numbers in Dhaka and Chittagong. Until the mid 1980s the number of new entrants in this industry increased rapidly. In the following year it increased by another 105 per cent (Table 1.1). During the last half of the decade, the entry of new industries slowed down drastically, the growth rate of industry fell below 1 percent for the three consecutive years. Many believe that many factors contributed to the phenomenal growth of this industry. Luckily, both domestic and international environment favoured the rapid growth of this industry in Bangladesh. Bangladeshi entrepreneurs got familiar with the world apparel market. They acquired the expertise of mobilising resources to export oriented RMG industries. The introduction of Back-to-Back L/C, innovated by the founder of Desh Garments, Mr. Nurul Quader Khan, not only solved the problem of working capital, it also facilitated access to the quality fabrics to be imported as the basic raw materials of the industry. The government also assigned a very high priority to the development of RMG industry, provided continued support to the entrepreneurs and took a number of pragmatic steps to streamline import-export formalities. The government introduced appropriate incentives for encouraging the use of local fabrics in the export oriented garments industry. The duties on all capital machinery in the export-oriented industries and on raw-cotton have been withdrawn; duty on cotton yarn has been reduced from 15% to 7.5%; on textile spares from 30% to 15%; and on dyes from 60% to 30% (Siddiqi, 1996). These are encouraging steps taken by the government.

Traditionally, textiles and clothing are not a technology generating sector but are situated downstream of the technological innovation process. Nevertheless, maintaining the competitive edge of the sector means constantly adopting production and distribution methods and designing new products (Menezes, 2000).

1.3 International Arena and Bangladesh RMG Industry

The history of the trade in textiles and clothing, from the inception of GATT in 1947 to the successful conclusion of the Uruguay Round in 1994, had been characterised by discriminatory use of projectionist positions of the developed world against the developing countries. Although GATT envisaged reciprocal and mutually advantageous arrangements and elimination of discriminatory treatment in international trade, which is often called most-favoured nation (MFN) principle, the textile and clothing sector dominated by the developing world, received no enthusiastic attention for inclusion in the GATT discipline (Dowlah, 1998). Worse still, while each of the GATT Rounds, prior to the Uruguay Round (UR), led to further trade liberalization in products of major exports interest to the developed world, trade in garments, a sector of increasing export interest to the developing countries, evolved in the opposite direction (Cable, 1987). Consequently especially since early 1970s, global trade in the textiles and clothing sector-characterised by multiple forms of restrictive measures such as Most Favoured Nation (MFN) and non-MFN tariff barriers, special bilateral and multilateral arrangements, quota restrictions, unrestrained safeguard actions had been governed by bilateral quotas negotiated under the Multi-fibre Arrangement

(MFA). MFA survive more than two decades in full sweep, until December 1994, when the restrictive and discriminatory regime began to crumble down under the auspices of the successful conclusion of the Uruguay Round.[7] The Agreement on Textiles and Clothing (ATC) of the UR calls for gradual, phase-wise and eventual elimination of all MFA restrictions in textiles and clothing, and complete integration of this sector into GATT 1994 by the year 2005.

From the Table 1.2 one can easily observe that the labour cost is the lowest in Bangladesh. They found Bangladesh as one of the most suitable countries. Despite the shock of September 11 bringing down RMG exports pitiably dusting the last fiscal year, the sector has made a remarkable recovery on its own steam, due to the increased demands in the US and European markets of dependable and fashion conscious Bangladeshi garments manufacturers. This sector is the only dynamic link of Bangladesh capable of claiming a share of global business on merit and experience albeit aided by Multi-Fibre Arrangement concessions.

Table 1.2
Comparative Average Hourly Wages in RMG Industry

Country	Average Hourly Wages (in US Dollar)
Germany	25.00
USA	16.00
South Korea	5.00
Hong Kong	3.90
Turkey	3.50
Mexico	2.40
Brazil	1.50
Malaysia	1.20
Thailand	1.00
India	0.60
Sri Lanka	0.45
Pakistan	0.40
Indonesia	0.40
Vietnam	0.40
Bangladesh	0.20

Source: 1. The Economist, October 1-7, 1998
2. Textiles and Clothing: An Introduction to Quality Requirements in Selected Markets, ITC/UNCTAD/GATT, Geneva, 1998

Liberalization of trade following the UR agreements presents opportunities as well as challenges for a developing country such as Bangladesh. In the post UR period, traditional trade policy such as tariffs, quotas, subsidies will become less

7 Centre for Policy Dialogue (CPD), Dhaka, Bangladesh (A Civil Society Think Tank), available at www.cpd-bangladesh.org

feasible and less relevant. In a liberalized trade regime, competition among textiles and clothing exporting countries is likely to become intense. For a developing country such as Bangladesh, low relative labour costs may not be sufficient for improving the competitive position of the clothing industry (Islam, 2001).

Export plays a very important role in the development and growth of any country. This is specially true about countries like Bangladesh aspiring to ensure an improvement in the standard of living of the masses (Bhuiyan, 1998). In fact, the message these days is "export and grow or perish". This is the Newly Industrialised Economics (NIEs) of Asia during the recent past bear ample testimony to this assertion. Infact, the tremendous development that has taken place in the economies like Taiwan, South Korea, Malaysia and Singapore during the past decades has been possible mainly because of the massive growth in their export sector (Ahmed and Khan, 1996).

Bangladesh trade in international arena encounters a constant deficit. As of financial year (FY) 1998-99, Bangladesh export earnings could effort only 66.36% of its import bills while the condition of other years being even worse (Ahmed, 2002). Country's internal resource mobilisation and industrial base is also weak. Agriculture is the spine of the economy, so far buttressing predominantly. Therefore, Bangladesh is dependent on foreign aid, loan, grants etc. This is certainly disgraceful and humiliating for an independent country. To achieve a satisfactory balance between its export income and import cost is, therefore, essential. Export oriented industrialization, preferably boosted by smooth growth and development is dispensable for the survival of the people of Bangladesh.

1.4 Causes of Development of RMG Industry in Bangladesh

Both domestic and international environment paved the way for rapid growth of this industry. These are:

i) usage of simple labour intensive, moderately sophisticated technology and lower level of skills. So initially the hitherto unemployed and illiterate rural population come up to constitute the required work force with comparatively lower wages;

ii) requirement of comparatively low capital investment;

iii) the gestation period is low as machinery is available at nominal lead time. Installation time required short and one can go to production within a period of 4 to 6 months;

iv) the turn over ratio is high as compare to investment and other conventional industries;

v) because of low gestation period and prospect of quick turn over the commercial banks come forward to finance garments enterprise;

vi) back to back letter of credit not only abolished the necessity of investing huge working capital but also facilitated access to the quality fabrics to be imported as basic raw material for RMG industry;

vii) bonded warehouse facilities is introduced and simplification of the formalities of this system were provided for this industry;

viii) government also provided many attractive incentives to the entrepreneurs and took a number of pragmatic steps to streamline import export formalities such as reduction of tax at source of Free on Board (FOB): value and allowing duty free import of capital machineries.

These encouraging factors fuelled the rapid expansion of RMG in Bangladesh. Added to this the international environment was completely favourable to the tremendous growth of this industry (Nath, 2001). By mid 70's the already established developed suppliers of apparels in the world markets viz. Hong Kong, China, South Korea, Singapore, Taiwan, Thailand, Malaysia, Sri Lanka and India were severely constrained by the quota restrictions imposed by their major buyers like USA, EU, and Canada.[8] To maintain their business and competitive edge in the world apparel markets, they followed a strategy of reallocation of RMG factories in those countries which were free from quota restrictions and at the same time had enough trainable cheap labour.

1.5 The Causes of Why Women are Larger Percentage in Garment Industry

In the following figure (Figure 1) it is shown why women are larger percentage in Bangladesh garment industry. These are:

a) female employees are docile and thus labour manegement are easier;
b) Female employees are not unionized;
c) they are most often secondary earners and their retrechment may be easier and
d) they have a weak burgaining power in the labour market, not only due to availability of large surplus of female labour but also because of the fear that loss of the job will lead to problems within the family (in the form of husband's ill treatment, children's frustration etc.)

8 "Textile Woes", Editorial, available at independent-bangladesh.com/news/oct/18/18102002.htm.: downloaded n October, 19, 2002

Figure 1.1
Why women are in larger percentage in garments industry

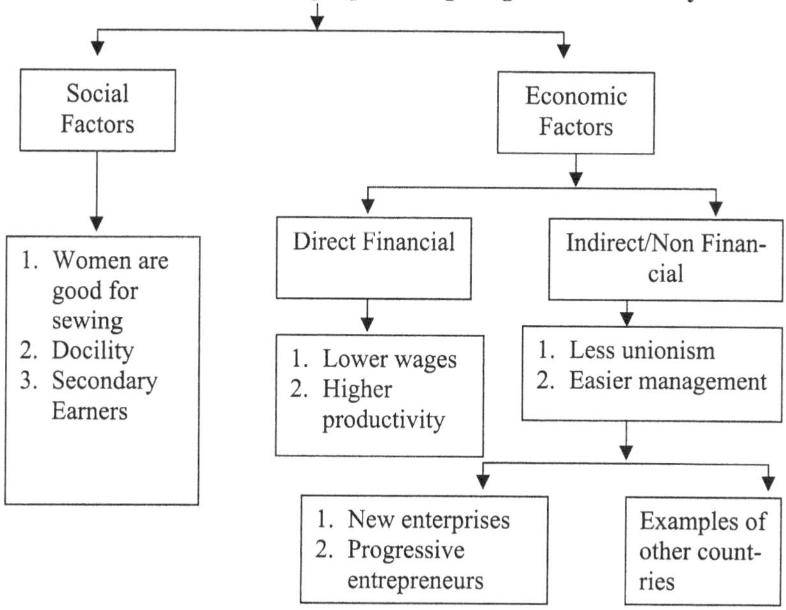

1.6 Trade Liberalization and Bangladesh

Bangladesh has been at the forefront in the last decade in embracing prescriptions for trade liberalization. It was praised in international forums-that espouse trade liberalization measures –for its relatively faster face of opening up its markets for barrier free trade. India, Pakistan, Sri Lanka and other regional countries have not been as enthusiastic about trade liberalization and these countries also did not have to play price like Bangladesh for its quicker pace of trade liberalization or rather one sided trade liberalization. However, Bangladesh's experience after such liberalization has not been a happy one. It suffers a huge trade imbalance with its biggest neighbour, India. Even European Union and the US have tended to discourage export of Bangladeshi products like RMG and Shrimps into their markets citing objections such as of child labour in Bangladeshi RMG industries and alleged catching of shrimps by violating so-called environmental standards.[9] But, we believed that, most of the foreign economists who have looked at the Bangladesh trade performance in the last 8 years have concluded that its trade liberalization since 1990 has been a textbook case of success. Exports have increased at double-digit rates, and imports have increased in parallel, leaving the trade balance largely unchanged in dollar terms. These exports have been heavily concentrated in the garment industry, which is an industry well-suited to Bangladesh's comparative advantage in view of its heavy use of abundant unskilled labour. GDP growth has accelerated. What more could anyone ask for, apart from more of the same? In this context Williamson,(1999) mentioned "Well, I suppose one could have asked for much more progress in establishing and enabling business environment, reforming the financial sector and state enterprises, and improving infrastructure, measures that would have been well worthwhile in themselves and would also have enabled Bangladesh to draw even greater benefits from trade liberalization."

What has surprised many of us is that it seems that public opinion in Bangladesh, and even some of its leading economists, do not see things the same way. They have complained of a flood of imports having a devastating effect on the import-competing industries, and reducing the breadth of the country's industrial base. They complain of the great trade deficit with India. They complain that the garment industry uses imported textiles, so that the value-added is much less than the gross value of exports. There are even complaints that smuggled imports from India are taking markets away from local industry, with an apparent belief that smuggling is stimulated by trade liberalization.

The study we are discussing today, Bangladesh trade liberalization concerning garments and other industries provides the best basis we have yet for evaluating these charges. It documents the parallel increase in exports and imports, and shows that the share of exports in GDP has more than doubled in the 1990s, compared to a 50% increase in the 1980s. It has a pioneering and most illuminating analysis of the microeconomic impact on the import-competing industries, and concludes that these experienced much more dramatic productivity gains than the export industries, but that their fortunes were far more varied than those of the export industries. These findings seem plausible. Export industries had to be efficient in order to be capable of exporting when there was a 66% bias against exporting, so they had little scope for productivity improvement after liberalization. Import-competing industries, in contrast, had an easy life under the ancient regime. After liberalization, some succeeded in modernizing under the stimulus of competition, but some were out-competed by imports, as we know must happen if exports and imports are to expand in parallel.

---

9 "WTO and Globalization of World Trade" by Anu Mahmud. Available at http://www.independent-bangladesh.com/news/oct/18/18102002ed.htm: Downloaded on October 19, 2002.

In case this does not reassure those who worry about deindustrialization in Bangladesh, let us look at the statistics on growth of the manufacturing sector. Manufacturing output grew at 3.0% per year in the 1980s and at 6.6% per year in the 1990s. Even if one excludes garments, growth was about 4.4% in the 1990s, i.e. faster than in the pre-liberalization years. Admittedly the growth of manufacturing value-added, at 4.7% per year, was faster than the 3% growth of gross production in the 1980s, and if one estimates that garments also contributed 2.2% to the 6.8% growth of manufacturing value-added in the 1990s, then the growth of value-added in the rest of manufacturing showed no acceleration in the 1990s. But neither did it decline, as the pessimists seem to believe. The accelerated growth of garments was a net addition to manufacturing growth, not something that displaced the rest of other manufacturing industries. It is of course true that, Bangladesh is a signatory to the WTO rules and the WTO rules required its members to remain steadfast in the path of trade liberalization. But under the WTO guidelines member countries are under no absolute compulsion to reduce their tariffs. They can go slow with the process or even revise tariffs upwards in some cases exceptionally in the backdrop of serious difficulties faced by them. Bangladesh could take advantage of the flexibility in the WTO rules to give legitimate protection to its domestic industries. Specially it could adopt an anti-dumping law to this end as was adopted years ago by its neighbours and even the developed countries. The net exports of the garment industry are substantially less than the gross exports, and it is worth knowing that in net terms jute is still Bangladesh's biggest export industry. That fact surely makes the case for an enquiry into the future of the jute industry, which I recently heard economist Prof. Dr. Rehman Sobhan plead for. But it does not constitute an indictment of the garment industry, which remains an invaluable national asset. The test of its value to the nation is a comparison of the value added with the value of the resources employed to produce it, and the fact that the industry generates good profits and many jobs implies that the industry passes the test.

The charge that trade liberalization is responsible for the smuggling from India is, as I have already implied, absurd. That said, the report is right to point out that smuggling is also encouraged by the failure to collect Value Added[10] Tax (VAT) properly in Bangladesh. If retailers were charged VAT on the value of their sales, and entitled to a rebate on the value of their purchases if and only if those goods could be shown to have already had tax paid on them, the distorted incentive to smuggle so as to avoid VAT would be elimi-

---

[10] "Value added" is defined as "the ex-works price minus the customs value of each of the products incorporated, which originated in another country of the original group". Ex-works price is defined as" the price paid for the product ex-works to the manufacturer in whose undertaking the last working or processing is carried out, provided that the price includes the value of the materials used, minus any internal taxes which are, or may be, repaid when the product obtained is exported".

nated. The worry about a bilateral trade deficit with India is of course misplaced: there is nothing wrong with triangular trade, which is often welfare-enhancing. But it may be acting as surrogate for a perfectly legitimate complaint, which is that Bangladesh's big neighbour India retains a very restrictive import regime. That regime hurts India as well as Bangladesh; its existence provides no rationale for Bangladesh to hurt itself as well as India by reciprocating.

Nothing in the above challenges my tentative conclusion that Bangladesh would be well advised to seek more of the same: more trade liberalization, leading to more trade, leading to faster growth. It would of course be better still if those reforms were supplemented by more reforms in the sectors where Bangladesh has lagged, like the financial sector and privatization and the civil service and infrastructure. Therefore, time has come for Bangladesh not to back pedal on trade liberalization. But, experience has shown that the country can benefit from trade liberalization even without these other reforms. Just think what it might accomplish if it had these other reforms as well.

1.7 Bangladesh Macroeconomy: A Glance

Bangladesh, the erstwhile East Pakistan, separated from Pakistan in 1971 through a civil war with a view to achieve political and economical independence for its citizens. Unfortunately, the country didn't achieve this latter objective even after thirty years of its independence. This failure is imputed to several fundamental aspects. Most significant of these are: political instability coupled with lack of vision, unbridled pervasive corruption, floods and cyclones, weak industrial base, gigantic size of population leading to massive unemployment, lack of natural resources, high illiteracy rate, weak revenue base, meagre domestic savings and investments etc. Bangladesh is, therefore, one of the poorest countries of the world which received a bulk of foreign assistance from various donors since her independence. But significant economic attainment is still far away. It is therefore, imperative to explore the loopholes of such failure.

1.7.1 Agriculture and Industry

Geographical location of Bangladesh is labelled as the semitropical climatic region. It is a land of numerous rivers and their tributaries that make up its soil exceptionally fertile. Agriculture is the spine of the economy of Bangladesh as opposed to its inadequate and feeble industrial sector. Approximately 82% of the total population of the country inhabit in rural areas and they earn their living from agriculture. The economy is now self-sufficient in food grains. Natural disaster, mainly flood almost every year and ruinous cyclone intermittently, results in colossal amount of damage to the economy of Bangladesh. However, agriculture accounts for 26% of GDP, down from about 40% in 1980's, and is

the primary occupation of about 70% of its population, mostly farmers or rural labourers. The growth rate of agricultural production accelerated from 5.0% in FY 1999 to 7.0% in FY 2000.[11]
The country was one of the major exporters of textiles, silk and sugar till the eighteenth century, but the industrial process was subsequently halted during the 200 years of colonial exploitation.

As a result, Bangladesh inherited a narrow industrial base when it become independent in 1971. It has a great number of large, medium and small sized industries in both public and private sectors based on both indigenous and imported raw materials. Among them are jute, cotton, textile, fertilizer, engineering, shipbuilding, steel, oil-refinery, paper, newsprint, sugar, chemicals, cement and leather (Figure-1). Jute industry has traditionally played an important role in the national economy. But in recent years RMG industry has replaced jute as the principal export earners of the country.

Figure 1.2
Export Sector Performance in FY 2000-2001

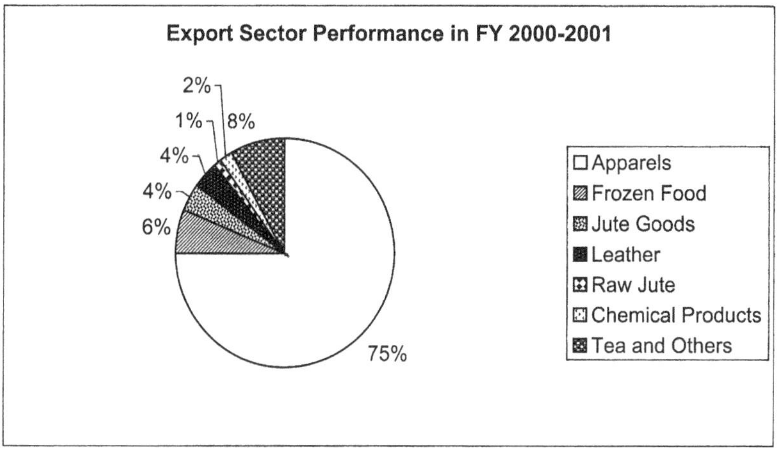

Source: Bangladesh Garments Manufacturers and Exporters Association

With the development of infrastructure, supportive policies for trade and investment and comparative advantage in labour intensive industries, excellent prospects for investment exists in Bangladesh today.[12]

---

[11] "Country Commercial Guide" (CCG) 2000-2001, US Embassy, Dhaka available at www.usembassy-dhaka.org downloaded on January 08, 2001.

According to the CCG, 2000-2001 of the US Embassy Dhaka, industry to the real GDP of Bangladesh is about 26% which comprises manufacturing, construction, power, and utilities. Industrial activity in the private sector remains constrained as consumer demand is weak, domestic and foreign investment is slow, import demand is slack, letter of credit openings are slow, and lack of confidence in business conditions persists among businessman. The culture of "hartals"[13] and strikes pose a serious threat to the Foreign Direct Investment (FDI) flow and impairs severely the industrial activity of Bangladesh.

1.7.2 Overall Economic Growth

A moderate growth was spectacular in Bangladesh economy over the last decade, which country commercial guide recorded meticulously as follows: "Bangladesh has experienced fairly robust economic growth during a decade, which saw restoration of a democratically elected government and a steady, albeit slow, liberalization of the economy."

Table 1.3
Plan Size, Actual Expenditure and GDP Rate of Past Plans
(At respective base year price)
(in Million Taka[14])

Plan	Plan Size			Estimated Actual Expenditure			Realised Growth
	Total	Public	Private	Total	Public	Private	
1	2	3	4	5	6	7	8
First Five Year Plan(1973-1978)	44,550	39,520	5,030	20,740	16,350	4,390	4.00
Two Year Plan (1978-1980)	38,610	32,610	6,000	33,590	24,020	9,570	13.50
Second FiveYear Plan (1980-1985)	172,000	111,000	61,000	152,970	103,280	49,690	3.80
Third Five Year Plan(1985-1990)	386,000	250,000	136,000	270,110	171,290	98,820	3.80
Fourth Five Year Plan (1990-1995)	620,000	347,000	598,480	598,480	274,083	324,397	4.15

Source: Ministry of Planning, Government of the People's Republic of Bangladesh p. 2

The average annual growth of GDP in the ten-year period from FY 1991 through 2000 was 4.8; the It is obvious from the Table 1.3 that the average annual growth rate during the fourth plan period was 4.15 per cent, which appears

---

12 http://www.discoverybangladesh.com/meetbangladesh/economy/commerce_industry.htm downloaded on May, 9, 2003.

13 Hartal is the strike called by opposition party when almost normal activity remains virtually stopped.

14 Taka is Bangladesh currency

as the maximum among the earlier plans. This low growth has been attributed to among stagnant agricultural production in the country. Again preliminary estimate for FY 2000 economic growth is 5.5%. However, these growth rates fall short of the levels needed to reduce significantly the poverty that afflicts one of three Bangladeshis."[15] It is righteous to say that the country voted for three free and fair general elections in 1991, 1996 and 2001 to place in power three democratic governments which might have positive impact on economic growth of the country. Moreover, liberalization of the economy commenced in the year 1992. Table 1.3 below shows the GDP growth rates of different five-year and two-year plans prepared by the Ministry of Planning of Government of Bangladesh.

Table 1.4 provides some insights about the sectoral rates during the Fourth Five Year Plan. The Table indicates that agricultural sector attained poor growth because this sector experienced trouble in fertiliser distribution and lack of adequate public procurement of food grain at support prices.

Table 1.4
GDP Composition and Growth Rate During Fourth Five Year Plan
(at 1984/85 prices) (In million Taka)

Sector	1989/90	1990/91	1991/92	1992/93	1993/94	1994/95	Annual Growth Rate Achieved
1	2	3	4	5	6	7	8
Agriculture	190,354	193,421	197,662	201,230	201,915	199,822	0.98
Industry	49,322	50,503	54,211	59,140	63,786	69,302	7.05
Elect, Gas and Natural Resources	5,561	6,704	7,876	8,933	10,184	11,339	15.31
Transport & Commu.	59,024	60,840	63,349	66,416	70,089	74,203	4.68
Trade & other Services	105,124	110,237	115,780	122,041	129,516	140,115	5.92
Construction	29,749	31,087	32,471	34,032	36,074	34,593	5.34
Housing	38,030	39,316	40,656	42,187	43,792	45,457	3.63
Public Services	20,363	22,334	24,184	26,240	28,484	30,962	8.74
Total GDP	497,527	541,442	536,189	560,219	583,840	609793	4.15

Source: The Fifth Five Year Plan 1997-2002, Ministry of Planning, Government of the People's Republic of Bangladesh p.3

1.7.3 Unemployment Situation

Unemployment is a constant problem of the country as it feeds a gigantic population of about 141 million, the most densely populated country of the world.

During the Fourth Plan period the situation seems to be improved as the fifth plan[16] reads: "The fourth plan (1990-95) laid specific emphasis on em-

[15] Op. Cit.
[16] The Fifth Five Year Plan 1997-2002, Ministry of Planning, Government of Bangladesh , p.8

ployment generation to alleviate poverty. The labour force has almost doubled since independence growing at a rate faster than the population. Against this, reduction of unemployment rate (including under employmet) from 38.78% in 1972/73 to 31.23% in 1994/95."

1.7.4 Foreign Aid

Since the independence of Bangladesh in 1971, it has accepted foreign assistance every year that constitutes a considerable part of its GDP. The country commercial guide of US Embassy report[17] reads as "The country historically had received annually the equivalent of close to 6% of GDP in foreign assistance disbursement, but this figure has declined to around 3-4% in recent years as GDP has increased while aid utilization has levelled off." But this aid has not been utilised in an efficient way heading to sustainable development. At present, aid flow has shrunk by significant amount. The Fifth Five Year Plan 1995-2000 outlines few reasons behind as "The global recession after the Gulf war, the emergence of independent states in the former Soviet Union, and above all, newly emerging donor priorities adversely affected the availability of external assistance and caused a decline in the flow of foreign aid to Bangladesh. Implementation problems also adversely affected aid disbursement." The report also adds that during the plan period, the total aid disbursement fell short of the target by 9.28% to $ 7.56 billion and accounted for 47.64 % of development expenditure at 1989/90 prices. This indicates that development works were excessively dependent on foreign aid.

1.7.5 Government's Role in the Economy

Government of Bangladesh has put together its privatization efforts to divert from the constantly inefficient State-owned enterprises. But still it has not gained full momentum. The country commercial guide 2000-2001 of the US Embassy, Dhaka stipulates as: "Although over the past decade the Bangladesh government has enacted policies to diminish bureaucratic requirements and open the economy to private sector development, these efforts at market-based reforms have only been partly successful. Trade has been liberalized and new sectors opened to private sector development; privatization, encounter stiff opposition from vested interest groups, such as public sector labour unions, bureaucrats or opposition political parties. The state, a major participant in Bangladesh's industrial sector, owns 40% of industrial capacity, primarily in jute, textile milling, steel, and chemicals. According to the World Bank, the state-owned enterprises (SOE's) accounted for over 25% of total fixed capital formation, but only 6% of GDP. Gross losses of these SOE's cost the government

[17] "Country Commercial Guide" (CCG) 2002-2001,The US Embassy in Dhaka, available at www.usembassy-dhaka.org downloaded on February 11, 2001.

several hundred million dollars each year, and continue to burden the budget and are a major drag on the economy". Strengthening private sector is, therefore, crucial for the country's economy.

1.7.6 Export Promotion

During the last decade the world experienced remarkable rise in openness to trade and investment flows. It was partly because of the fall of communism and the old ideas of self sufficiency, partly because of the liberalization agreed upon during the Uruguay Round (UR) and partly because of spread of new information technology. Although globalization and openness to trade were taking shape, the financial crisis and its contagion effect, which hit South-East Asian economies, has spread over other parts of the world during the year 1998 causing a drastic fall in commodity prices. Given the global economic turmoil, Bangladesh economy has overcome this crisis by the far-sighted economic and fiscal policies of the government as envisaged in the annual report of the Export Promotion Bureau (EPB) of Bangladesh. Given the circumstances as above, Bangladesh export sector has achieved considerable growth during the years 1995-2001 despite the world-wide downward trend. As a result, depletion of foreign exchange reserve did not occur during the years. Devaluation of the currencies did occur to boost export but it was less in comparison with the neighbouring countries, for instance, India and Pakistan.

1.7.7 Export Promotion Bureau (EPB) and its Features

By the promulgation of a Presidential Ordinance in 1977, EPB emerged as a semi-autonomous body with a view to promoting export and improving plan and policies to assist the private sector.[18] Honourable Minister for Commerce is the ex-officio Chairman of the Board of Management, which comprises a Vice-Chairman, a Director- General, four private sector members, and six high officials of the Ministry of Commerce, Industry, Agriculture, Jute, Textile and Foreign Affairs. The Vice chairman acts as the Chief Executive of the EPB. The main features of the EPB is to suggest the government for efficient, adequate, economic and co-ordinated plans and policies for the promotion of exports; to assess the export potential of Bangladesh products and services and ensure appropriate quality control with regard to export goods, to co-ordinate the export efforts of Bangladesh private and public sector organisations and provide necessary advice, information and assistance to such organisations so as to enable them to maximise their export potential; to explore and examine markets of other countries with a view to promote of raw, semi-finished and finished products from Bangladesh to such countries.[19]

---

18 Annual Report 1997-98, Export Promotion Bureau, Government of Bangladesh, p. 11

19 Annual Report 1997-98, Export Promotion Bureau, Government of Bangladesh, p. 11 & 12

1.7.8 Objectives of the Export Policy

Increase of export in regional and international markets with a view to achieve optimum national growth is one of the main objectives of the export policy 1997-2002. For attainment of this, narrowing the gap between import payments and export earnings is extremely important. Export policy aims at timely production of exportable items at competitive price because it is essential for sustaining existing markets and its further expansion. It also aims at reaping the benefits by taking advantages of global trade liberalization after the Uruguay Round environment. The objectives of the export policy 1997-2002 also incorporates such agenda as product diversification, quality improvement, establishment of backward linkage to export-oriented industries and service sectors, introduction of newer products for export, exporting high value added products, developing infrastructure for export performance, creating skilled man-power in the export sector etc.

1.7.9 Incentives Provided by the Government to Support Enhanced Export

Government provides some incentives to the 100% export-oriented industries, for example, tax exemption, bank credit etc.[20] The annual contribution of leather sector of Bangladesh to its total export is highly significant. To boost up export activities, government has declared that leather-manufacturing firms exporting at least 80% of their products will receive similar benefits as that of 100% export-oriented industries. Other industries exporting 80% also reap like benefits except those customs and taxation incentives as meant for 100% export oriented industries. In addition, these industries are allowed to sell 20% of their products in the local market, subject to paying normal duties and taxes. Moreover, leather industries are provided with supervised bonded warehouse facilities.

To promote export of software, Bangladesh Telegraph and Telephone Board takes immediate steps for installation of adequate number of high speed dedicated lines to facilitate the export of 100% export oriented software and data entry service industries. The government also offers supervised bond facilities for duty free import of computers and other accessories. Moreover, 50% of the income arising out of any export business is exempted from income tax. Under the provision of Duty Drawback system, all duties paid can be pulled back subject to repatriation of sale proceeds in the form of foreign exchange for all exports other than deemed export through the commercial banks. Civil aviation authority has withdrawn the royalty on the landing of cargo flights of the foreign airlines to facilitate the transportation of air borne export goods at competitive price. Moreover, government provides bonded warehouse facility for import-dependent export industries, treats small and medium export oriented agriculture

[20] Ibidem, page 17-22

firms as industries, provides import facility for packaging materials, facilities for handcrafts through establishment of craft village, boosts jewellery export, among others.

1.7.10 Review of Export Performance FY 1998-99 Compared to Preceding Years

During the fiscal year 1998-99 export from Bangladesh in total amounted to US$ 5312.86 million as against US$ 5161.20 million during 1997-98 showing an increase of US$ 151.66 million i.e. 2.94%. A picture of total export earnings over the years might be obtained from the Table 1.5 below:

Table 1.5
Total Export Earnings Since Fiscal Year 1988-89
(Million US$)

Fiscal Year	1988-89	1990-91	1995-96	1996-97	1997-98	1998-99
Export Earnings	1291.56	1717.55	3882.42	4418.28	5161.20	5312.86

Source: Export Promotion Bureau (EPB), Government of Bangladesh, 2000

Table 1.6
Commodity-wise Export Earnings of FY 1998-99
(Million US$)

Commodity	Export Earning	% of Total Earning
Woven Garments	2984.81	56.18
Knitwear Garments	1035.42	19.49
Jute Good	303.85	5.72
Frozen Food	274.32	5.16
Leather	168.25	3.17
Chemical Products	79.25	1.49
Raw Jute	71.75	1.35
Tea	38.56	0.73
Agricultural Product	22.09	0.42
Others	334.56	6.29
Total	5312.86	100.00

Source: Annual Report of EPB 1998-99, Government of Bangladesh, page 28

The principal commodities that marked an increase in the export earnings during the year 1998-99 compared to preceding years are: Chemical products (6.78%), Jute goods (7.97%), handicrafts (27.05%), knitwear garments (10.11%), woven garments (4.98%), electronics (94.12%), and other products (1.29%).[21] The commodities which caused recession in export earnings are frozen food (6.64%), tea

[21] EPB, Op.Cit, page 28

(18.77%), agricultural products (43.56%), raw jute (33.42%), petroleum by products (51.97%), leather (11.57%), engineering commodities (44.65%).[22]

Out of the total export earnings of US$ 5312.86 million during the FY 1998-99, the share of primary commodities was 422.33 million and that of manufactured products stood at US$ 4890.53 million i.e. 7.95% and 92.05% respectively as against US$ 501.93 million and US$ 4659.27 million i.e. 9.73% and 90.27% respectively during the FY 1997-99.

As we look into export pattern according to destination during the FY 1997-98, USA appears first followed by Germany and U.K as the second and third. France, Italy, the Netherlands, Belgium, Japan, Canada, Hong Kong, India, Spain, China, Sweden, Pakistan, Denmark, Australia, Iran, UAE, and Singapore are also the principal importers of Bangladeshi products as evident from the Table 1.7.

Table 1.7
Bangladesh Export According to the Destination
(Million US$)

Countries	1996-97	1997-98	1998-99
U.S.A	1432.15	1929.21	1968.46
Germany	428.29	510.93	625.13
U.K.	437.69	440.00	491.34
France	312.65	369.07	135.36
Italy	203.62	270.47	270.01
Netherlands	208.59	236.08	251.61
Belgium	210.57	211.40	227.62
Canada	69.12	106.84	104.91
Japan	114.05	112.00	92.76
Hong Kong	109.18	87.39	79.19
Spain	55.01	60.56	76.58
Sweden	38.13	48.27	62.50
India	46.25	65.64	59.72
Denmark	51.24	43.77	51.84
Thailand	12.05	16.56	40.70
Pakistan	38.97	44.67	38.10
Iran	53.00	35.76	36.67
Australia	28.48	35.43	35.61
Turkey	17.08	23.35	25.94
Switzerland	10.13	16.55	22.37
Others	542.03	497.25	406.44
TOTAL	4418.28	5161.20	5312.86

Source: Export Promotion Bureau (EPB), Government of Bangladesh

[22] Ibidem, page 28

If we compare the import figures of Bangladesh of different years with those of export, trade deficit appears to be a permanent feature although it varies from year to year. This indicates that export promotion is crucial to boost the country's economy. In 1998-99, export earnings afforded only 66.36% of import bill. Export showing as a percentage of country's import over the years from 1982-83 to 1998-99 is furnished in the Table 1.8.

Table 1.8
Export as percentage of Import
(Million US$)

Fiscal Year	Export	Import	Export as Percentage of Import (%)
1982-83	687	1823	35.73
1985-86	819	2120	38.63
1990-91	1718	3511	48.93
1995-96	3882	6827	56.40
1997-98	5161	7545	68.40
1998-99	5313	8006	66.36

Source: Annual Report of EPB, 1998-99, Government of Bangladesh

Table 1.8 provides that export has increased over the years corresponding to imports. Now, we can look into the export of Bangladesh to the outside world focusing on different regions. It is evident from the data of the EPB that the EU countries topped the list registering 46.36% of the total export of Bangladesh in the year 1998-99. American region and Asian region appeared as the second and third important region of Bangladesh's export, which accounts for 39.50% and 7.68% respectively for the same year. Countries from the Organisation of Islamic Conference (OIC) play also an important role in the export earnings of Bangladesh. During the financial year 1996-97 export earnings from these countries was US$ 244.00 million. If we consider Bangladesh export to SAARC[23] countries, we find a frustrating picture. In FY 1996-97, this earning was only 2.10% of the total export.[24]

1.7.11 Imports vs. Exports-a Nexus

Bangladesh trade in the international arena encounters a constant deficit as evident from the data of Bangladesh Export Promotion Bureau. As of the financial

---

23 South Asian Association for Regional Co-operation (SAARC) consists of Bangladesh, Bhutan, India, Maldives, Nepal, Pakistan & Sri Lanka and it was formed in 1985 under the aegis of Government of Bangladesh.

24 Bangladesh Export Statistics 1996-97, EPB.

year 1998-99, Bangladesh export earnings can afford only 66.36% of its import costs while the condition of previous year being even worse. As we know that Bangladesh's import cost is always higher than its export earnings. In recent years, "exports have increased at double-digit rates, and imports have increased in parallel, leaving the trade balance largely unchanged-if not, improved in dollar terms.[25] This parallel fashion could apparently, be attributed to the highly import dependence of garments industries of the country. This garment sector, as I have mentioned earlier, fetches roughly 76% of the export earnings of Bangladesh. Because of the country's gross deficiency in supplying fabrics and other accessories to feed these export-oriented clothing industries, it has to spend almost 75% of foreign exchange earned through garments exports for importing fabrics and related items. This matter could more easily be understood from the following: "It is important to raise that fast rate of growth of exports (average annual rate being 25% from 1991-92 to 1995-96) has necessitated almost an equally fast rate (23.6% in the same period) of growth of imports, which are almost mandatory".[26]

Government of Bangladesh through its EPB is striving for higher export earnings to reach a balance with its import bills in the near future. Bangladesh has a large population of about 141 million, the density of population is more than 900 persons per square kilometre. As the land for agricultural production is limited, rather gradually decreasing due to new habitats and various establishments, the basic need of these gigantic population is almost impossible to meet up with the agricultural production. Export oriented cum labour incentive industries like RMG, boosted by up-to-date policies and strategies in the area of economic and social aspects for meeting the challenges of trade liberalization, is therefore, essential for the survival of the people of Bangladesh.

1.7.12 Readymade Garments as a Multidisciplinary Field of Inquiry

Over the last decade a range of studies appeared focusing on the readymade garments industry. These studies were indeed diverse. Some are related to hard core economics studies focused on the growth of the sector, located at the technological capability and backward linkages and attempted to assess its growth potentials in the face of post-MFA challenges. Some are related with industrialization possibilities of various proto-types, prospects in a "labour-surplus" economy, potentialities for an export-led growth and what it means to be industral-

---

25 "Trade Liberalization in Bangladesh, Who Gained, Who Didn't, and Why" by Tercan Baysan and Zaidi Sattar, available at The Daily Star website http://www.dailystarnews.com/200003/29n0032909.htm downloaded on April 2, 2000. Feature page Volume 3, Number 209, March 29, 2000

26 Sources of Export Growth in Bangladesh, The Daily Star, Editorial Page, Volume 1, Number 54, October 07, 1999. Available at http://www.dailystarnews.com/199710/07/n7100502.htm#BODY4

ized in the era of liberalization, globalization, and late capitalism. RMG is Bangladesh's gateway to the world of trading nations, the world that is out there, of commerce and communication, of trade negotiations and trade wars, competitive and comparative advantages, the Uruguay Rounds and WTO, the world of dependencies and bilateral and multilateral arrangements. RMG is also our best placed hope of trading out of hope of poverty. Some other considered outside the sphere of conventional economics. Some are thinking the demographic implications as well as who participates and why participates in this sector. Some considered the economic and social well-being using quantitative and qualitative indicators. The modernity/tradition debate raised afresh the question about the "*Purdah*"[27] and the silent transformation within society and tradition and many questions of factory norms and legal rights for workers recruited from the pre-modern periphery. In the still dominating traditions in social sciences in Bangladesh where each discipline claims exclusiveness and near monopoly over truth there is little interaction between economics and anthropology, between demography and politics, between gender studies and history. RMG enjoyed having the advantaged position of receiving a rare multidisciplinary attention.

1.8 Statement of the Problem

Industrial development is essential for the strength and stability of a country. It is also vital for improving the quality of life of general masses as well as to put the economy to the path of development. Bangladesh, being a labour-abounded country, started the process of industrialization by concentrating on labour- intensive products such as textiles and clothing. Since clothing is more labour intensive than textiles, it is logical for Bangladesh to demonstrate its comparative advantage in readymade garments. Over the last decade or so Bangladesh has substantially liberalized its trade regime, moving away from costly protectionst policy toward a more export- friendly trade regime.

The Uruguay Round presents opportunities for Bangladesh by liberalizing trade in textiles and clothing over a ten year transition period. Several factors however, generate uncertainty and present challenges for Bangladesh: trade diversion induced by regional trade blocs, special trade relationships between trade blocs and some non-member countries, safeguard mechanisms and stringent "rules of origin" introduced by developed countries, China's accession to the WTO and greater competition from major developing countries such as China and India which have a well-integrated textiles and clothing in-

[27] Purdah means curtain or veil (covered face and body with a piece of cloth). A muslim women above 13 years has to maintain the purdah to preserve herself.

dustry. But most challenges and threats will come after phasing out of MFA after 2004 which is now guaranteed by MFA for decades through quota[28].

Currently, clothing exports from Bangladesh enjoys unrestricted entry into EU market and restricted market to the US and Canadian markets. Cheap unit labour cost constitutes the main comparative advantage for Bangladesh compared with other garment exporters (Hasan, 2000). But these advantages are exposed to a number of serious challenges. Firstly, with the gradual phasing out of the Multi- Fibre Arrangement, 33% of trade volume has already become integrated into WTO rules, and by January 01, 2005, the remaining portion 67% would be integrated. Consequently, all preferential treatment (such as quota, GSP etc) would be phased out and the competitors of Bangladesh will have quota free access to EU, US and Canadian market. This would put Bangladesh in a serious competitive situation with other textile and clothing rich countries with better backward linkage. Another consequence of implementation of WTO rules is the gradual reduction of tariffs by EU countries along with other developed countries. In addition to this, the quota levels are being gradually increased by quota countries (USA, Canada etc.) during transition period (1995- 2005). Consequent upon this, increased for our competitors would put them in a better position due to their fairly well-developed backward linkage industries. This in effect means more stiff competition and probable loss of market for Bangladesh.

From the above discussion, we can say the country must confront two central question: First, what are the challenges for the Bangladesh RMG industry in the long – run when the quotas will be finally eliminated and unrestricted trading in textile and clothing takes place in the post-ATC world ? Second, what economic and social impact Bangladesh has to face in the textile and clothing sector due to trade liberalization globally?

1.9 Synoptic View of the Study

The study is divided into ten chapters. The first chapter provides an information covering the macro-economic indicators of Bangladesh economic situation, the evaluation of the readymade garment industry in Bangladesh with background of the study, trade liberalization and Bangladesh development. This chapter also covers the definitional issues regarding trade liberalization and Bangladesh readymade garments industry, the problem statement with interim concluding remarks.

The second chapter is concerned with the through review of the existing literature of trade liberalization and Bangladesh readymade garments industry, particularly general textile and garments studies, social dimension of RMG in-

[28] "Relax rules of origin for LDCs to absorb post MFA shock-Dhaka urges European Commission", The Daily Star Business Report, available at http//:www.dailystarnews.com /200305/12/n3051205 downloaded on 12th May 2003.

dustry and the international regime in textile and clothing and the association of Bangladesh.

The following chapter deals with the objectives, hypothesis, scope of the study, methodology used in the study.

The fourth chapter provides an overview of the trade and industrial policy concerning textile and clothing in the international arena.

Chapter five is composed of current Bangladesh RMG industry condition which includes trade performance, industry structure, industry characteristics, and development contribution due to this sector in Bangladesh economy.

The sixth chapter provides review of world production and Bangladesh performance which covers global market analysis, leading clothing and textile export markets, cost structure, network of world trade as well international comparison is analysed.

The seventh chapter contains social dimensions of Bangladesh RMG which includes positive and negative effects of working conditions, i.e. establishment of export processing zones, wages, housing, health care, issue of child labour, non-formal education, earn and learn programmes, changing characteristics of labour force, education and marital status, access to income, participation in decision making, household conflicts and co-operation, incidence of illness, modes of commuting etc.

The chapter eight consists of migrating to work which deals with female labour migration and urban adaptation, socio-economic background before migration, motives for migration, poverty and economic dimension of adaptation, women's attempt to change their working condition, and strategies workers adopt to cope with urban environment.

The following chapter is dedicated to case studies of woven garment and knit garment. Five case studies have been undertaken. Each of these case studies covers wide range of issues, namely type and nature of business, management, employee strength, production, export, product range, export market network, sourcing of raw materials, problems and types of raw-materials, changing patterns of raw-materials, problems and critical issues, and impact of trade liberalization.

Finally, the last chapter contains the main economic and social findings of the study with the major conclusions, suggestions, policy implications and directions for further research.

1.10 Concluding Remarks

This study will be an attempt to describe the present scenario of Bangladesh garments industry in the context of globalization of the world economy and liberalization of world trade and its possible economic and social effect. To the best of my knowledge, no serious study on the above stated objective is yet undertaken. I believe that this study will certainly go a long way in making a significant contribution to the existing knowledge and remarkable addition to the present stock of international trade literature including Bangladesh, which would be discussed in the subsequent chapters.

CHAPTER TWO
REVIEW OF THE LITERATURE

2.1 Introduction

Literature review has been divided into three parts. The first part comprises the general trade liberalization concerning GATT/WTO with respect to readymade garment industry in Bangladesh, the second part covers the review of social aspects and migration issues concerning RMG industry in Bangladesh and the third part consists of international regimes in textiles and clothing and association of Bangladesh studies. Until now several studies have been done in the area of textiles and garment, but very few studies are in the area of global trade liberalization concerning garments industry in Bangladesh covering its impact on the economic and social aspects upto the recent period. Whatever little has been attempted in this context is so scanty and wanting in many respects.

2.2 Review of Literature Concerning General Trade Liberalization (GATT/WTO) with Respect to Bangladesh Readymade Garment Industry

Bangladesh along with other developing countries joined the WTO at the culmination of the Uruguay Round (UR) in order to avail the advantages of an open and liberal trading system. This was to strengthen the domestic production base and competitive position and to, inter alia, avail the opportunity to negotiate for enhanced market access in major developed and newly industralized countries. In Bangladesh, the trade liberalization process started in the mid 1980s (GATT, 1984). The Government has since undertaken a number of steps, which include liberalization of the trade and foreign investment regime, strengthening the financial sectors, legislative and regulatory framework, closing and privatising some loss-making state-owned enterprises (SOEs), adjusting or abolishing some administered prices, broadening the base of VAT collection and taking steps to improve governance (Hossain, 1990; EPB, 1990).

In respect of trade liberalization, export diversification and import liberalization received the highest priority in the earlier years. This consisted in permitting the exporters of non-traditional items to convert some of their export earnings at the higher exchange rate in the secondary market, reduction of the tariff level and tariff dispersion, simplification and rationalisation of the tariff structure, and deregulation of the import process etc. (Dowlah, 2000).

Trade liberalization in Bangladesh appears to have progressed at a faster rate than in many neighbouring countries. Bangladesh exporters have been very successful in penetrating the highly competitive markets of the European Union and the United States. In some cases the quota utilization rate for different categories of apparel has recently been nearly 85% in Bangladesh. Over the years, Bangladesh has been able to improve product quality and has gained greater acceptance in international markets, with apparel exports increasing from 5.2% of total world imports in 1995 to 6.8% in 1997. Garment exporters have gradually moved up-market in recent years and are increasingly exporting sophisticated items like high quality suits, jackets and branded items (Siddiqi, 2000). In recent years some exporter have also been successful in penetrating Japan's extremely quality conscious market. As a result, merchandise exports, led by the garments industry, grew at an impressive annual average rate of 17% in US dollar terms between 1990/91 and 1999/2000. However, the export base has been very narrow, with bulk of the foreign exchange earnings coming from a few sectors (BATEXPO, 2000). The removal of the Multi-Fibre Arrangement (MFA) quotas in 2004, under the Uruguay Round Agreement on Textiles and Clothing, might result in Bangladesh losing its preferential access in these markets. While Bangladeshi exporters have started competing effectively in global markets, the phasing out of preferential access and the abolition of quotas, scheduled for 2005, will require them to increase their efficiency, improve product quality and ensure that their products are competitively priced (WTO website[29]).

During the early 1990s, Bangladesh made considerable progress in stabilising and liberalizing its economy. As a result, inflation was much lower than previously, and average annual real GDP growth in 1992-98 was above 5%, largely led by exports involving ready-made garments (Abdullah, 1997). Indeed, one of the most striking features of Bangladesh's trade is that textiles and particularly clothing dominate exports: their combined share grew from 70.4% in 1992 to 83.5% in 1998; by contrast, jute, which had previously been Bangladesh's main export, comprising around half of total exports through the mid-1980s, accounted for only 6% in 1998. This dramatic change in the composition of exports is the consequence of Bangladesh's increased integration into the multilateral trading system. Agriculture still accounts for 30% of GDP while employing 63% of total labour force. The RMG-dominated manufacturing sector and services, accounting for 9% and 61% of GDP, respectively, have been the sources of the economy's growth (CPD, 1999).

On the structural policy front, the Government has continued to pursue, inter alia, trade liberalization, financial sector reform, and privatization, while maintaining in legislative terms one of the most liberal Foreign Direct Investment (FDI) regimes in South Asia (Islam, 1996). However, in the face of severe political difficulties and civil unrest, which manifested themselves in frequent nation-wide strikes ("hartals") costing the country at least 30 working days in 1999 alone, the impetus for structural reform seems to have waned. Moreover, between 1997/98 and 1998/99, real GDP growth dropped from 5.3% to 4.2%. This was partly the consequence of a sharp drop in export growth (from 17.1%

---

29 WTO website available at www.wto.org

to 2.9%), which was initially due to the devastating floods that covered a third of the country, but exacerbated by recurrent power shortages, inadequate port facilities, and other infrastructural bottlenecks, as well as disruptions owing to nation-wide strikes. At the same time, inflation increased owing to a surge in food prices, again caused by the floods. As the food supply situation improved and non-food inflation moderated, inflation began to fall (Rahman, & Rahman, 2001).

Given Bangladesh's high incidence of poverty, its dense population, and its vulnerability to natural disasters, including periodic flooding and cyclones, food security is a major policy objective of the government. Bangladesh is a large recipient of foreign aid, a substantial portion of which entails food (Ahmed, 2002).

Bangladesh extends most-favoured-nation (MFN) treatment to all trading partners and has taken steps to amend its legislation in the light of its obligations undertaken in the context of the Uruguay Round, including in the areas of customs valuation, anti-dumping and countervailing measures, and protection of intellectual property rights. However, Bangladesh has found it difficult to meet its WTO notification requirements. Bangladesh is a leading voice among least-developed members in the WTO as regards their specific needs and concerns as well as the difficulties they face (WTO, 1998).

While Bangladesh has escaped the worst effects of the Asian crisis, the depreciation of the crisis-hit countries exchange rates may well mean that it will face intensified competition from these and other countries, particularly in respect of labour-intensive RMGs (Bow, 2000) With textiles and clothing dominating its exports, and the bulk of those exports going to the European Union and the United States, there is a need for Bangladesh to diversify both its export base and export markets. At the same time, the phasing out of preferential access to these markets and the full integration of all textile and clothing products into the GATT 1994, scheduled for 1 January 2005, will require Bangladeshi RMG exporters to increase efficiency, improve product quality, and ensure that their products are competitively priced.

A brief review of the literature regarding impact of MFA phasing out reveals that there are considerable differences of views among textile experts and economists about the nature of the consequences of the impact of MFA elimination for developing countries (Greenway, 1993; Martin & Winters 1996; Hertel, (ed.) 1997; and Yang, Martin, & Yanagishima, 1997; John & Arther, 1998 & Mitchell, 2001). A number of studies (Hamilton, 1990; Ahmed and Warr, 1994; Chowdhury 1994; Rahman, 1994; Ahmed & Giasuddin, 1996; Siddiqi, 1998; CPD, 1999; IFC, 1999; Bow, 2000; Spinanger, 2000; Afroz, 2001; Bhattacharya, 2001; Bhattacharya & Rahman, 2002 & Kamal, 2002) suggest that the vast majority of these countries will gain from the removal of trade restrictions on textile and clothing, with some gaining proportionately more than others through increased market share. Conversely, some estimates indicate that the distribution of welfare gains from trade liberalization in readymade garments will be very skewed. According to these estimates, China, Indonesia and South Asian countries stand to gain more compared to countries from Latin America and Sub-Saharan Africa. At the same time, the higher cost exporting countries (e.g. Hong Kong, South Korea and Taiwan), which controlled the largest share of exports to the developed country markets under the MFA, are likely to cede ground to lower cost suppliers (e.g. China and India). However there is an apprehension that the relatively new and low-cost sources (Bangladesh and Sri Lanka) may be squeezed out of the market because of their small size, lack of product diversification and low productivity.

It is also reckoned that the phasing out under the MFA may prompt the flow of the foreign direct investment from quota restricted to non-quota restricted or less restricted countries. This implies that elimination of MFA may even cause a reverse flow of investment from relatively new suppliers (Bangladesh) because the sourcing of textiles may tend to gravitate back to the larger and more efficient exporters like Hong Kong, South Korea and Taiwan. (Dowlah, 1999).

A number of studies (Jared, 1989; Borawice, 1992; Hyvarien & Lipman, 1992; Bhuiyan and Shaw, 1994; Haque, 1994; Blackhurst et al, 1995; Rahman, 1995; EPB, Kitty, 1996; 1999; Bhattacharya & Rahman, 2000; Cookson, 2000; IBC & UIL 2000; CPD, 2001; Haque, 2001; Ministry of Commerce, 1996 & 2001; Ahmad, 2002; Hasan, 2002 & Jabbar 2002) raised a question which is being increasingly in the current context is whether Bangladesh will be able to eke out a share in the incremental gain from the future expansion of the global RMG market. The answer of this questions will be defined by the extent to which the MFA phase out may impact on the performance of the textile and apparel sectors of Bangladesh. With the phasing out of MFA and elimination of quotas, some of the traditional RMG exporters like Bangladesh are expected to face serious competition from exporting countries which is now very restricted because of the quotas imposed in US and Canadian markets .

At present, export quota is imposed on Bangladeshi RMG in only two of the nine countries who were original signatories to the MFA, viz., US and Canada. As far Bangladesh is concerned, market access is restrained on thirty one categories in the U.S. market and nine categories in the Canadian market. These two markets currently provide about 50 percent of the total RMG exports from Bangladesh (Baysan & Sattar, 2000[30]). Quota utilization of the USA and Canada had been on an average 85 per cent and 65 per cent respectively. This would suggest that quotas did not initially have a restrictive impact on RMG export from Bangladesh (World Bank, 1993 & 1997; Nath, 1993). However, in recent

[30] Website, www.dailystarnews.com/200003/29/n0032909htm. Feature page, volume 3, Number 209, March 29.

times quota fulfilment by Bangladesh has been substantial and Bangladesh was also able to expand its export to non quota markets as well.

On the otherhand, the patterns of comparative advantage and hence the structure of exports and imports depends on the stage of economic development (Balassa, 1979). A country's comparative advantage is expected to change as a result of changes in factor endowments, accumulation of human capital, and technological innovations. Countries move along a ladder of comparative advantage as development proceeds: relatively advanced countries will lose competitive advantage in product groups intensive in unskilled labour and will shift to products and processes intensive in capital, skilled labour, and innovations.[31] The experience of many countries, specially Japan and other East Asian countries appears to support the dynamic aspects of comparative advantage.

Raw materials (grey fabrics) for Bangladesh's RMG industry is generally sourced from the countries such as China, India, Thailand, Hong Kong under back-to back Letter of Credit (L/C) facilities. Under a quota free regime these countries likely to substitute export of grey fabrics to countries such as Bangladesh by export of RMG to North American and European markets.(Bhuiyan, 1997) This study also supported development of linkages among major subsectors of textile and clothing industries. Evidently, Bangladesh will face a dual challenge: accessing raw materials at competitive prices and competing with hitherto restricted countries under a quota free-context (Islam, 1992). Whether the Bangladesh RMG export sector will be able to withstand the challenge posed by these newly emerging competitors in the post-MFA phase is an issue of critical importance for the future of its RMG industry (Menezes, 2000). The key issue here is the competitive strength of the Bangladeshi textile sector in general and the RMG sector in particular. Finally, this study however tries to find out the challenges and opportunities facing the country now in view of the phasing out of MFA, US-TDA 2000 and terrorist attacks of 11 September 2001 and attempts to sketch a number of policy implications and suggestions for the development of the sector in the context of present trade liberalization scenario.

2.3 Review of Social Dimensions and Bangladesh RMG industry

The rapid growth of the RMG industry in Bangladesh since mid 1980s has generated considerable female employment in the formal export-oriented manufacturing sector. This has made women visible in statistics and brought a social change in Bangladesh. At dawn and dusk one can see a stream of girls and women passing through the streets of Dhaka, the capital of Bangladesh. They are on their way to or from one of the innumerable garment industries which have springing up like mushrooms in the last decades (Bachmann, 2002). The products of the increasing garment sector represent the major part of the coun-

[31] For further discussions on this topic, see Greenaway and Milner (1993)

try's export volume, about 80 percent of the industry workers are female.[32] According to the BGMEA report in 2001, there are over 1.5 million women workers in the about 3500 RMG industry, and they contribute 90% of the total work force. Working in the garment industry brings status for women because it provides a certain freedom which the housemaids and the rural poor housewives lack (Siddiqui, 1999).

The rapid increase of the foot-loose industries created much employment opportunities for women, not only in Bangladesh women entered in large number of shop floors. Since the seventies a relatively fast growth of women's industrial employment in several South-East/East-Asian and Latin American economics has occurred. For instance, in Malaysia, Korea and Singapore women's industrial employment grew more than twice the rate of growth of men during the seventies (Banerjee, 1990). This phenomenon is described as feminisation of labour (Standing, 1989). Nevertheless, studying women's work in Bangladesh and elsewhere we have to keep in mind that women always have worked hard inside and outside the households. In rural Bangladesh women work for example as seasonal labourers in agriculture or as stone breakers in the construction sector. Many women in rural and urban areas are engaged as servants in prosperous families (Hossain et. al. 1990).[33]

Although female economic activities do not appear in the statistics, they are always a significant part of the rural and urban economy (Abdullah & Sondra, 1982). In this context Lachenmann (1998a & 1998b) indicated that the labour of women is to regard as always socially and economically embedded. In Bangladesh, it was the crisis following the Liberation War in 1971 which leads to the first strikingly growth of the number of women who seek gainful employment. Due to economic problems in that time the landlessness increased, many men were not in the position anymore to support their wives (Rozario, 1998). Thus, the traditional family system of support eroded, as Kabeer (1995) argues.[34] Due to its rapid increase the garment sector generated within the eighties employment opportunities for women in the formal sector in great numbers.[35]

But women's visibility is contradictory to that what is widely known about Muslim gender culture in the West. In accordance to that, the spaces of

32 "Impact of international trade regime on the female garments workers in Bangladesh" by Mashuda Khatun Shefali, available at www.sdnbd.org/sdi/news/general-news/ 14-11-2002.

33 For the topic of women's integration in the global economy see also Lachenmann, 1998a, 1998b.

34 In this time development organisations and aid agencies became for the first time for women's issues. Through the influence of the United Nations Decade of Women and Development from 1975 until 1985 several government and non-government organisations focused women and integrated them in the projects as "target group" as they named it (For the discussion on this topic see for example Lachenmann, 1998b, Jahan et al, 1995).

35 Also government and non-government organisations have generated employment opportunities for women, specially for educated middle-class women.

living and working of men are separated from the women's sphere and thus, the world is divided in a male and female area. The female domain is said to be the home, they are responsible for family and household. As a complement the public space is the male sphere. Therefore, women and their reproductive work is invisible. As part of the gender order the interactions between women and men are limited and regulated. However, everyday the female workers are on the streets, visible, impossible to ignore, they leave the domestic places for employment, work together with male colleagues and superiors. So evidently everyday the women workers violate gender conventions, that lead to them having to cope with contradictory social expectations and claims. These ambivalences and conflicts aroused many interest. How they manage the rising inconsistency, and moreover, how can they manoeuvre between confronting social expectations? This is very important to know, how the working women try to improve their positions (ibid., p.2).

Some studies have argued that women employment in the manufacturing sectors improves women's economic status and mobility, and expands individual choices (Joekes, 1987; Lim, 1990; Menezes, 2000). Others (Elson and Pearson, 1981a; 1981b) have shown that it is more complex depending on the forces of three tendencies: the possible intensification of existing forms of gender subordination, a decomposition of existing forms and the decomposition of new forms of gender subordination.

There are small scale qualitative studies on women garments workers in Bangladesh based on in-depth interviews analysing intra-household power relations (Kibria, 1995; Kabeer, 1997; Khundker, 2001). Others have used questionnaire survey to look into intra-household relations (Zohir and Paul-Majumder 1996; Afsar, 1998). But none of these studies relate systematically to male-female differences in many cases over a time period to see how the intra-household relations have changed. The minimum legal age of admission to employment in Bangladesh has been variously defined as between the age of 12 to 16 years of age under different labour laws. But to facilitate international comparisons, analysis in this study will refer to persons aged 15 years and above.

On the other hand, various surveys have shown that migrant workers have dominated the garment industry in Bangladesh. The BIDS 1990 survey showed 83% of the male workers and 69% of the female workers originated from the rural areas (Zohir and Paul-Majumder, 1994).

Existing studies also focussed on causes and processes of female labour migration. Some of the studies examined the impact of women's entry into formal sector employment on their status (Zohir and Majumder, 1995, Afsar, 1995). The literature on rural to urban migration in developing countries describes migrant adjustment to urban life as a problematic process. (Stark, 1976; Baden, 1993; BIGWUP, 1999). Their adjustment is heavily influenced by two basic tasks: obtaining a suitable job and finding accommodation. Considering the fact that many migrants had few or no economic resources for establishing themselves in the new factory and urban environment, it is important to focus on their adjustment process. More so because RMG factories started purely with profit motive in Bangladesh, and Dhaka city remained largely ill- equipped to house female migrants and respond to their needs.

On the other hand, the country side of Bangladesh is no longer confined to food production but is now a source of labour for urban areas (Toufique and Turton, 2002). Even since the emergence of the RMG sector as the major employer of the female labour force in the urban areas, a few number of studies are conducted on this sector and the female labour (Chaudhury and Curlin, 1975; Chaudhury, 1978; Islam and Begum, 1983; Hossain & Bar, 1988; Afsar, 2000; Hossain et. al. 2003). On the background characteristics of female labour some of these studies suggest that more than 90 percent of the garment factory workers are migrant from rural areas and the bulk of them (three-quarters) migrated from land-less families. These studies demonstrated that female labour migration still remained a first generation phenomenon and it is important to know women from rural landless families are coping with rapidly changing urban sector.

Migration is one of the major contributors to urban growth in Bangladesh. Study on the internal migration clearly demonstrated that greater job opportunities in the cities and metropolitan areas "pulled" migrants from rural areas (Skeldon, 1997; Hugo, 1991).In the past century, the urban population grew by about 35 million, an increase of more than three-fold (from 28.2 million to 103.1 million). Rural areas are still home to most of the total population. Migrant accounts for about two-third of the urban growth seen in Bangladesh since independence. The proportion of people living in urban areas rose from 6.2% in 1965 to 9.9% in 1975 and reached 25% in 2000 (UN, 2002).

It is widely believed that in the Indian Sub-Continent including Bangladesh, women's autonomous migration from rural to urban areas is low, compared to Sri Lanka and South East Asian countries, largely due to low economic growth and rigid norms of Purdah (Yousef, N., Buvinic and Kudet, 1979; Findely and Williams, 1991). Notwithstanding such a negative image, with the emergence of the RMG sector, there has been a boost in independent migration by young women in Bangladesh. This is reflected in the urban sex-ratio and specially that of metropolitan cities, which became more balanced in 1994 (Mitra et.al.1994) from being male dominated in the previous census years 1991 and 1981 (Afsar, 1995). For example, the sex ratio of the Dhaka city dwellers declined from 150 to 105% between 1961 and 1993-94. Particularly, the sex ratio obtained for the 15-34 age group in the urban poor agglomerations, where the large majority of the garment factory workers live has gone more in favour of women, from 103 to 65% between 1991 and 1996 (Thwin et. al.1996). While describing the restrictive role of Purdah in Bangladesh, Cain et. al.(1979) observed that Purdah restrictions on the movement of outside home excluded them from access to such economic opportunities as paid agricultural work and petty trading. However, empirical studies done in 1980s and 1990s (Rothschild & Mahmud, 1989; Afsar, 1990, 1996) suggest class differences in women's participation as wage labourers. While alluding to the role of poverty in breaking Purdah and enhancing women's mobility, elsewhere Afsar wrote (1998) "In Bangladesh, seclusion of women was observed in the case of landless families only. For the large majority of landless families, women always contributed to families income, whether directly through harvesting or indirectly through post-harvest and other income generating activities." Thus, when the demand for female labour was generated through RMG sector as a result of export promotion by the private entrepreneurs, it was met with the help of loyal kinship network support from landless families of the village who are either kin members or neighbours or embedded in a patron-client relationship with the entrepreneurs. On the above literature review regarding social context, the studies did not come forward to investigate working condition, changing characteristics of the workers, their health conditions, migration and adaptation process of female migrants from rural areas to Dhaka city as well as recommendations on the above issues of RMG industry in Bangladesh.

2.4 International Regimes in Textiles and Clothing and Association of Bangladesh

As the domestic productions and exports of any country are affected by the development in international environment, it is indispensable that the country is abreast of these evolutions absolutely. Specially, it is demanding in the context of complex features of international regimes in RMG industry. The present review touches all these developments from the time before World War II to the integration into WTO under the Agreement on Textile and Clothing.

2.4.1 Historical Development

It is extensively believed that India is the birth place of the cotton manufacture where this industry stayed in a high state of perfection at least three thousands years ago (Ellision, 1968). It is also factual that the industrial revolution was mainly the revolution of the cotton industry in Britain (Blokker, 1989). Moreover, cotton industry in Japan witnessed a rise in mid-eighteenth century followed by other East Asian States. It is therefore, obvious that expansion of textile and clothing industries was not ubiquitous. In this context, here we will concentrate only on the historical development of textiles and clothing from the perspectives of innovations of devices, its expansions and Bangladesh association.

2.4.2 Chronological Innovations and Devices in Textiles and Clothing Industries

Historical evidence dictates that the "Charka" was the first hand mill which was utilised to make cotton threads in India in ancient past beyond known history and at that time cotton was cleaned from dirt by means of vibrating bow and the term "bowed cotton" has been derived from it.[36] Again the term "manufacture" has been originated from the time of "arrival of a number of Flemish immigrants during the reign of William the Conqueror" and the "art of spinning and weaving wool were introduced into England by the Romans."[37] The Spartacus Internet Encyclopedia home page about the British History (1700-1950) supplements that the handloom was devised about 2,000 years ago. But these were primeval innovations which couldn't assist in a faster process with large output. At a later stage, "after the invention of the fly-shuttle by Mr. John Kay, of Bury, in 1738", the weavers could turn out twice as much cloth as before in a given space of time.[38] The improved variety of this primitive wheel was the "spinning jenny" invented by James Hargreaves in 1764.[39] Before this innovation, in 1730, John Wyatt created a device which was known as spinning by rollers and it provided a footing to Richard Arkwright's "spinning-frame" in 1768. Later, this spinning frame was perfected at a mill at Cromford, Derbyshire in 1771 that took up the name "water frame."[40] In fact these two machines Spinning-Jenny and the water-frame initiated a new era in the history of cotton trade as well as cotton manufacture, as a separate and distinct industry.

Unifying the principles of both Hargreave's Jenny and Arkwright's water-frame machine, called "mule", was devised in 1779 that enabled production of finer and more uniform yarn. After that, Dr. Cartwright invented a power-loom in 1785.[41] Moreover, abreast the development of spinning and weaving, technological development also took place with the invention of cylinder printing by Bell of Glasgow, in 1783.[42] Innovations did not come to an end rather it continued in other segments of textile industry. For example, in 1748, a carding machine was brought out by Lewis Paul of Birmingham to replace the hand one, which was improved upon by Mr. John Lees of Manchester, in 1772.[43] As these developments so far were not entirely flawless, Mr. Roberts, in 1825, patented the new "self-acting mule" which eliminated the difficulties of earlier one and

---

36 "International Regulations of World Trade in Textiles", Neils Blokker, Published by Martinus Nijhoff Publishers, 1989. P.4

37 Ibidem p.4

38 Ibidem p.15

39 Ibidem p.19

40 Ibidem p.19

41 Ibidem p.20

42 Ibidem p.24

43 Ibidem p.20

its refined variety came out in 1830. Almost concurrently, a very important improvement was made in the "water frame" whereby the quality of the yarn spun was improved, the quantity produced increased, and the cost of production diminished. The new machine was called "Throstle."[44]

The Woollen Industry was established in the Middle Ages.[45] At that time, this industry used home-grown wool where production was based on the domestic system. Leeds in Yorkshire then became the centre of such product market. On the other hand, opening of silk production dates back to ancient China. Subsequently, the art of producing silk cloth reached France, Spain and Italy in the 12th century. The weaving of silk was introduced to England by Flemish refugees in the 16th century and was greatly developed after 1685 when the Huguenots from France established themselves at Spitalfields in London. The main centres of the silk industry in England in the 16th century were London, Coventry and Norwich[46]. More recently, silk loom was invented by Joseph Jacquard in the early 19th century, who was a silk weaver in France and with the widespread application of this loom in the 1820s imparted the textile industry a tremendous boom in Britain[47].

In addition, since the Second World War three types of technical change have had an important impact on the textile industry. These are rapid progress in transportation and telecommunication combined with the development of mass retailing that facilitated the global rise in production and distribution of clothing, astounding advancement in synthetic fibre technology that revitalised the textile industry in developed countries in the 1960s and early 1970s, and important process innovations such as introduction of rotor spinning and shuttle looms, increased automation in various stages of production etc. Specially, computerised production management and application of microelectronics to new machinery became prominent by the end of 1970s, which increased the capital-intensive character of the textile industry leading to a shift in competitive advantage between developed and less-developed countries. A citation regarding such advancement in spinning in the US textile industries would be noteworthy as below[48]:

"The development of open-end (OE) spinning technology in the 1960s started a new era in yarn manufacturing. This advance provided spinners the opportunity to increase output per production unit by more than two-fold. Current OE systems operate at rates six times that of ring spinning, while the newer air jet systems are more than eight times as fast."

---

44 Ibidem p.32

45 "The Textile Industry, The Spartacus Internet Encyclopedia, The British History 1700-1950" Op. Cit (www.spartacus.schoolnet.co.uk/Textiles.htm)

46 Ibidem

47 Ibidem

48 "American Association of Textiles Chemist and Colourists" (AATCC) homepage at www.aatc.org/may 1997/p29-35

2.4.3 Expansion of Textile and Clothing Industries

Manufacturing process, in general, appeared in Italy in the fourteenth century. By the middle of the sixteenth century it was established in Germany, Prussia, Saxony, and the Netherlands. A little later came England, France followed in the seventeenth century and Russia in the eighteenth (Ellision, 1968). This development in manufacturing is not anything discrete from the development in the textile and clothing industries because, as mentioned earlier, the industrial revolution of Britain in eighteenth century was basically the revolution of textile and clothing industries. However, an interesting feature of this development in this sector is that it was not ever escalating in a country as mentioned by Blokker (1989):

"World manufacturing production doubled between 1911-13 and 1936-38; the increase in world textile production was less than 40 per cent during this period. After the Second World War, this trend continued; whereas in all market economies, in 1953, production of textiles amounted to 13.6 per cent of total manufacturing production, this share had decreased to 8.7 per cent by 1980." (GATT, 1984)

Again Blokker (1989) added that this decline in developed countries is tagged with a rise in Japan, East European and less developed countries, as it carried out almost the same take off function that occurred previously in developed market economies (Noman, 1940), which resulted in a slump in textile exports from developed market to domestic markets of these new producers (Jurgen, 1983). A confrontation of textile industries in developed market economies cropped up with textile products of the new comers[49] in other markets as well as in their own domestic market (Maddison,1969, Aspand & Edward, 1997).

In a cyclic order, these newcomer countries share of textiles in total production of manufacturers also dropped between 1953 and 1980, in Japan from 18.1 per cent to 5.8 per cent and in the group of less-developed countries from 30.3 per cent to 16.0 per cent. Only for Africa this share rose (GATT, 1984). Now, we can move to scrutinise the reason behind this rise and fall in the relative importance of textiles and clothing industries. Certainly, it is linked to the shift in comparative advantage i.e. from labour intensive to capital intensive products of the concerned countries as their economy get matured with strides toward high-tech industries. According to this cycle, it could be anticipated that countries, like Bangladesh, would be turned to the similar competitive edge in textile and clothing industries for their comparative advantage in cheap labour provided that other relevant factors stay favourable.

---

[49] Taiwan, Hong Kong, South Korea, Singapore and later on Japan

2.4.4 Some International Developments Before World War II

As mentioned earlier, Japan achieved a spectacular growth between the two world wars and it began to export cotton textile products at this time. But these exports were soon confronted with a number of restrictions: in 1936, they were subjected to quantitative restrictions in 40 out of 106 markets apart from protective and discriminatory tariffs and exchange control measures.[50] Particularly, Japan had to conclude some arrangements "under the American threat to take more restrictive unilateral measures if no agreement could be arrived at". Another agreement between the US and Japan was concluded in 1935 on the condition of Japanese control of exports of cotton fabrics to the Philippines which was then ruled by the United States (Blokker, 1989. p. 90).

2.4.5 International Textile Trade Policies Before 1960

After the Second World War, liberalized framework of GATT and of the OEEC (Organisation for European Economic Co-operation) facilitated diminution in restrictions in international textiles trade. But North America and West Europe harvested the benefits stemming from this liberalization. In contrast, restrictions on imports from Japan, East European countries and many less developed countries turned out to be, in many instances, "more restrictive in the course" of the 1950s (GATT,1984 p.63). Although less "developed GATT members were allowed to bring in restrictions under Article XVIII [51] of the General Agreement to stimulate import substitutions, the upsurge of cotton textile production in these countries entailed in enhanced exports to developed countries, obviously raising confontration with the products of developed countries in the international markets as well as in their domestic markets." Therefore, developed countries "defended in a way or other their domestic cotton textile industry that asked for protection".

Most West European countries invoked provisions of the General Agreement in Article XIX[52] of GATT, 1994. Moreover, "the cotton trade association" of Germany, Austria, Belgium, the Netherlands, Italy, France, Switzerland and Norway concluded in 1958 the so called "Noordwijk Agreement", with a view to check "undermining of existing quotas through re-exporting to other participating countries of grey cloth, admitted temporarily on a duty- free basis for finishing" (Aggarwal, 1985). On the other hand, the US "took up the same arms

---

50 Monthly Record, Manchester Chamber of Commerce, 30th September 1936.

51 "Government Assistance to Economic Development" through imposing tariff protection and quantitative restriction to stimulate import substitutions in the less developed countries allowed by the contracting parties to GATT, 1994.

52 Permitting importing countries to take the safeguard measures (tariff and quotas) under certain condition. when domestic producers suffers serious injury from increased imports to justify quantitative restrictions on their textile imports.

as before the war" i.e. Voluntary Export Restraints (VERs) to restrict cotton textile imports from Japan (1st VER November 1955 and 2nd VER 1956) and Italy (Velveteen exports to the US for 1957) and an abortive attempt with Hong Kong. Thus, imports from Hong Kong increased while the same from Japan stabilised. However, "Hong Kong had to pay its price later, when it became the main target" for new American restrictions during the Short- Term Arrangements.[53] After the Second World War, British industry[54] asked for protection and during 1959-1960 the British government reacted positively to this call agreeing to the Lancashire Pact.[55] Selective restrictions, thus, were effective against low priced imports of cotton textiles starting off from "newcomers" both within as well as outside the framework of GATT. Ultimately, "selective safeguard measures" entered the GATT legal order in 1961, when the Short-term Arrangement entered into force.[56] Thus, The General Agreement on Tariffs and Trade was the only multi-lateral legal framework governing world trade in textiles from its provisional entering into force in 1948 until 1961.[57]

2.4.6 Textiles and Clothing Arrangements from 1961 to 1973

The Short-Term Arrangement (STA) and the Long-Term Arrangements (LTA) were concluded in 1961 and 1962 respectively to set up separate rules for international trade in cotton textile and in 1973, the Multi-fibre Arrangement (MFA) extended this special treatment to trade in textiles produced from man made fibres and wool.[58] These arrangements swerved from the General Arrangement principally in two fundamental aspects. These are quantitative restrictions were allowed and these restrictions could be introduced on a discriminatory basis. But these textile arrangements "never covered all world trade in textiles. Never all textile exporting and importing countries were party to the arrangements."[59] Moreover, apart from these textile arrangements, there were some other trade policy instruments that were different from textile arrangements but could affect the world trade in textiles and had their legal basis as well. These are tariffs, preferential tariffs (by virtue of Generalised Systems of Preferences, GSP), sub-

53 Blokker (1989) Op.CIt. p 96.

54 The British cotton textile industry had traditionally enjoyed a commanding position but it shrank extremely. In the nineteenth century, "it exported 75% of world exports, in 1913 50%, and in late 1950s the UK became a net importer of cotton textiles." (Blokker, 1989, p. 97)

55 A series of inter- industries agreements affecting imports from Hong Kong, India and Pakistan. In agreeing to this Pact the British Government not only violated the General Agreement, it also contravened the Ottawa Agreement, containing the preferential system of the Commonwealth countries. Op.CIt. (Blokker, 1989, p. 97).

56 Blokker (1989),Op.Cit, p. 97

57 Ibidem, p.41

58 Ibidem, p.2

59 Ibidem

sidies and countervailing duties, and anti- dumping duties.[60] Again, agreed cotton textile arrangements obviously diverged from the basic rules of the GATT i.e. non- discrimination, prohibition of quantitative restrictions and particular Articles XIX, (as mentioned earlier). The first objective of the 1961 arrangement was "to provide growing opportunities for exports of these products provided that the development of this trade proceeds in a reasonable and orderly manner so as to avoid disruptive effects in individual markets and on individual lines of production" while the second objective was "to facilitate economic expansion and in particular to promote the development of the less-developed countries by providing increasing access for their exports of manufactured products."[61] Again, both the STA and LTA encompassed only cotton textile products, which is contrary to the Multi- fibre Arrangement (MFA) as it incorporated man- made fibres and wool too. The 1961 arrangements were effective for one year. Thereafter, LTA came into force on October 1962 and remained in force for five years. Later, LTA was extended three times without any amendment to its basic rules. The first two Protocols extended the LTA each by three years and the third extension was only for three months to let the MFA emerge in 1974.[62]

2.4.7 The Multi-fibre Arrangement (MFA) from 1974 to 1994

As mentioned in the preceding paragraph, the MFA commenced its drive in 1974. MFA-I remained in force for four years with effect from 1 April 1974 and MFA-II from 1978 to 1981 followed by MFA-III continued for four years and seven months and then MFA-IV covered the period from 01 August 1986 up to 01 August 1991.[63] The MFA terminated on 31 December 1994 upon the entry into force of the WTO and its Agreement on Textiles and Clothing from 1 January 1995.[64] During the period of 21 years, from 1974 to 1994, the MFA experienced numerous amendments with regard to new provisions and new products. Moreover, six per cent growth rate in quotas, as predicted in the MFA, "was in many cases sharply reduced in practice in bilateral agreements."[65] With reference to the objectives of the MFA, Article 1.2 from its text read as :

"The basic objectives shall be to achieve the expansion of trade, the reduction of barriers to such trade and the progressive liberalisation of world trade in textile products, while at the same time ensuring the orderly and equitable development of this trade and avoidance of disruptive affects in individual markets and on individual lines of production in both importing and exporting countries."[66]

---

60 Ibidem, p.3
61 Ibidem, p.109
62 Ibidem, p.117
63 Ibidem, p.163
64 World Trade Organization (WTO), homepage www.wto.org
65 Ibidem
66 Blokker (1989), p.157

From this Article it appears that the first main objective, trade liberalization, encompasses three more precisely defined objectives, i.e. to achieve the expansion of trade; to achieve the reduction of barriers to such trade and to achieve the progressive liberalization of world trade in textile products. Again, the second main objective in it may be splited into two objectives: ensuring the orderly and equitable development of this trade; ensuring the avoidance of disruptive effects in individual markets and on individual lines of production in both exporting and importing countries. Obviously, these two objectives are partly conflicting. In addition, Article 1.3 contains a third main objective, namely to promote the development of less developed countries which reads as following:

"A principal aim in the implementation of this Agreement shall be to further the economic and social development of developing countries and secure a substantial increase in their export earnings from textile products and to provide scope for them in world trade in these products."[67]

The third main objective also breaks down into three more detailed objectives, i.e. to further the economic and social development of the developing countries; to secure a substantial increase in their export earnings from garments products; to provide scope for a greater share for them in the world trade in these products. This is also conflicting. Through restrictions of quota in developing countries, who have higher potential for export, found contracted market in developed countries which appears in disparity to the objective of economic and social development of developing countries owing to trim down of their export earnings.In relation to the Product Coverage allowed under MFA Article 12.1 of the MFA stipulates as follows[68]:

"For the purpose of this Arrangement, the expression "textiles" is limited to tops, yarns, piece-goods, made-up articles, garments and other textile manufactured products (being products which derive their chief characteristics from their textile components) of cotton, wool, man-made fibres, or blend thereof, in which any or all of those fibres in combination represent either the chief value of the fibres or 50 per cent or more by weight (or 17 per cent or more by weight of wool) of the product."

As mentioned earlier, MFA had larger product coverage than its predecessors STA and LTA. It covered not only cotton textiles, but also, as mentioned earlier, man-made fibres and wool. In addition, handloom textiles from less developed countries were excluded from the scope of MFA. The MFA, like the preceding cotton arrangements, granted provisions for "the imposition of quotas, either through bilateral agreements or unilateral actions, when surges of imports caused market disruption or threat thereof in importing countries" whereby importing countries were required to discuss with exporting members "both in determining a situation of market disruption" as well as introducing and maintain-

67 Ibidem, p.158
68 Ibidem, p.161

ing restrictions.[69] Normally, importing countries allowed "annual growth rate of six per cent in the quotas" and a statutory body, the Textiles Surveillance Body (TSB), was entrusted with monitoring and reporting functions and settlement of disputes.[70] Ironically, application of the MFA was not even handed. WTO homepage provides further that "apart from restrictions on former state trading countries, the MFA was used almost exclusively to protect against imports from developing countries". But Switzerland and Japan were exceptions. Although these two countries were parties to the MFA, "they had no restraint agreements" and "Sweden dropped all of its restraints and withdrew from the MFA in 1991."[71]

2.5 Research Gap

It is quite clear that a number of studies conducted so far in the field of Bangladesh readymade garments industry have covered different aspects, but global trade liberalization as well as impact on the RMG sector are very limited in number. Majority of these studies are referred to were either related to general textiles and clothing industry or about a particular situation of the industry but none of them were specific in solving global trade liberalization problems and little attempt has been made to study the various impacts like economic, social and legal aspects as a whole. Their findings did not reveal the impact on this industry. In the view of the limitations of these studies and the developments that have recently taken place at the national and international levels, the underlying reasons need to be explored as their remains a gap for making a study of the global trade liberalizaton, trade and industrial policy in garments sector, trade performance of Bangladesh in readymade garments and possible economic and social effects as well as policy recommendations.

2.6 Concluding Remarks

The discussions made in this chapter clearly show that Bangladesh has been at the forefront in the last decade in embracing prescriptions for trade liberalization as Bangladesh is a signatory to the WTO rules and the WTO rules required its members to remain steadfast in the path of trade liberalization. The development of world textiles and clothing industries through the ages obviously triggered the opportunities for its trade in the international arena. The textile and clothing industries has traversed a long way of its development through diverse innovations in its vast domain. From 'Charka' to 'automation'-it's really an astounding progress. As an LDC, Bangladesh has not been entirely familar with the latest tech-

69 Ibidem, p.163
70 WTO Homepage, www.wto.org
71 Ibidem

nologies. On the other hand, the rapid growth of readymade garment industries in Bangladesh since the mid 1980s has generated considerable female labour migration and their employment in the formal export-oriented manufacturing sector. Now, before we turn to the Bangladesh perspective in textiles and clothing sector, it is imperative that we look into the experience of other contemporary leading countries. The next chapter would, therefore, focus on the methodology of the study.

CHAPTER THREE
METHODOLOGY OF THE STUDY

3.1 Introduction

This study is concerned with global trade liberalization and its impact on Bangladesh garments industry. The study is exploratory in its basic nature. But while analysing certain decision variables it is descriptive and suggestive as well. The overall design of the study follows the steps of setting objectives, defining scope, and specifying methodology.

3.2 The Objectives

The clothing products of Bangladesh, at present, have restricted and reserved access (quota) to the readymade garments (RMG) markets of developed countries, particularly the, United States and the European Union. From 01 January 2005, as per the provisions of WTO Agreement on Textile and Clothing (ATC), garments and textile manufacturers of Bangladesh will have to cope with steep competition from such countries as India, Pakistan, China, Thailand, Taiwan, and Vietnam, from which Bangladesh now imports raw materials to satisfy the demand of its textiles and clothing sector. All these countries will be able to inflate their RMG exports, now limited by quotas, when the WTO establishes its free market in 2005. Consequently, these countries are likely to utilise more of their locally produced yarn and fabrics internally, resulting in the rise of prices for such raw materials. As Bangladesh imports such materials from these countries, the rise of prices may have many impacts on the textiles and clothing industry of the country, as well the whole economy of Bangladesh. Another important reason for growing concern for this sector is that it opened up a huge opportunity for labour specially the women in Bangladesh to be gainfully employed. The garment industry alone employs about 73 percent of working women in the formal manufacturing sector of Bangladesh. Considering the above two types of scenario, this study has been undertaken with the following objectives:

1. To review the evaluation of readymade garments industry in the context of Bangladesh macroeconomic indicators
2. To present an overview of international trade in textiles and clothing
3. To examine the implications of globalizations and international trade policy regimes for textile and clothing
4. To review the current Bangladesh RMG industry condition
5. To examine the competitive positions of Bangladesh in the global market
6. To analyse the changing characteristics of the workers as well the conditions of workers

7. To analyse the changing characteristics of labour force
8. To understand the female migration process, motives and adaptation.
9. To see the in-depth case studies on RMG industries
10. To drawing upon the major findings as well recommendations and policy implications in view of the above objectives

3.3 Hypotheses

It is assumed that several of the policy decisions and strategic actions have been playing a key role in the trade liberalization and its impact on the readymade garments industry in Bangladesh. The extent and kind of this impact made by these hypotheses is to be considered while analysing the economic as well social aspects. In order to analyse, examine and explore the above objectives, following (null) hypotheses will be always in my mind when writing of this study.

- Global trade liberalization doesn't impact on the Bangladesh economy in the context of readymade garments industry of Bangladesh.
- Global trade liberalization doesn't impact on the social aspects of the workers in the context of readymade garments industry of Bangladesh.

3.4 Research Design

The research design is consists of scope of the study, the methodology, the approach, data sources and method of collection and analysis of data and literature. These are as follows:

3.4.1 Scope of the study

The scope of the study is limited in terms of two aspects

- The liberalization of trade in the context of Bangladesh readymade garments industry and
- Social dynamics and migration issues in context of growth of garments industry in Bangladesh.

The liberalization of trade and the Bangladesh RMG industry consists with the relevant Bangladesh general macro-economic indicators and the international regimes in textiles and clothing and association of Bangladesh (already partly discussed in the literature chapter). These are the situation before World War II, international textile trade policies before 1960, textiles and clothing arrangements from 1961 to 1973, the Multi-fibre arrangements (MFA) from 1974 to 1994, effects of Multi-fibre arrangements and Bangladesh, The agreement on textiles and clothing (ATC) under GATT and Bangladesh, Trade policy instruments of the European Union, United States, and Japan, Regional trade blocs, US Trade and Development Act 2000, world production and Bangladesh performance with current Bangladesh RMG conditions and finally impact on

Bangladesh garments industry. On the other hand, household dynamics and the growth of garments industry is another concern i.e. social dimensions of the RMG 1995-2000, female labour migration and urban adaptation as well the impact of garments work on quality of life measures are being considered.

3.4.2 Methodology

The present study is based on certain objectives as mentioned earlier. In the light of these objectives the techniques of investigation to be adopted, tools have to be used and the pattern of statistical analysis have to be followed. Both the descriptive and the analytical techniques have been used in the course of study. The statistical tools are to be applied at the social aspects of the study while the economic aspects are totally based on secondary data from both the national and international sources.

Figure 3.1
The Approach

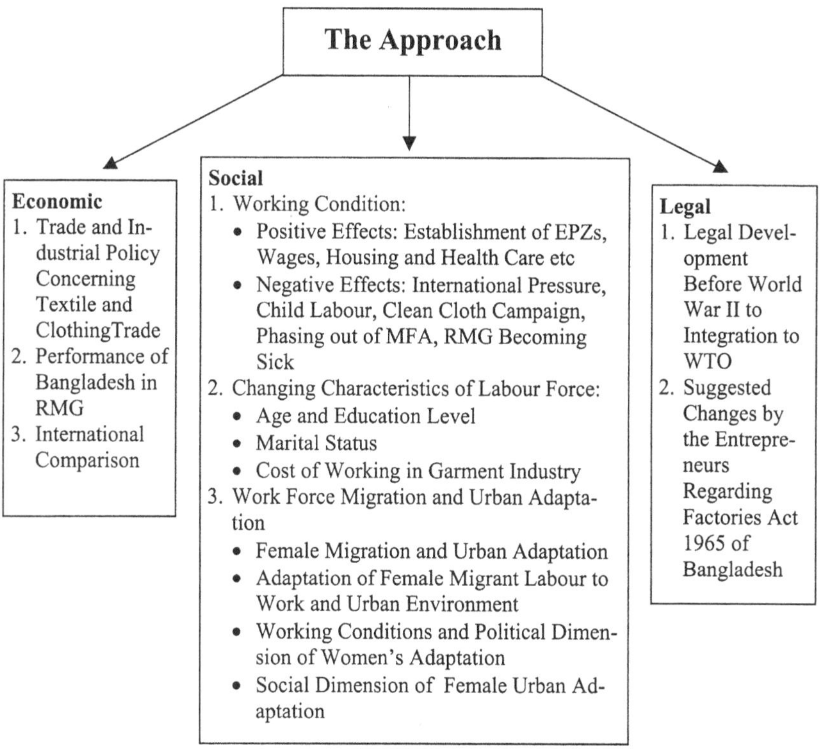

3.4.2.1 The Approach

With a view to achieving the objectives of the study mostly secondary data have been used. However, the major reliance on secondary data and published and unpublished materials available both at national and international level. The data has been culled out from research reports, market surveys, feasibility studies, seminar papers, journals, bulletins, newspapers and specialised studies made by private as well as semi-government government and international bodies.

The books, acts, annual reports, agreements, directories, arrangements, speeches at national parliament, budgets, trade commissions and statistical year books were consulted to supplement the available information. Very recent data and the latest information regarding trade liberalization and the impact on the Bangladesh garments industry as well as world market conditions were discussed and have been collected from the Internet sources.

3.4.2.1.1 Economic Analysis

A major concern of the study is economic analysis, which is based on trade and industrial policy in garments sector related with trade performance of Bangladesh, industry structure of RMG, its contribution in the economy, global market analysis, market access of Bangladesh and the world etc.

3.4.2.1.2 Social Analysis

Another major concern of the study is social analysis. Mostly it is based on the garments workers' positive and negative effects of working conditions, i.e. establishment of export processing zones, wages, housing, health care, issue of child labour, non-formal education, earn and learn programmes, changing characteristics of labour force, education and marital status, access to income, participation in decision making, household conflicts and co-operation incidence of illness, modes of commuting, motives of female labour migration and adaptation, income spending and savings, health and well-being and policy implications.

3.4.2.1.3 Legal Framework

As the domestic production and exports of any country are affected seriously by the developments in international environment, it is indispensable that the country is abreast of those evaluations absolutely. Specially it is demanding in the context of complex features of international regimes in textiles and clothing. Legal framework touches all these developments from the time before World War II to the integration into World Trade Organization (WTO) under the Agreement on Textile and Clothing (ATC), i.e. Short term agreement (STA) and Long term agreement (LTA), The Multi-Fibre Arrangements (MFA), The

Agreements on Textiles and Clothing (ATC), EU, US and Japan trade policy instruments, regional trade blocs, along with its impacts on Bangladesh. However, a list of existing labour laws concerning garments industry and suggested changes by the entrepreneurs (the entrepreneurs were asked to give their opinion on them) have been duly incorporated at appropriate places.

3.4.3 Data Sources and Method of Collection

With a view to collect and know the information and data about global trade liberalization and Bangladesh readymade garments industry, I used the secondary sources of data by reviewing available literature from both national and international level.
The necessary quantitative and qualitative information has been obtained from the secondary sources at both national and international level. The main sources are :

3.4.3.1 National Level

Ministry of Textiles (MOT), Dhaka, Bangladesh
Ministry of Commerce (MOC), Dhaka, Bangladesh
Ministry of Planning (MOP), Dhaka, Bangladesh
Export Promotion Bureau (EPB), Dhaka, Bangladesh
Bangladesh Bureau of Statistics (BBS)
Bangladesh Garments Manufacturers and Exporters Association (BGMEA)
Bangladesh Textiles Mills Association (BTMA)
Institute of Fashion Technology (IFT)
Bangladesh Institute of Development Studies (BIDS)
Government of Bangladesh Annual Budget
Bangladesh Bank (BB)

3.4.3.2 International Level

World Bank
World Trade Organization (WTO)
General Agreement on Tariffs and Trade (GATT) Secretariat
Global Trade Analysis Project, USA
United States Development Agency, Foreign Agricultural Service
The World Trade Analyzer
The Economist
International Finance Corporation (IFC)
Joint International Weather facility (USDA/NOAA)
The United States International Trade Commission (USITC)
United Nations Monthly Bulletins of Statistics
United Nations Industrial Development Organization (UNIDO)

Country Commercial Guide (CCG), US Embassy, Dhaka
Ministry of International Trade and Industry, Japan
The General Agreement on Tariffs and Trade (GATT)
United Nations Conference on Trade and Development (UNCTAD)

Besides the secondary sources, some first hand information has also been collected from the primary sources through in-depth interviews and discussions with garments workers, exporters, entrepreneurs, experts, Bangladesh garments manufacturers and exporters' association and government agencies. The discussions with them proved helpful and some relevant suggestions were very appreciative which have been duly incorporated at appropriate places. In fact all these primary sources of data were tapped only to fill the gap in secondary data.

3.4.4 Analysis of Data and Literature

In order to analyse, process and present the available data from both levels, I followed the principles of quantitative and qualitative methods. Wherever necessary, various statistical measures such as sample, surveys, in-depth interviews, quota sampling as well multi-stage random sampling procedure have been applied for analysis and interpretation of data. However, some narratives about the female factory workers' perspective on the factory work, migration, problems of living in the city and other issues have been incorporated. The details of data analysis have been discussed in the social dimensions chapters of the study.

3.5 Case Studies

In order to get insight about the Bangladesh readymade garments industry both from woven and knit sectors, five case studies have been undertaken. Each of these case studies cover a wide range of issues, namely type and nature of business, management, employee strength, production, export, product range, export market network, sourcing of raw materials, problems and types of raw- materials, changing pattern of raw materials, problems and critical issues and impact on trade liberalization.

3.6 Limitations of the Study

The data and the literature related to trade liberalization and garments industry have been gathered in a truly scientific specification. Therefore, the present study should not be considered as a mathematically accurate measure of the problem studied. Findings might be verified and tested through further conclusive investigations. The main limitations of the present study are:

1. It was difficult to collect all the necessary data from the grass-root level. Although I tried my level best but the latest information on the world production, world consumption and world demand could not be obtained.

2. Different sources of information give different data, hence there was no uniformity in the data. Frequently, the data are of poor quality and inconsistent. For example, the data on the RMG consumption of local fabric provided by BTMA (supplier) and BGMEA (consumer) differ by almost 100 per cent. On the other hand, government and private sector decisions based on unreliable data could be counter-productive. For overcoming this problem, I have to depend on international sources.
3. As far as the scope of the study is concerned, the study has covered only garments industry concerning the trade liberalization which is selected in the present scenario. Given the scope of the study a broader treatment of every aspects of other industries was not possible. Thus the real picture of total impact of Bangladesh trade liberalization is absent here.
4. Five case studies on the selected woven and knit RMG industries have revealed the true picture of the management, production, export, import and their concern about trade liberalization is duly incorporated in the relevant chapter. But in-depth case studies on the labour is absent in the study. Thus the total picture about the RMG industry was not possible.
5. Most of the export and import organisations regarding RMG industry neither publish the information nor do they allow the outsiders get an access to their records, internal working etc. on the pretext of maintaining secrecy. This restricts the data availability.

3.7 Concluding Remarks

With the above objectives and research methodology as well limitations in mind now, we can look into the economic and social implications of trade liberalization in the readymade garments industry in Bangladesh. In this context, chapter four is, therefore, aimed at the international trade and industrial policy toward textiles and clothing sector of Bangladesh.

CHAPTER FOUR
TRADE AND INDUSTRIAL POLICIES TOWARD TEXTILES AND CLOTHING

4.1 Introduction

International trade involving textiles and clothing represents a classic example of managed trade. Bangladesh is one of the few developing countries which have emerged as significant exporters of clothing within a short-period of time. During the last decade or so, Bangladesh has substantially liberalized its trade regime, moving away from costly protectionist policy toward a more export-friendly trade regime. The current industrial policy (1999) and the export policy (1999-2002) have identified the textile and clothing sector as the trust sectors in Bangladesh. On the other hand, during the 1974-94 period, international trade in textiles and clothing were negotiated bilaterally and govern by the rules of Multifibre Arrangement (MFA). Anyway, it should be noted that only a part of international trade in textiles and clothing were governed by MFA. International trade in textiles and clothing among developed and among developing countries were outside the scope of the MFA. Some developed countries such as Japan and Switzerland were members of MFA, but did not maintain quotas (Islam 2001, Wohn, 2001). However, before looking the Bangladesh situation in the RMG sector, present chapter touches all the developments from the MFA to ATC and the EU, US, China and Japan's trade policy instruments concerning textiles and clothing including regional trade blocs.

4.2 International Trade in Textiles and Clothing: An Overview

International trade in textiles and clothing has changed substantially since 1980.

Table 4.1
World Trade In Textiles and Clothing: Selected Years

SITC[72] Codes	1980	1990	1997
26 (Textiles fibres)	19,124.0 (.95%)	23,077.4 (.66%)	25,468.6 (.45%)
65 (Yarn, fabrics, made-up articles)	57,091.0 (2.83%)	113,455.7 (3.27%)	167,210.9 (2.95%)
84 (Articles of apparel)	39,621.0 (1,97%)	110,603.0 (3.19%)	195,934.0 (3.45%)
Total (26+65+84)	115,837.0 (5.57%)	247,136.9 (7.12%)	388,613.0 (6.85%)

Source: The World Trade Analyser.
Note: Figures in parentheses are percentages of total world trade.

[72] SITC codes refer to the Standard International Trade Classification

Table 4.1 represents data on world trade in (1) textiles fibres, (2) yarn, fabrics, made-up articles; and (3) apparel for selected years.

As reported in Table 4.1, the share of textiles fibres in the world declined from .95% in 1980 to .45% in 1997. In contrast, the share of apparel increased from 1.97% in 1980 to 3.45% in 1997. The share of yarn, fabrics and made-up articles increased from 2.83% in 1980 to 3.27% in 1990 but declined to 2.95% in 1997. Table 4.2 presents data on market shares of developing countries and the composition of textiles and clothing exports from developing and developed countries. It can be observed easily from Table 4.2 that the market shares of developing countries increased for (1) textiles fibres, (2) yarn, fabrics, made-up articles, and (3) clothing. The share of developing countries in yarn, fabrics and made-up articles increased substantially from 31.60% in 1980 to 49.22% in 1997. The market share of developing countries in apparel rose from 50.84% in 1980 to 64.47% in 1997. Table 4.2 also reports data on the composition of textile and clothing exports for developing and developed countries. For the developing countries, the proportion of textile fibres declined significantly during the 1980-97 period, while the proportion of clothing increased from 44.2% in 1980 to 57.77% in 1977.

Table 4.2

Developing Countries in World Trade in Textiles and Clothing

A. Market Shares of Developing Countries (%)

SITC CODES

Years	26 (Textiles fibres)	65 (Yarn, fabrics, made-up articles)	84 (Articles of apparel)
1980	38.64	31.60	50.84
1990	38.53	41.29	59.34
1997	39.31	49.22	64.47

B. Composition of Textile and Clothing Exports From Developing Countries (%)

SITC CODES

Years	26 (Textiles fibres)	65 (Yarn, fabrics, made-up articles)	84 (Articles of apparel)	Total
1980	16.22	39.58	44.20	100
1990	7.33	38.60	54.08	100
1997	4.58	37.65	57.77	100

C. Composition of Textiles and Clothing Exports from Developing Countries (%)

SITC CODES

Years	26 (Textiles fibres)	65 (Yarn, fabrics, made-up articles)	84 (Articles of apparel)	Total
1980	16.70	55.58	27.72	100
1990	27.65	38.60	33.75	100
1997	9.09	49.95	40.96	100

Source: The World Trade Analyser

The proportion of yarn, fabrics, and made-up articles has changed little. For developed countries, the composition of exports presents a different picture. For these countries, the dominant category is yarn, fabrics and made-up articles. The share of this category declined from 55.58% in 1980 to 38.60% in 1990 but increased to 49.95% in 1997. It is noteworthy that the share of clothing increased from 27.72% in 1980 to 40.96% in 1997. However, table 4.3 presents data on the network of trade in textiles fibres for selected years.

Table 4.3
Network of Trade in Textile Fibres (millions of US $ and in %)

From /To Countries	Developing Countries	Developed Countries	All Countries
A. 1980			
Developing Countries	3,310.3 (44.80%)	4,079.5 (55.2%)	7,3989.8 (100%)
Developed Countries	5,661.5 (48.25%)	6,072.8 (51.75%)	11,7734.3 (100%)
All Countries	8,971.8 (46.91%)	10,152.3 (53.09%)	19,124.1 (100%)
B. 1990			
Developing Countries	4,941.2 (55.58%)	3,949.7 (44.42%)	8,890.9 (100%)
Developed Countries	5,976.2 (42.13%)	8,210.4 (57.87%)	14,186.6 (100%)
All Countries	10,917.4 (47.31%)	12,160.1 (52.69%)	23,077.5 (100%)
C. 1997			
Developing Countries	6,656.1 (66.48%)	3,356.8 (33.52%)	10,012.9 (100%)
Developed Countries	8,729.7 (56.48%)	6,726.0 (43.52%)	15,455.7 (100%)
All Countries	15,385.8 (60.41%)	10,082 (39.59%)	25,468.6 (100%)

Source: The World Trade Analyser.

As reported in this table (Table 4.3), inter-developing country trade in textile fibres increased during the 1980-97 period. In 1980, 44.8% of exports of textile fibres from developing countries were destined for developing countries. The figure increased to 66.48% in 1997. The table also shows that in 1997, 56.48%

of exports of textile fibres from developed countries were destined for developing countries.

In Table 4.4, the same pattern can be observed for yarn, fabrics and made-up articles: the share of developing countries in exports of yarn, fabrics and made-up articles from developing countries went up from 52.39% in 1980 to 65.01% in 1997.

Table 4.4
Network of Trade in Yarn, Fabrics and Made-up Articles
(millions of US $ and in %)

From /To Countries	Developing Countries	Developed Countries	All Countries
A. 1980			
Developing Countries	9,450.3 (52.39%)	8,587.9 (47.61%)	18,038.2 (100%)
Developed Countries	11,638.4 (29.92%)	27,370.3 (70.08%)	39,053.7 (100%)
All Countries	21,133.7 (37,02%)	35,958.2 (62.98%)	57,091.9 (100%)
B.1990			
Developing Countries	29,336.6 (62.62%)	17,510.7 (37.38%)	46,847.3 (100%)
Developed Countries	15,383.6 (23.1%)	51,224.9 (76.9%)	66,608.5 (100%)
All Countries	113,455.8 (39.42%	44,720.2 (60.58%)	68,735.6 (100%)
C. 1997			
Developing Countries	53,506.3 (65.01%)	28,800.9 (34.99%)	82,307.2 (100%)
Developed Countries	29,332.0 (34.55%)	55,571.6 (65.45%)	84,903.6 (100%)
All Countries	167,210.8 (49.54%)	82,838.3 (50.46%)	84,372.5 (100%)

Source: The World Trade Analyser

Inter developing country trade in yarn and fabrics is dominated by East Asian countries (Islam, 1996). Furthermore, in 1980, about 29.9% of exports of this category from developed countries were destined for developing countries. The figure decreased to 23.1% in 1990, but rose again to 34.55% in 1997.

In order to explore the international division of labour concerning textiles and clothing, it is useful in examining not only international trade in these products but also trends in production in the relevant sectors across different regions. Table 4.5 shows trends in index numbers of production of textiles and wearing apparel and leather products.[73] In North America, the quantity of output of textiles shows an upward trend. The upward trend in textiles in North America may be included by the NAFTA. For wearing apparel and leather products, no clear trend is evident. By contrast, in Europe and Caribbean, Central and South America levels of output in both sectors show a downward trend. In Asia, the index of output shows an upward trend for textiles but a downward trend for wearing apparel and leather products.[74]

Table 4.5
Index Number of Production of Textiles and Wearing Apparel and Leather Goods

1990=100

Year	Textiles					Wearing apparel, leather and footwear				
	NAm.	Euro	Asia	Ccs.	World	NAm.	Euro	Asia	Ccs.	World
1989	103.1	113.5	97.0	104.8	101.3	103.4	110.0	100.7	108.0	104.5
1990	100.0	100.0	100.0	100.0	100.0	100.0	100.0	100.0	100.0	100.0
1991	98.8	91.5	103.1	104.0	100.8	97.9	94.3	100.3	96.9	97.90
1992	107.1	84.0	104.9	101.7	102.2	99.5	88.8	97.4	95.5	95.50
1993	112.7	75.7	103.3	97.2	101.1	101.6	83.0	92.6	97.7	93.60
1994	118.8	69.3	105.8	101.0	104.6	104.1	77.0	89.4	100.0	94.10
1995	119.1	66.1	108.8	96.9	105.4	104.2	74.0	87.4	94.2	93.10
1996	117.9	61.4	113.3	99.5	106.2	101.8	70.3	85.1	96.6	91.10
1997	122.0	62.6	116.5	98.5	109.3	100.3	68.1	81.5	96.3	89.30
1998	122.2	61.4	112.2	94.9	106.9	96.7	65.0	74.8	96.3	85.60

Notes: NAm: North America
Euro: Europe
Ccs: Caribbean, Central and South America
Source: Monthly Bulletin of Statistics, November, 1999, United Nations

[73] Data on wearing apparel excluding leather products were not available from the Monthly Bulletin of Statistics. The weight of leather products is considerably smaller than that of wearing apparel.

[74] The data for Asia include Japan. If Japan is excluded, textiles in Asia would show a strong upward trend and the downward trend in apparel would be much less pronounced.

4.3 Explanation of the WTO Agreement on Textiles and Clothing

After the Second World War, liberalized frameworks of GATT and of the OEEC (Organisation for European Economic Co-peration) facilitated the diminution in restrictions in international textile and clothing trade. But North America and West Europe harvested the benefits stemming from this liberalization. In contrast, restrictions on imports from Japan, East European countries and many less developed countries turned out to be, in many instances, more restrictive in the course of the 1950s (GATT, 1973 & 1984) The Agreement on Textiles and Clothing is a transitional trade regime from 1995 to 2005. Before explanation of the WTO agreement on textiles and clothing, we have to concentrate on the MFA (Multi-fibre Arrangement).

4.3.1 The Multi-fibre Arrangement (MFA) from 1974 to 1994

As mentioned in the preceding paragraph and also in the chapter two, the MFA commenced its drive in 1974. MFA I remained in force for four years with effect from 1 April 1974 and MFA-II from 1978 to 1981 followed by MFA-III continued for four years and seven months and then MFA-IV covered the period from 01 August 1986 up to 01 August 1991 (Blokker, 1989). The MFA terminated on 31 December 1994 upon the entry into force of the WTO and its Agreement on Textiles and Clothing from 1 January 1995 (WTO, 1995). During the period of 21 years, from 1974 to 1994, the MFA experienced numerous amendments with regard to new provisions and new products. Moreover, six per cent growth rate in quotas, as predicted in the MFA, "was in many cases sharply reduced in practice in bilateral agreements" (WTO, 1998a). MFA sets terms and conditions for governing the imposition of quantitative restrictions on textile and clothing exports of developing countries either through negotiations or bilateral agreements or on unilateral basis. It promises that freer trade under the strengthened GATT rules and disciplines will increase annual world income by more than US$ 500 billion by the year 2005 (Table 4.6). It has also been postulated that the revenues of developing countries as a group from exports of textiles and clothing are likely to rise when MFA is phased out, despite the loss of the quota rents that accrue to exporting countries under MFA. Several studies indicate that effects of removing MFA quotas and reducing tariffs on textiles and clothing products increase in the value of imports of textiles and clothing by 244 per cent in the United States, 214 per cent in Canada, and 264 per cent in European Community (ITC of US 1999). A UNCTAD study (1986), for example, found that complete non-discriminatory liberalization trade involving both tariffs and MFA quotas could increase the developing country exports of clothing by 135 per cent, and textiles by 78 per cent. An earlier study by Kirmani, Molajani and Mayer (1984), found that developing country exports to the major OECD countries could increase by 82 per cent for textiles, and 93 per cent for clothing if tariffs and quota restrictions are removed. Some recent studies suggest that with the elimination of both MFA quota and tariff restrictions, developing country exports of textiles and clothing will increase substantially.

Table 4.6
Estimates of the Annual Benefits of Uruguay Round Trade Liberalization (in billion of US $ at 1992 prices)

Model/variant	Year	World	Industrial	Developing
WTO (Francois, McDonald, Nordstorm)				
A. Static, perfect competition	1992	40 (0.17)	27 (0.16)	13 (0.30)
A. Static Imperfect competition	1992	99 (0.44)	40 (0.23)	59 (1.23)
B. Induced Investment, Imperfect competition	1992	214 (0.94)	90 (0.50)	125 (2.6)
World Bank (Harrison, Rutherford, Tarr)				
A. Static,perfect competition	1992	93 (0.40)	75 (0.41)	18 (0.38)
D. Static, imperfect competition	1992	96 (0.42)	77 (0.42)	19 (0.42)
E. Induced Investment, Imperfect competition	1992	171 (0.74)	115 (0.61)	55 (1.20)
GATP (Hertel, Martin, Yanaiahima and Dinaranan)				
Liberalization in projection to 2005, Perfect competition	2005	258 (0.89)	172 (0.72)	86 (1.56)

Notes: a: Percentages of GDP in parentheses
b: Definitions of developing countries differ slightly between models
Source: Reproduced from Martin and Winters (1996)

According to Yang et. al. (1997), exports from MFA exporters (developing countries) to MFA importers (industrialised world) would increase by 26 per cent for clothing and 10 per cent for textiles. Trela and Whalley (1990) estimated that individual developing countries could increase their exports by 190 per cent to 305 per cent if both quota and tariff restrictions were removed.

4.3.2 Explanation of Agreement of Textiles and Clothing (ATC)

The WTO Agreement on Textiles and Clothing (ATC) has been concluded by the member states for a period of ten years (1995-2004). It is a transitional instrument step into the quota free trade in the international market. But it will not be the duty free regime, for which further negotiations might be necessary. The ATC has been framed by the following key facets:[75]

(a) The product coverage, basically encompassing yarns, fabrics, made-up textile products and clothing;
(b) a programme for the progressive integration of these textile and clothing products into the GATT 1994 rules;
(c) a liberalization process to progressively enlarge existing quotas (until they are removed) by the increasing annual growth rates at each stage;
(d) a special safeguard mechanism to deal with new cases of serious damage or threat thereof to domestic producers during the transitional period;
(e) establishment of a Textiles Monitoring Body (TMB) to supervise the implementation of the agreement and ensure that the rules are faithfully followed; and
(f) other provisions, including rules on circumvention of the quotas, their administration, treatment of non-MFA restrictions, and commitments undertaken elsewhere under the WTO's agreements and procedures affecting this sector.

ATC provides for the elimination of the quotas and the complete integration of textiles and clothing into the WTO regime over a 10 year period ending on January 1, 2005. All WTO members are subject to ATC disciplines, and only member countries are eligible for the ATC benefits. In contrast only 55 countries were members of MFA with only four members (Canada, European Union, Norway, and the USA) maintaining import restrictions. The product coverage of the ATC covers all products which were subject to MFA quotas. A number of products which were not covered by the MFA have been included in the ATC, such as umbrellas and garments for dolls. The ATC provides for the elimination of the quotas through two mechanisms: product integration and acceleration of growth rates for quotas still in effect during the transition period. As specified in the ATC, WTO countries integrated 16 per cent of their textile and apparel imports into the WTO regime on January 1, 1995, and another 17 per cent on January 1, 1998, based on the 1990 import volume. The ATC requires the importing countries to integrate another 18 per cent in 2002 and the remaining on January 2005. The TMB reported that all the products integrated by the importing developed countries in the first stage were not subject to quotas. The TMB also stated that during the first and second stages together lower value-added goods (such as yarns, and fabrics rather than apparel and made-up goods) accounted for 76% of the import volume integrated by the European Union, 65% for the United States, 60% for Norway, and 47% for Canada.

---

[75] The Agreement of Textile and Clothing (ATC,), WTO home page (http.://www.wto.org/english/tratope/textie/texintro.htm downloaded on 23 October, 2000

For products still under quota during the transition period, the ATC required importing countries to increase the quota growth rates for major supplying countries by 16% on January 1, 1995, 25% on January 1, 1998 and by another 27% in 2002. For small suppliers (countries accounting for 1.2% or less of an importing country's total quotas in 1991), quota growth rates were increased by 25% in 1995 and 27% in 1998. The increased quota growth, known as the growth on growth provision has significant implication for the market access of textiles and clothing. For instance, with a MFA quota growth of 7% for Bangladesh in the US market, quota growth was 8.12% by January 1, 1995, 10.15% by January 1, 1998 and 12.9% by 2002. The ATC allows WTO countries to set new quotas during the transition period on imports of goods that are yet to be integrated into the WTO regime and which are not already under quota through the transitional safeguard provision. In the application of safeguard provision, the least developed country members and the small suppliers shall be accorded favourable treatment.

Apart from the Agreement on Textiles and Clothing, the World Trade Agreements contain several features which have implications for textiles and clothing. The Agreement on subsidies concerning manufactured goods, in Articles 3.1 (a) prohibits subsidies contingent upon export performance and Article 3.1 (b) prohibits subsidies contingent upon the use of domestic over imported goods. The prohibition mentioned in Article 3.1 (a) however does not apply to a number of other developing countries which includes Bangladesh. This prohibition also does not apply to a number of other developing countries including Pakistan, India and Sri Lanka provided the levels of per capita GNP do not exceed US$ 1,000. Other developing countries shall phase out their export subsidies within a period of 8 years from the date of entry into force of WTO Agreement.

4.4 European Union Trade Policy Instruments Concerning Textile and Clothing

The European Union (EU) is the leading market for apparel. The share of the EU, including intra-EU imports, of world apparel imports in 1997 was 42%, compared to 47.5% in 1990. As in most other industrialised countries, the textiles and clothing industries account for a declining share of EU manufacturing value added and employment. However, textiles and clothing remain important in certain local areas in such countries as Italy, Spain, Portugal, Belgium, France, U.K. and Germany. Import penetration for textiles and clothing in the EU increased substantially during the last 15 years.

The main trade policy instruments concerning exports of textiles and clothing to the EU are quotas and tariffs. Currently the EU maintains 209 quotas on textiles and clothing from 21 countries including 5 non-WTO countries. The WTO countries facing quota restrictions include India, Pakistan, Sri

Lanka, Indonesia, Thailand and Vietnam. The EU imposes no quotas on textiles and clothing from least developed countries including Bangladesh. However, three product groups (4, 6 and 8 according to the combined nomenclature code) from Bangladesh are subject to the system of double-checking surveillance. Category 4 includes knitted shirts, T-shirts, and certain other products belonging to Harmonised System (HS) chapter 61. Category 6 includes men's and women's trousers and shorts made from cotton or man- made fibres, covered in HS chapter 62. Category 8 includes non-knitted men's shirts made from cotton or man-made fibres. In 1998, only 33 out of 209 quotas were used by 95% or more. During the same year, products under quota represented about a quarter of the textiles and clothing imports into the EU. The European Union has opted for a stage-by-stage approach toward integration of textile and clothing in the WTO framework, unlike other members (e.g., the United States) which has submitted a programme for the entire transition period. The EU notified the second lists of products for integration, effective from January 1, 1998 representing 17.99% of 1990 import volume covered by the ATC. In the second list, tops and yarns accounted for 11.63%, fabrics for 2.22%, made up goods for 2.06%, and clothing for 2.09%. Thus far the EU has not invoked the transitional safeguard mechanism to prevent import surges. However, the EU has taken anti-dumping actions affecting textile products such as polyester yarns and fibres, with 24 measures in force.

The European Union has a common external tariff policy. The average applied advalorem tariff rates in 1999 for knitted apparel (HS chapter 61) and non-knitted apparel (HS chapter 62) were 12.3% and 12.4% respectively. The average tariff rates on fabrics covering HS chapters 58, 59, and 60 range from 6.8% to 9.9%. The GSP of the EU, unlike that of United States covers textiles and clothing and provide tariff concessions to eligible developing countries. Furthermore, eligible textiles and clothing from the least-developed countries[76] under the GSP or under the Lome convention [77] enter the EU duty free, with restrictions linked to rules of origin. From January 1999, the EU has relaxed rules of origin for textiles and apparel. The new GSP is based on a two-stage derogation for knitwear and one stage derogation for woven garments, instead of a three-stage, respectively. Knitwear manufacturers in Bangladesh can therefore buy yarns abroad and woven garment markets can buy fabrics produced with foreign yarns. The new GSP rules are likely to increase Bangladeshi garment

[76] Bangladesh belongs to the least-developed countries

[77] The European Union and the ACP (African, Caribbean and the Pacific) countries have recently concluded an agreement to replace the Lome convention. There are 39 least developed countries among the 71 ACP countries. The new agreement has signed in May 2000 in Fiji, and is known as the Fiji convention.

exports to the EU. However, the new rules would have adverse effects on Bangladeshi yarn manufacturers.[78]

In the recent years, a major phenomenon has been the rapid rise of bilateral trade between the EU and the countries in Central and Eastern Europe, and the Mediterranean region, reflecting the growing importance of out-ward processing trade (OPT). The OPT with these regions more than doubled in value during 1990-97. This type of trade, similar to that of the production-sharing provision in the United States, consists of exporting fabric to low-cost labour countries to be made into finished apparel for re-import into the EU, with EU tariffs applied on the value-added only. Consequently, while the market share of big suppliers of East Asia and China have declined, the shares of Poland, Turkey, Tunisia and Morocco have increased in the EU. In 1997, the OPT accounted for about 17% of total EU external trade. About 70% of OPT imports originate in the Central and East European countries. Germany and Italy are the major users of the OPT provision, accounting for 58% and 11% of EU OPT apparel imports in 1997. For Germany, more than two thirds of total trade in textiles and clothing products with the Central and East European countries are part of OPT. The tariff difference for imports from the Central and East European countries and imports from other countries is significant. For instance, while imports of textiles and clothing from Poland, Bulgaria, Hungary, Romania, the Czech Republic, and the Slovak Republic have entered duty-free since January 1, 1997, imports from MFN sources were subject to average tariff rates of 9% and 12% respectively. There are now EU-wide rules and quotas for OPT, with harmonised rules of origin.[79]

The European Union established, in 1996, a Customs-Union agreement with Turkey, which allows Turkey to export textiles and clothing to the EU duty-free. The EU has concluded a free-trade agreement with Mexico in November 1999. According to the agreement tariffs on Mexican goods will be eliminated before 2003. This is likely to further promote foreign investment in the textiles sector of Mexico and help transforming Mexico into a world textile production centre. The EU has started free trade negotiations with Mercosur countries.[80] Although belated, the European Commission on 20 September, 2000 adopted a ground breaking plan to provide full access to the world's 48 poorest countries. The proposal would cover all goods except the arms trade. This initiative pioneered by the EU in the run up to the WTO Ministerial meeting in Seattle in 1999 could go beyond all previous community commitments. The proposal reflects the Union's belief that all WTO members can and should benefit from

---

78 "Quota system Bangladesh to face 1m job in RMG sector", reported by Bangladesh News Agency available at http://www.nation.ittefaq.com/artman/publish/article_1258.shtml, downloaded on May 12, 2003.

79 WTO, Trade Policy Review of the European Union, 1998

80 Argentina, Brazil, Uruguay and Paraguay

trade liberalization. The EU signed an agreement in June 2000 in Cotonou Benin with African, Caribbean and the Pacific (ACP) countries triggering a process that will ensure free access for essentially all products from all the LDCs[81] by 2005 at the latest. On the other hand, the EU has initiated negotiations with 12 countries of Central and Eastern Europe and the Mediterranean region which are interested in joining the EU. In the EU 2002 summit, EU have taken decision that 10 Eastern and Central European countries will join the EU in 2004. Imports of textiles and clothing from many of these countries already enter duty-free. However, accession of these countries to the EU is likely to promote further trade and investment relations involving the current EU members and the new member countries. On the other hand, phasing out of MFA will pose serious threat to the textile and apparel exports from the LDCs like Bangladesh. It will lead to huge losses of employment, resulting in adverse socio-economic impacts on LDCs. Bangladesh has raised these issues while representing the LDCs in the May 5-6, 2003 global conference on the future of textile and clothing, organised by the EC in Brussels. In that conference, Bangladesh urged the European Commission to introduce a new GSP (Generalized System of Preference) with relaxed rules of origin for LDCs, and devise an effective capping mechanism for protecting the market share of apparel exporting LDCs.[82] The rules of origins adopted by Switzerland and Norway are exactly the same as those of the EU. To satisfy the rules of origin the goods have to be either wholly produced in the beneficiary country or they must have undergone working or processing criteria laid down in the regulations.[83]

4.4.1 General Principle of Generalized System of Preferences (GSP)

According to the GSP rules, the Generalized Tariff Preferences (GTP) are granted by the community to certain products originating in developing countries based on the following conditions (except where the products are obtained in the community countries):

a) Products wholly obtained in the country such as mineral products, vegetable products, live animals or products obtained from live animals, product ob-

---

81 Least Developed Countries (LDC) is used by UNDP to identify the countries having lowest GNP per capita. In the 'World Development Report 1998-99' of the World Bank , 'low income' economics refer to the countries with GNP per capita US $ 785 or less. The LDCs are the countries with the lowest GNP per capita of this group.

82 "Impact of Quota Elimination on Developing Countries and Strategies for Industrial Restructuring" A conference on Future of Textile and Clothing held at the European Commission in Brussels in May 5-6, 2003, available at http://www.dailystarnews.com/200305/12/n3051205.htm, downloaded on 15th May, 2003.

83 Generalized System of Preferences: The Swiss Scheme, Federal Office for Foreign Economic Affairs, Bern, Switzerland , 1998

tained by hunting or fishing, sea fishing or other products taken from the sea by its vessels or products, made thereof in factory ships etc.

b) Products obtained in that country in the manufacture of which products other than those referred to in a) are used, provided that the said products have undergone sufficient working or processing.

It may be noted that working or processing carried out in the country must go beyond minimal operations such as assembling of different parts of garments into sets or sample mixing of salt and water into saline solution. In case of processed articles of textiles (RMG) if the fabrics are manufactured in a third country and RMG are made in GSP beneficiary country, it is a non-originating product. But in case where yarn, fabrics and RMG are processed and manufactured in GSP beneficiary country, it is an originating product.

For the purpose of distinguishing between non-originating and originating products the EU has prepared a Logical Tree work which is presented in a diagram. (Figure 4.1)

Figure 4.1

RECAPITULATION- LOGICAL TREE

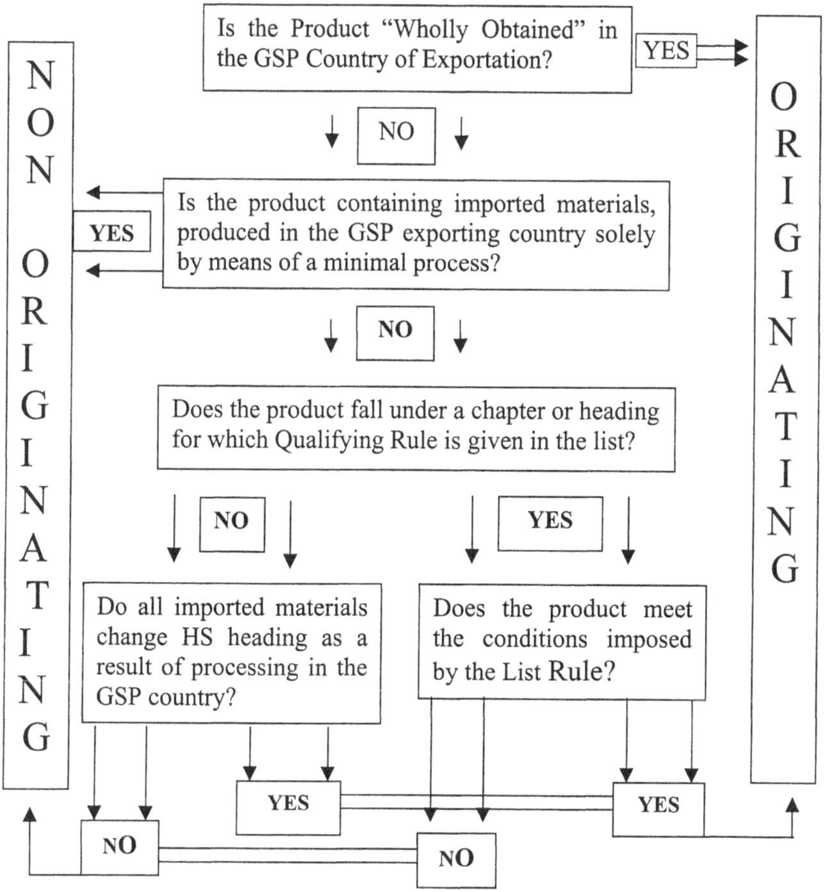

4.4.2 Main Features of GSP

Generalized System of Preferences (GSP) is a commercial policy instrument by the EU which allows preferential treatment to developing countries by giving "Tariff Preferences" to the product exported from the developing countries over those from the developed countries. This allows exports from developing countries an easier access to the community markets. Its aim is to promote industrialization in the developing countries through allowing opportunities for diversification of their export and thereby increasing their export and income. Thus, it is found that GSP provides commercial advantage and gives priority to community importers and thereby this encourages them to import from the developing countries. GSP also provides exporters easier access to community markets.The community provides assistance through trade promotion and extends technical and financial co-operation to the partners in the developing countries.

4.4.3 Preference for Least Developing Countries (LDCs)

Consequent upon commitments made in 1967, in the Tokyo Round, the community has accorded special treatment to the countries designated by the United Nations as "The Least Developed" of developing countries. Under the programme, besides majority of such countries, which are beneficiaries under the LOME Convention, special arrangements have been made for countries like Bangladesh, Afghanistan, Yemen, The Maldives, Nepal, Bhutan, Myanmar, Laos and Cambodia. These LDCs arrangements encompass exemption from all preference limits for industrial and textile products, and also for a large number of agricultural products.

4.4.4 Rules of Origin

Generalized System of Preferences (GSP) is subject to strict rules with regard to the origin of products seeking benefits through the export to EC countries. Detailed legislation has been enacted which has been adopted by the EC after assent of a Regulatory Committee (Committee of Origin) which provides for the Rules of Origin of products and also control mechanism. In a situation where two or more countries are involved in a manufacture of products, the country which finally exports the goods in question to the EC can only benefit from the GSP provided the manufacturing undertaken is sufficient to be considered as the country of origin. The processing can be considered sufficient if it gives rise to change in tariff heading HS Code between the imported item and finished products. However, there are numerous exceptions to this rule, which involve supplementary or alternative processing conditions, expressed either by a description of the type of processing or in terms of a maximum percentage of imported matter. There are special provisions which permit derogation from these conditions where a good has been subject to successive processing within a regional group of beneficiary countries. The aim of these provisions, known as regional cumulation, is to encourage the regional integration of the developing countries.

4.4.5 SAARC Cumulation and GSP Issues with European Union

In the new system, if a fabric of any SAARC (South Asian Association for Regional Co-operation) country is used in the making of garments in Bangladesh, the RMG products, if exported to the EU countries, will receive the duty-free GSP facility if certain other conditions are met. Originally, Bangladesh, as a member of LDCs, enjoyed a facility of tariff reduction while exporting its commodities in EU markets including RMG products. The condition was that these garment products would be made from yarn and then fabrics produced both in the country and 12.8 per cent tariff reduction would be accorded in doing so. But this system did not bring much benefit to the country as a few entrepreneurs used indigenous fabrics. The SAARC Secretariat, therefore, requested EU headquarters to provide SAARC cumulation facility under which fabric would be imported from any SAARC countries, in contrast to the earlier case, instead of obligatory domestic production. The condition here was that 12.8 per cent tariff reduction facility would be provided if local value addition to any product were more than 50 per cent. Otherwise, this privilege would be reduced to 15 per cent of that 12.8 per cent i.e. overall 1.92 per cent. The SAARC cumulation came into effect on October 1, 2000.

Now, according to the SAARC Cumulation proposal, the government of Bangladesh is under tremendous pressure from two conflicting groups. The Bangladesh Garments Manufacturers and Exporters Association (BGMEA) stands in favour of SAARC cumulation while the Bangladesh Textile Mills Corporation (BTMC) resists the move on ground that SAARC cumulation would seriously impair the growth of backward linkage industry in the country which is regarded as extremely important to survive in the post-MFA era, starting from January 01, 2005. However, a recent World Bank study reveals that the prospects of benefits accruing to Bangladesh RMG sub-sector from SAARC cumulation is very scanty.[84]

4.5 United States Trade Policy Instruments Concerning Textiles and Clothing

The United States is a leading exporter as well as importer of textiles and clothing. The share of the United States in the world apparel imports in-

[84] The Daily Ittefaq homepage, a national daily of the country in Bengali 27 January, 2001 issue, available at http://www.ittefaq.com/current/special/news3.pdf, downloaded on January 28, 2001.

creased from 16.4% in 1980 to 22.9% in 1997. The US trade deficit in apparel amounted to over $40 billion dollars in 1997. Imports now supply more than 50% of the US apparel market and are likely to continue to increase as quotas as gradually eliminated. During 1993-97, US consumer spending on apparel has increased faster, at an average annual rate of 5.5%, than overall consumer demand, which increased at the rate of 2.8%. In recent years, because of increasing imports, a number of phenomena are occurring in the textiles and apparel sector of the United States: (1) restructuring operations in the form of consolidations of production, divestiture of non-core product lines, mergers, and acquisitions; (2) increased global sourcing, including the use of assembly operations in Mexico and the Caribbean countries, (3) adaptation of the quick response manufacturing, marketing, and distribution systems; and increased power of big retail companies which are taking on production responsibilities in their private level product lines (Dickerson, 1999).

4.5.1 Historical Cotton Production in the United States

Southern parts of the United States are cultivating cotton and textile products for many years. This part comes up as a historical location of cotton production of the country, which, in turn, is corroborated by the literature in Hammond (1897) as "of the original thirteen states of the American Union, the only two which have become great cotton producing regions are South Carolina and Georgia."[85]

As of December 2000 (MY 2000/2001), an estimate of USDA shows that the country's total production of cotton is 3,778,000 metric tons, being the second highest of the world. In addition, as revealed by the time series data in Table 4.8, US cotton has augmented its production in the late 1990s although a decline is noticed in 1998/99. Again, United States import figures are very less as compared to those of exports. The United States introduced new rules of origin for textiles and apparel on July 1, 1996, to prevent the avoidance of U.S. import quotas by foreign suppliers which were dividing their production operations among various countries.[86]

85 "The Cotton Industry: An Essay in the American Economic History", by M.B. Hammond, Ph.D., Macmillan Company, New York, 1897, p.11

86 The WTO is carrying out a programme on harmonising non-preferential rules of origin to be applied by all member countries. However, the programme has not been completed yet.

Table 4.7
United States Cotton Production, Yield, Supply and Utilization
(In Thousand 480-Lb.Bales, MY 1966-2000/2001)

Mktg. Year	1.000 Hec.	Yield Kg/Ha	Beg. Stocks	Product.	Import	Total Supply	Con-sump	Loss	Exports	Ending Stocks
1966/67	3,866	538	17,028	9,555	105	26,688	9,574	(62)	4,832	12,344
1970/71	4,514	492	5,843	10,192	37	16,072	8,204	(232)	3,897	4,203
1975/76	3,560	508	5,708	8,302	92	14,102	7,250	(140)	3,311	3,681
1980/81	5,348	453	3,000	11,122	28	14,150	5,891	(335)	5,926	2,668
1985/86	4,140	706	4,102	13,432	33	17,567	6,413	(154)	1,960	9,384
1990/91	4,784	711	3,000	15,505	4	18,509	8,657	(285	7,793	2,344
1995/96	6,478	602	2,650	17,900	408	20,958	10,647	(27)	7,674	2,609
1998/99	4,324	701	3,887	13,918	443	18,248	10,401	(436)	4,344	3,939

Source: USDA, Foreign Agricultural Service, 2000

Under the new rules, the country of origin for apparel assembled in the country from parts cut to shape in another country would be the country where assembly occurs, rather than the country where the cutting took place, as was the case under the rule 1985 rules of origin. Under the previous rules, for instance, major Asian suppliers such as Hong Kong, Taiwan, and South Korea could cut garments in their home countries and send cut pieces to be sewing in lower-wage neighbouring countries like China. The product then could be shipped to the United States using the home country's quota. However, elimination of quotas by the year 2005, may lead to relocation of various textile components in different countries. The new rules led to trade dispute between the European Union and the United States, because these rules restricted export of silk scarves from the European Union made from Chinese fabrics. The United States agreed to allow an exception for silk goods but the relevant bill is yet to be passed by the US Congress (Aspand & Edward, 1997).

The principal trade policy instruments of the United States affecting textiles and clothing are quotas, tariffs, and rules of origin. The United States currently has import quotas on textiles and apparel from 47 countries, of which 37 are WTO members. For Mexico, the only quotas now in place cover non-originating textiles and apparel which contain non-NAFTA materials. The quotas for non-originating goods from Mexico will be phased out by January 1, 1995 as specified by ATC. Under the 1985 United States-Israel-Free-Trade-Area-Agreement, the two countries phased out all tariffs and quotas involving apparel and other industrial goods over a ten year period. With the passage of US Trade and Development ACT-2000 (TDA-2000) US Congress has made duty free and quota free access for 48 countries of Sub Saharan Africa (SSA) and 24 countries of the Caribbean Basin. Among these 72 countries, 34 countries are Least Developed Countries (LDCs). Due to this decision, another 14 LDC countries including Bangladesh are deprived from the advantage. It is important to remember that US TDA-2000 came into existence following the North American Free Trade Agreement (NAFTA) which granted Mexico an unrestricted access to the US market and allowed her to increase her share in US apparel market from 4.6% to 14.1% over a six year period between 1994 to 2000.

4.6 Japan Trade Policy Instruments Concerning Textile and Clothing

Japan is the third largest market[87] for textiles and clothing of Bangladesh, after the European Union and the United States. Japan's share of world apparel imports increased from about 3.8% in 1980 to 8.3% in 1997. The commencement of Cotton spinning machinery in Japan happened in the neighbourhood of 1866 while no machine method was adopted in cotton weaving until 1888. On the other hand, in the cotton weaving industry, the tempo of employment of the machinery was dawdling "that in 1894, at the time of Sino-Japanese War, which opened a new era in the industrial development of Japan, there were only 420 power looms in the entire country."[88] By the period of World War I, the cotton weaving industry had fostered a modern system of industrial organisation and could adopt large-scale production methods. Conversely, the spinning industry expanded very fast during the late 1880's which is substantiated by the data below.[89] "In 1886 there were 81,000 spindles in operation, producing 16,000 bales of yarn per annum. By 1890 there were 358,000 spindles, producing 108,000 bales of yarn. By 1896 there were 959,000 spindles, turning out 428,000 bales of yarn." This was a tremendous achievement in a remarkably short space of time.

However, the Japanese textiles industry began to develop intensely around 1887 and by 1894 as the dominant manufacturing industry in terms of using up of its product as well as the number of workers.[90] Japan embarked on exporting her cotton goods in the world market by the 1897 and the Japanese cotton industry, like Indian cotton industries, strengthened coarse cloth production rather than fine.[91] Thereafter, Japanese textiles industry, expanded further and in 1937, Japan possessed 215 mills in operation and the average number of spindles per mill was 57,482. Again, it is amazing that the size of an average mill in Japan

---

87 "MFA Phase out after 2004, Critical Challenges await the economy's thrust sector" available at www.independent-bangladesh.com/news/may15/15052003pd.htm

88 "The History of Early Cotton Industry in the Far East", In Stages of Industrial Development in Asia, A Comparative History of Cotton Industry in Japan, India, China and Korea. By Sung Jae Koh, Philadelphia. University of Pennsylvania Press, 1966

89 Ibidem p.23

90 Ibidem p.62

91 Ibidem p.61

was twice that of an average mill in India.[92] On the other hand, Japanese textile industry has responded to changing market conditions by shifting its product mix to more technologically sophisticated items and by upgrading products, particularly in new synthetic materials and high quality textiles. Another important facet of Japanese textile industries is its interior textiles.

Formal research efforts also stimulated the productivity in the textile. For instance, the Japanese textile industry exported 182 technologies and received more than 4 billion yen in royalties. More than 70 per cent of those technology exports were purchased by neighbouring Asian countries. Moreover, the Japanese textile industry has responded to changing market conditions by shifting its products mix to more technologically sophisticated items and by upgrading products, particularly in new synthetic materials and high quality textiles.[93] Another important facet of Japanese textile industries is its interior textiles, [94] the market size of which was US $ 3,775 million at 131 yen/$ in 1998.[95] In recent times, Japanese textile industries seem to be dwindling in terms of number of establishments, number of employment, exports which is evident from Table 4.8.

Table 4.8
Textile Industry (1985-99) of Japan (persons)

Year	No. Establishment	No. Employees	Value of Shipment
1985	35,424	609,462	8,086,962
1990	30,515	530,736	7,838,171
1995	16,045	264,528	4,230,099
1999	12,309	201,264	3,236,317

Source: Ministry of International Trade and Industry, Japan, 2000

In addition, Table 4.9 provides data on employment in the textile and clothing industries, which again exhibits the similar trend as the preceding one. This declining trend in employment might be imputed to the rising force in East Asia in these industries, namely, of Hong Kong, Taiwan, Korea and more recently China. China and Japan's parallel move to even high-tech industries is coupled with rising labour costs in its capital-intensive edge.

---

92 Ibidem p.111

93 "The Experience of Japan in the Historical and International Perspective" by Young-II Park and Kym Anderson, Cambridge University Press, 1992

94 Carpeting, curtains and other products

95 INTERIOR TEXTILES http://www.tradeport.org/ts/countries/japan/isa/isar0011.html Downloaded on 12 November, 2000.

Table 4.9
Employment in Japanese Textile Industries (000' persons)

Year	Mfg.	Man-made Fibre	Spinning	Weaving	Knitting	Dyeing and Finishing	Textile	Apparel
1990	11,788	25	57	141	192	102	625	621
1995	10,880	23	31	93	16	84	327	644
1998	10,399	19	23	76	14	70	272	544

Source: Ministry of International Trade and Industry, Japan 2000

In recent years, Japanese textiles companies have increased investments in Asian countries such as China and Vietnam. The leading apparel exporting countries to Japan are China, South Korea, Thailand, Hong Kong, France and Italy. China's market share in Japan for apparel increased from 14.1% in 1980 to 25.4% in 1997. The corresponding for South Korea are 15% and 23.2%. The market share of Thailand and Indonesia have increased substantially during the 1980-97 period: for Thailand from 2.0% to 10.9% and for Indonesia from 1.9% to 7.6%. It is instructive to note that Italy and France also have significantly increased their market shares of apparel in Japan. Italy's share increased from 2,6% in 1980 to 7.6 % in 1997, while for France, from 3.2% to 7%. The market share for Bangladesh in Japan's apparel imports in 1997 was only 0.6%. The market shares of India, Pakistan, and Sri Lanka in the same year were 2%, 0.6% and 1.1% respectively.

Japan has no quota restrictions, unlike the EU and the United States, on imports of textiles and clothing. However, Japan's markets are often characterised by informal non-tariff barriers involving unclear requirements and procedures, a complex distribution system, and technical barriers. The tariff rates on apparel in Japan range from 4.5% to 13.9%, while the rates on fabrics range from 4.2% to 12%.

4.6.1 The GSP Scheme of Japan

The government of Japan had initiated tariff preferences for selected industrial products including textiles on August 1, 1971. As per the GSP scheme of Japan (revised as of 1995) most of the RMG and clothing items and accessories are granted tariff preferences with quantitative ceilings. In order for goods exported from a preference-receiving country to be eligible for the preferential tariff treatment, they must be recognised as originating in that country under the origin criteria of the Japanese GSP scheme, and transported to Japan in accordance with its rules for transportation.

4.7 China Trade Policy Instruments Concerning Textiles and Clothing

China badly needs "hard currency export earnings" to purchase essential imports as well as for servicing China's sizeable foreign debt. As Chinese farmers are unlikely to put in much to the basket of foreign exchange earnings and the demand for mineral and energy products are likely to grow faster than domestic supply in China's industrial development process, textile and clothing industries contribution is crucial to its economic growth and development.[96] China ranks as the largest producer of cotton clothing and the second largest producer of synthetic fibres in the world. It is also believed that China is one of the most important producers and exporters of clothing and textiles in the world. China owned about 54,000 textile and clothing factories in 1995 of which more than 90% were small and medium sized enterprises (SMEs).[97] Some 80% of the fibres consumed in China in its textile and clothing is cotton.[98] In addition, other natural fibres such as wool, jute, mulberry worm silk, hair etc. are also used. Synthetic fibres constitutes a significant component in its total fibre consumption. Moreover, the textile and clothing industry in China provides opportunity for large employment. The industry employed 22.43 million employees in 1995. The total value of output was 703.5 billion Yuan RMB in the same year. As mentioned above, China's textile industry is mostly in the type of SMEs and so compatible the technology and the techniques are at the level of the Europe-American textile industries in the 1970s and 1980s. In spite of its rear position in technological advancement, the textile industry of China enjoys a competitive edge in the global market owing mainly to its "comparative advantages" in low labour costs, available raw materials, and low manufacturing costs.[99] Further, its domestic market is quite large due to the gigantic size of its population, more than 1.2 billion. Being a traditional industrial sector, detailed standards have been formulated in Chinese textile industry, specially raw material standards, yarn and fabric standards and clothing processing stands.[100]

The textile industry in China reached a stage by the middle of the eighteenth century through a "putting out" system.[101] By this system merchants could easily take a leading part in the further growth of the textile industry, providing the operating funds for the weavers and by providing a system to put out raw cotton as well as some other materials. Obviously, this method assisted the cotton producers and weavers at the time in these countries. But, unlike India and

[96] "Will China's experience be different?" by Kym Anderson. In: Anderson, Op.Cit, p. 197-98.
[97] "Profile of China's Textile Industry", available at http:// www.cestt.org.cn/acca21/online sercices/sectors/Textile%20Industry.htm, Downloaded on 15 October, 2000.
[98] Ibidem
[99] Ibidem
[100] Ibidem
[101] Sung Jae Koh, Op.Cit. p. 111

Japan, the merchant class in China was less likely than ever before to provide dynamic and progressive leadership to play a pioneer role in the development of textile industries.[102] Although the Opium War (1840-42) and the European industrialism and commercial activities exerted a thrust to traditional Chinese society, this external stimulus could in no way convert the merchants into industrial leaders.[103] The bureaucrats, therefore, began to emerge themselves as industrialists under the mountain pressure of foreign industrial development. Although they had a great role in the development of the modern textile and cotton industry in China, soon the bureaucratic industrialists revealed the management problems, such as the cost structure, the pricing of the product, and the profitability of the enterprise etc. Most of these mills eventually underwent change of ownership or failed altogether.[104] When the industrialisation was in progress in India and Japan in the 1850's and 1860's respectively, China lagged far behind of these two countries that successfully dominated the Chinese market and thereby stimulated their domestic industries. Moreover at that time, "China was opened to a flood of Western influence" and the Chinese government felt an urgent need to reinforce the industrial sector.[105] The first Chinese textile mill, however, was not erected before 1890 and by 1930, there were fifty-nine textile mills in Shanghai including thirty-two Japanese, three British and the rest Chinese (Blokker, 1989). Onward looking policies during the 1980s had led clothing industries of China expand very fast, and are becoming more dependent on imports of fibres. However, the emergence of China specially as a major exporter of textile products is now putting competitive pressure on Asia's advanced developing economics as well as adding pressure on manufacturers in high-income countries.[106] It is interesting that China has established "Hi-Tech-Parks" for China's textile industry (HPCT) which would impart, no doubt, a new momentum to China's textile and clothing.[107] As stated earlier, demand for natural fibres is increasing, notwithstanding the huge natural fibre production. It is therefore, perceived that, "expanded production and exports of finished textiles and standard clothing are leading to increased imports of fibres, both natural (from the United States and Australia) and synthetic (from Japan and newly industrialised East Asia)."[108] Further it is to be mentioned that China has already achieved the most difficult tasks required to emulate its East Asian neighbours.

[102] Ibidem, p.183

[103] Ibidem, p.221-222

[104] Ibidem, p.254

[105] Ibidem, p. 182

[106] Introduction and summery, by Kym Anderson in: Anderson, Op.Cit

[107] "International Hi-Tech Park for China's Textile Industry" U.C. Computer (Shanghai) Co. Ltd. 568 Ou Yang Road, Shanghai, 200081, P. R. China; Available at http://www.sh.com/zone/other/textile.htm, downloaded on 16 November, 2000.

[108] "Effects of China's dramatic reforms on its neighbours and on world markets", Kym Anderson and Young-II, Park, In: Kym Anderson (1992), p.48

Chinese raw cotton production, even earlier, during the period 1975-79 was a 14.8 per cent world total by volume and the same was 5.2 per cent for raw wool (Anderson, 1992). This obviously demonstrates China's continued dominant position in world fibre production from a far-off past. In the year 1996-97, China topped the list as cotton lint producing country. On a recent statistics of the USDA regarding textile production, supply and marketing by country, it is shown that China's stock up to December 2000 (Marketing year 2000/2001) was 2,276,000 MT, being again the highest all over the world. However, statistics show that, Chinese textile and garment industries exported $52.1 billion, worth of products in 2000. The export of RMG totalled $ 36.1 billion production, 18.1% of world's total.[109]

The accession of China[110] to the WTO is likely to have significant implications for textiles and clothing exporting countries. In November 1999, China has reached a WTO agreement with the United States. According to the agreement U.S. quota restrictions on textiles and clothing from China will be phased out by the year 2005, China became a member of WTO. However, the U.S.-China WTO agreement provides for a special safeguard mechanism which will remain in place for 12 years following China's accession to the WTO. The agreement also provides for a special anti-dumping provision which will take into account non-market characteristics of China's economy when identifying and measuring possible subsidy benefits. A study by the International Trade Comission, U.S.A. (ITC of US, 1999) on the impact of China's accession to the

Table 4.10
Historical Cotton Production Statistics of China

Year	Area ('000 Hectares)	Yield (Metric Tons/Hectares)	Production ('000 Metric Tons)
1980	4,920	0.55	2,700
1985	5,140	0.81	4,137
1990	5,588	0.81	4,507
1995	5,422	0.88	4,768
1996	4,722	0.89	4,202
1997	4,500	1.02	4,594
1998	4,900	1.23	4,759

Source: Joint Agricultural Weather Facility(USDA/NOAA) Website

[109] "Experts on China's Garment Industry with WTO Entry"; available at http://www.intextile.com/htmlib/english/news/02040101.htm downloaded on 17th January, 2003.

[110] China is now member of WTO, from Doha Conference, 2002.

WTO suggests the following points: First, the short-run impact in the US market will be small because of low base quota growth rates for China established in the bilateral agreement in 1997. Second, China's wool's market share for apparel would rise by more than 6 percentage points in 2006, maintaining its position as the world's largest exporter of apparel products. The gain of China is at the expense of the other restricted exporters whose market shares would increase considerably less than under the scenario where China remains a non-member. The disparity between its textiles and apparel exports reflects the difference between its textiles and apparel industries. Textile production is relatively capital intensive while apparel production is relatively labour intensive and more consistent with China's comparative advantage. As the world's largest clothing manufacturer and exporter, China will face both opportunities and intense competition now that it is a WTO member.[111] So one can easily say that China's World Trade Organization (WTO) entry has boosted its economic growth and advanced its legal and governmental reforms.[112]

But today, China's presence into the WTO will definitely change the world scenario of textiles and clothing in apparel markets. Reduction of tariff and non-tariff barriers for textiles in China is likely to benefit textiles exporting countries such as South Korea, Taiwan, Japan, the EU, and the United States.

4.8 Regional Trade Blocs Concerning Textiles and Clothing

International trade in textiles and clothing as well as location of textiles and clothing industries are affected not only by multilateral trade rules but also by regional trade blocs often with different degrees of trade barriers for non-member countries. The following section briefly covers regional trade blocs concerning textile and clothing.

4.8.1 North American Free Trade Agreement (NAFTA)

In order to stem ever greater export outflows from Asia, in January 1995, the North American Free Trade Agreement-comprising the US., Mexico and Canada came into existence.

Apparel made in any NAFTA country, from NAFTA originated yarn and fabric, can be shipped to any NAFTA country quota and duty-free. In one fell swoop, the US government sacrificed its dwindling domestic apparel industry and massively consolidated its powerful textile sector. Mexico, which in 1990 was ranked as 26th largest importer into the US for apparel, became North America's low-cost offshore for RMG production. Early sceptics, including many from Asia, doubled Mexico's ability to train masses of skilled labour and

[111] Ibidem

[112] "WTO Entry Boost China's Economy" available at http://www.china.org.cn/english/49058.htm, downloaded on August 12, 2002

speculated that only low difficulty items would go to Mexico while complicated orders would still be placed in Asia. Yet by 1998, Mexico alone was shipping in more units into the US than Hong Kong and China combined. The combination of fast delivery coupled with no quota or duty worries and reasonable costs has proven unbeatable. Mexico's labour costs are four to five times those of Bangladesh. Here is a clear-cut case of low macro costs clearly win out over low direct costs.

Textile goods under NAFTA, which came into effect on January 1, 1994 include those items listed in chapters 50 to 60, chapter 63, most of chapters 65 and 66, and specific items of chapters 30, 39, 42, 64, 70, 87, 88, 91, 94, 95 and 96 of the Harmonised System (HS). Tariffs on originating textiles products and apparel involving Canada and the United States have been eliminated by January 1, 1998. Most textile tariffs between the US and Mexico will be phased out over a period of six years, while between Canada and Mexico over a period of eight years. US tariffs on originating apparel from Mexico have been phased out by January 1, 1999. Virtually all tariffs on originating textiles and clothing being traded between Canada, the United States, and Mexico will be eliminated by January 1, 2004. According to managers of industry surveyed, NAFTA seems to have provided opportunities for major US companies and retailers to engage in direct investment, sourcing and off-shore contracting with Mexico, with relative loss to distant suppliers in Asia.[113] While each member country of NAFTA maintains its own external tariff, the NAFTA preferential tariff is extended only to goods originating from a member country. For apparel the "yarn forward" or "triple transformation" rule must be met in order to obtain NAFTA preferential treatment. According to this rule, for apparel, the yarn, fabric, and garment must be made in NAFTA countries to qualify for NAFTA preferential duties. The agreement provides a *de minimis* rule for apparel, that is, apparel goods qualify as originating if the non-NAFTA content is 7% or less. The *de minimis* rule, on a weight basis, applies, that to goods covering HS chapters 50 to 63. For goods outside these chapters, the value based *de minimis* rule applies. The agreement however, exempts certain apparel products from the triple transformation rule if they are made from certain imported fabrics which are in short supply in the NAFTA countries, for example, silk fabrics and dobby weave fabrics. The agreement requires that for cotton and man made fabrics, the fibres used to manufacture the thread, yarn, and fabric must also be made in NAFTA countries, known as the "fibre forward" rule.

NAFTA provides preferential quotas for apparel and textiles, known as Tariffs Preferential Levels (TPLs). TPL allow the import of a fixed quantity of certain non-originating goods into Canada, the United States, and Mexico at the

113 "Crisis in the US Textile and Apparel Industry: Is it Caused by the Trade Agreement and Asian Currency Meltdowns", by W.A. Amponsah & V.O. Boadu, May 22-24, 2002 available at http://www.cnas.edu/publication/Power Point/amponsh.ppt

NAFTA rate of duty. The United States has TPLs for imports of cotton or man-made fibre apparel from Canada and Mexico. Textiles and clothing entering a NAFTA country above the TPLs are subject to the higher Normal Trade Relation (NTR) rate of duty (previously called Most Favoured Nation), usually applied to non-NAFTA countries. It should be noted that, as stated in the NAFTA, if there is any inconsistency between the NAFTA and the World Trade Agreement concerning textiles and apparel, the NAFTA shall prevail, unless the NAFTA members agree otherwise. Moreover, NAFTA has created additional opportunities for US textile manufacturers to take advantage of US advanced technology in producing yarns and fabrics in manufacturing apparels at relating lower labour costs in Mexico that are shipped back to the US market in faster response times.[114]

The stringent rules of origin for textiles and clothing may be responsible for significant trade diversion in the US market in the form of increased imports from Mexico at the expense of Asian exporting countries. Recently, negotiations have been initiated to establish the Free Trade Area for the Americas (FTAA) for the western hemisphere covering North, Central and South America, and the Caribbean region by the year 2005.

4.8.2 Caribbean Basin Initiative (CBI) and Sub- Saharan Africa (SSA)

With the passage of TDA-2000 U.S. Congress has made duty free and quota free access for 48 countries of Sub-Saharan Africa (SSA), and 24 countries of the Caribbean Basin. Furthermore, the recently enacted Trade and Development Act 2000 (TDA-2000), which provides tariff and quota references for apparel produce in the Caribbean Basin and Sub- Saharan Africa (SSA), could significantly change US trade in cotton apparel. As the result of NAFTA, Mexico has become the dominant supplier of apparel to the US market, at the expense of Asian suppliers. Now, speculation centres around whether, with the new legislation, the Caribbean will emerge as a key supplier of apparel to the United States, further eroding Asia's share.[115]

The CBI countries also benefit from preferential treatment into the U.S. under what is known as item 807. If yarn and fabric are of U.S. origin and the fabric is cut in the U.S. and assembled in any CBI country, upon return to the US, duty is levied only on the processing work carried out in the CBI country.

Duty on most cotton apparel into the U.S. ranges around 18% while synthetic fibres are taxed at 28% or higher, representing significant savings generated by not paying duty on perhaps 80% of the garment's FOB value. The CBI

---

114 Ibidem

115 "The Caribbean Basin Initiative: What will it mean for US cotton apparel trade?" Available at http://www.ptj.com.pk/1-2002/caribbean.htm

countries of the Dominican Republic, Honduras, El Salvador, Guatemala and Costa Rica all figure in the top 20 importers into the U.S. by volume. But 807 conditions are more difficult to comply with than NAFTA, meaning that export growth in the region has been as explosive. In the year 2000, the U.S. Congress finally passed a bill which grants 48 countries in sub-Saharan Africa as well as those in the CBI essentially the same privileges as NAFTA countries, provided yarn and fabric are of U.S origin or, to a certain degree, of local origin, and that certain social and labour standards are met.

4.9 Transitional Period

As mentioned earlier, the ATC allows a 10 year (1995-2004) transition period during which most of these restrictive and discriminatory regulations will remain in force. It is a transitional instrument to set into quota-free trade in the international market. But it will not be a duty free regime, for which further negotiations might be necessary. The integration process allows the restraining countries to select their own products, and it keeps 49 per cent of the trade in this sector for integration on the very last day of the transition period. Moreover, the provisions of the transitional safeguard bear a strong resemblance in criteria and procedures to the MFA and it left some of the vital concerns of the developing countries unaddressed.

4.10 Concluding Remarks

From the preceding discussion it is obvious that elimination of quotas by the year 2005 and reduction of tariffs present opportunities for export of increased labour-intensive apparel products from Bangladesh. However, liberalization of trade regimes also implies that competition in RMG exports is likely to be more intense. Furthermore, Bangladesh is located far away from major markets such as EU, US and Japan. The existence and possible expansions of free trade blocs like the EU and NAFTA provide opportunities through increased trade and investment relationship to Central, East European, Mediterranean countries, Mexico and Caribbean and Central American countries but challenges to a country like Bangladesh. So, the Bangladesh industrial and trade policy concerning textile and clothing sectors must be formulated from an international dynamic perspective. However, attention to the next chapter, therefore, would cover the current Bangladesh RMG industry conditions and its future perspective.

CHAPTER FIVE
CURRENT BANGLADESH READYMADE GARMENTS INDUSTRY CONDITION

5.1 Introduction

The Readymade Garments Industry of Bangladesh tells an impressive story about leadership of a private enterprise in the successful conversion of the country to a major export oriented country. Bangladesh registered its first apparel export in 1978, but the progress since early 1980s has been simply phenomenal. It has by now become the colossus in industry, earning the country's lion's share of foreign exchange and providing the nation's women with the highest formal employment. Within a very short period of time, it has attained prominence in terms of its contribution to Bangladesh's gross domestic product (GDP) and other macro economic factors. The industry has flourished because of its cheap and predominantly female labour market and the favoured international textile and clothing regime under the Multi-Fibre Arrangement. The present chapter examines the trade performance of Bangladesh in the RMG sector based on elements of the industry, its organisational set-up, contribution of the sector and its growth, role of internal and external factors as well as value addition and importance of backward and forward linkages for the development of this industry.

5.2 Standard Trade Theory and Bangladesh Textiles and Clothing Sector

Kym Anderson (1992) illustrates the standard theory in relation to the textile and clothing industry as follows:[116]

"A poor country opening up to international trade will tend to specialize in the export of primary products, though less so the more densely populated the country. If the domestic outcomes grow more rapidly then the rest of the world's, its export specialization will gradually switch away from primary products to manufacturers. The manufactured goods initially exported will be more labour-intensive, the more resource poor or densely populated the country. Since many processes in textile and clothing production tend to be intensive in the use of unskilled labour, they will be among the items initially exported by a newly industrializing, densely populated country. And as the demands for textile raw materials by that country's expanding textile industry grow, so the country's net export of natural fibres will diminish, or net imports of natural fibres will increase, *ceteris paribus.*[117] On the other hand, since syn-

[116] "New Silk Roads, East Asia and World Textile Markets", edited by Kym Anderson, Cambridge University Press (1992).

[117] Ceteris paribus, i.e. other factors remaining constant

thetic fibre production is an extremely capital-intensive activity, its products will tend to be imported by the newly industrializing country from relatively capital-abundant industrial countries. If this newly industrialising country is growing more rapidly then other countries, it will initially increase its share of world production and exports of textiles and clothing and of world imports of fibres at the expense of more mature industrial economies. In time, another generation of newly industrializing countries will duplicate this process, so gradually displacing the former in those world markets, but providing them with the growing export market for capital-intensive manufactures including synthetic fibres."

He adds further that Japan was primarily an agrarian economy before the 1870s and it transformed as of 1992, within "into one in which the primary sector accounts for less than one tenth of employment and one-thirtieth of GDP and exports." The shares of textiles and clothing in GDP, employment and exports increased from squatting levels in the 1870s to sizeable peaks in the middle of the twentieth century as "comparative advantage switched to manufactured that were intensive in more abundant human and physical capital." Consequently, natural fibres export share dropped down almost zero and the fibre import share in Japan's total imports grew initially. Subsequently, decline in Japan occurred first for labour-intensive apparel and last for capital-intensive synthetic fibres as envisaged in standard trade theory. Bangladesh, like Japan and NICs such as Hong Kong, Taiwan, and Korea, can traverse the same trajectory as the key factors envisaged in trade theory fully coincide with those prevalent in the country. Though, Bangladesh remains at the initial face of this trajectory, therefore trade liberalization has long way to go for which its impact in the economy will be necessary.

5.3 Trade Performance of Bangladesh in Readymade Garments

Few sectors in Bangladesh promise greater potential than the textile and clothing sector in terms of import-substitution, import-promotion, intra-industry linkage, employment generation and economic growth. The readymade garment's (RMG) industry - a prime component of the textile sector and the flagship of Bangladesh - now earns more than 75% of the country's total export income and directly employs about 1.8 million workers, of whom 80% are women workers. Besides it helps generating several million jobs in linkage industries, such as garments accessories, spinning, weaving, dyeing, printing, finishing, shipping, stevedoring, road transports and real estate development. Thanks to a burgeoning but highly promising entrepreneur class and an abundance of cheap labour, the RMG industry demonstrates the capability to emerge as the prime engine of economic growth, as happened in the newly industrialised economics (NIEs) in the seventies and eighties. But the fullest realisation of the possibilities of the garments sector on a sustained basis would depend on how skilfully Bangladesh can equip itself to operate in a restriction free international trading regime in textile and clothing scheduled to be in place by the year 2005 under the Uruguay Round. The challenge is enormous, multi-dimensional, wide-ranging and far-reaching, therefore this is one that this country can hardly over-emphasize. (Dowlah, 1998)

Bangladesh textile industry accounts for 45% of all the industrial employment in the country and contributes 5% of the total national income.[118] This industry is also facing serious problems, principally because Bangladesh does not produce enough raw materials necessary for this industry, unfavourable trade policies, inadequate incentives etc, and MFA phasing out after 2004.[119] The RMG industry owners, relevant ministries of the government and potential investors, should have finalised a plan of action long ago designed to hedge the RMG sector through establishment of linkage industries. Government should have created a special fund for the purpose to receive annually a big enough sum from the national budget for utilization by intending entrepreneurs in linkage industries. It should specially invite or take initiative to channel foreign investments in RMG linkage industries. Many economic impacts are going on in this industry due to globalization and trade liberalization in the Bangladesh economy.

5.4 Korean Involvement in Bangladesh Clothing Industry at the Beginning

Koreans were some of the first foreign investors to come to Bangladesh. Owing to the labour shortage in the Korean garment factories, Korean entrepreneurs selected Bangladesh as one of its overseas production base "because of its relatively low labour costs."[120] Garment industry of Bangladesh started its production in 1978 and it owes much to Korean entrepreneurs. Koreans were active in teaching Bangladeshi workers both in technical and the business sides of the garment industry over the years. As stated in the home page, a report written by the World Bank in 1989 stated that the Bangladesh garment industry had virtually begun by the *Daewoo* Corporation of South Korea. Many of the Koreans doing business in Dhaka still feel that garment industry in Bangladesh will help eliminate its poverty as they did once in their own country.

---

118 "The Textile Industry of Bangladesh" by Azizur Chowdhury: available at http://www.ais-dhaka.net/SENIORS/textileazizur; downloaded on October, 26, 2000.

119 Ibidem

120 "Korean Involvement in Bangladesh's Garment Industry", American International School, Dhaka, website available at http://www.ais-dhaka.net/SENIORS/Nackhoonkoreangarment, downloaded on 24 October, 2000.

5.5 Organisational Set up of Bangladesh Textiles and Clothing Sector

The textile industry of Bangladesh may be divided into three main categories namely, the public sector, the handloom sector and the organised private sector.[121] Presently, the organised private sector takes over other sectors and is growing at the fastest rate. According to June, 2000 statistics, there are 148 spinning units, 105 weaving, 282 dyeing-printing-finishing, and 155 knit, knit dyeing and finishing units in the country. On the other hand, there are more than 3500 RMG units now under operation in Bangladesh.[122] According to Bangladesh Textile Mills Association (BTMA), the textile industry of Bangladesh now comprise more than thirty sub-sectors. The existing structure of textile industry, according to BTMA, are shown in figure 5.1

5.6 Distribution Channels of Garments Product

An export channel of distribution is the chain of marketing agencies linking the producers to the final buyers of his product in the foreign target market. In the garment exports, if the manufacturer/exporter collects exports orders directly from the importer, after manufacturing the final knit/woven products they perform the packaging function and then handover those packaged knit/woven garments to the shipping lines through the local C & F agent according to the importer's specification. On the other hand, if the manufacturers/exporters collect export order through the buying houses or local agent of the importer (where direct supervision by the buying houses exists), manufacturing garments are handed over to them or to airline or shipping lines after necessary custom clearance through C & F agents according to the importer's direction. After obtaining the imported garment products from the exporters/agents/buying houses, importers sell those to the wholesalers who in turn supply directly to the department stores, chain stores, super markets, mail-order houses or textile super markets of the importing countries (Bhuiyan, 1998). The export Chain of garments is shown the figure 5.2.

[121] Azizur Chowdhury Op.CIt

[122] Shahriar Karim, ' Rejuvenating the textile sector, More mills are going for BMRE to grab the post-MFA opportunity ', The Daily Star, Business Page, Volume 3, Number 637, June 18, 2001

Figure 5.1
Structure of the Textile and Clothing Industry

		TOTAL
1. Spinning Sub-sector		
a. Ring spinning (Private sector)	83	
b. Ring spinning (Public sector)	27	
c. Ring with open-end (Private sector)	24	
d. Open-end (Public sector)	14	
		148
Installed Capacity		
a. Spindles (Private sector)	3 million	
b. Spindles (Public Sector)	0.6 million	3.6 million
c. Rotors (Private sector)		0.05 million
Annual Production Capacity		
a. Private sector	400 million	
b. Public sector	43 million	443 million kg
Production Capacity of export quality yarn		
a. Knit	119 million	
b. Woven	54 million	
c. Terry Towel, Socks and others	21 million	
d. Synthetic	10 million	204 million kg
Quantity of yarn exported (Jul.99- Jun.2000) only to EU		90 million kg
Raw Material Requirement		
a. Raw Cotton		
b. Man-made fibre		1 million bales
2. Weaving Sub sector		
Installed Capacity		
a. Shuttleless loom	3,715	
b. Shuttle loom	27,785	31,500
Annual Production Capacity (Fabric)		830 million mtr.
Fabric quantity exported to only EU (Jul.1999-Jun.2000)		109 million mtr.
3. Dyeing- Printing- Finishing		
a. Semi –mechanised	183	
b. Mechanised	99	282 million mtr
Annual Processing Capacity (Fabric)		680 million mtr.
4. Knitting, Knit Dyeing & Finishing Sub-sector		
a. Knitting & Hosiery (Domestic)	23	
b. Knitting, Knit Dyeing & Finishing (Export - oriented)	132	155
Installed Capacity		
a. Knitting and Hosiery	339	
b. Knitting, Knit Dyeing and Finishing	1709	2048 (Knitting machine)
5. Readymade Garment Sub-sector		
a. Garment Factory (Export oriented)		3500
b. Production Capacity (RMG)		165 million dozen

Source : Bangladesh Textile Mills Association, 2001

Figure 5.2
Distribution Channel of Export Garment Products

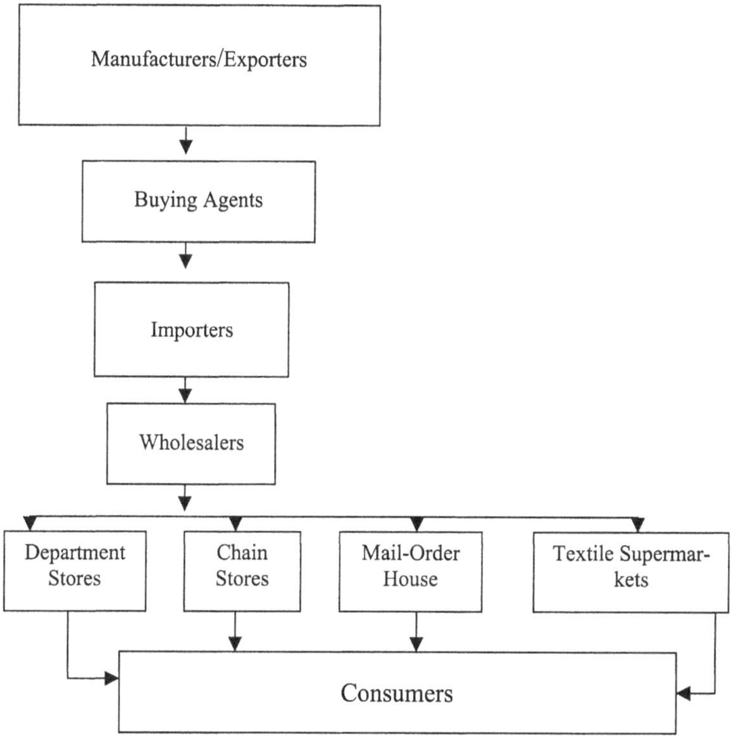

Figure 5.2 shows that buying agents, importers, wholesalers and department stores are the middlemen in the distribution system. That means, too many middlemen are involved in the export chain of this industry, which represents that many economic activities as well as impacts are going on due to the development of this sector.

5.7 Lead Time for the Export of RMG Product

For the survival of the RMG industry after 2004, Bangladesh must try to reduce the lead time,[123] i.e. the time it takes to process and complete an order. The following cycle indicates the typical lead-time in Bangladesh readymade garments industry (Figure 5.3). Even countries like Vietnam have a shorter lead time. All Caribbean countries have shorter lead time which is half the Bangladesh lead

123 Time left in hand for executing an RMG export order after accepting the same.

time. For this reasons, the US buyers rely upon CBI nations as primary apparel sources. Bangladesh will not be able to retain its leading position, or even may not survive in the post-MFA era if it cannot reduce the lead time substantially. Many important buyers have already diverted some of their sourcing from Bangladesh to Mexico and CBI countries. In the near future, they may prefer China and Vietnam to Bangladesh. An excerpt from a popular Daily in Bangladesh reads as following[124]: "For reducing the lead period, the government can allow private bonded warehouse to store raw materials, establish direct shipping link with major Southeast Asian ports and deep sea port." It takes around 20-25 days for raw materials to reach Chittagong port[125] from major South Asian ports. If a deep sea port is established at a suitable place for berthing mother vessels, the raw materials would reach within 8 to 10 days. On the other hand, the private bonded warehouses can collect raw materials and supply it to the garment manufacturer according to their requirements, which would make the execution process faster. There should be transparency about the capacity of the existing port and the proposals from a foreign country for establishing a private port there.

Figure 5.3
Typical Manufacturing Cycle

(A Breakdown of a typical lead-time)

Opening of Letter of Credit (L/C)	---	5-7 days
Confirmation by Bank	---	5-10 days
Fabric Production	---	30 days (Hong Kong)
Shipping Time	---	15-20 days to Chittagong
Clearance etc	---	2-3 days
Overland to Dhaka	---	4-5 days
Garment Manufacturer	---	1-2 Weeks
Overland to Chittagong	---	1-2 days
Clearance etc	---	1-3 days
Shipping time	---	25 days to New York
Total Lead Time Required	---	95 to 120 days

Source: Export Promotion Bureau of Bangladesh

124 "No Policy Guidelines yet to Face the Quota-Free Regime", The Daily Star, available at http://www.dailystarnews.com/200004/20/n00422005.htm, on the Business Page, Volume 3, Number 229, April 20, 2000

125 The biggest port city of Bangladesh

5.8 Raw Material Availability in Bangladesh

Although, in textiles and clothing, the term raw material can signify different materials or products in relation to its different stages of manufacture, here it is meant for the beginning stage. For instance, cotton yarn may be manufactured from cotton fibre by spinning but it is the raw material for weaving or knitting sub-sector which is the second stage in the textiles and clothing chain and the same is true for subsequent stages. Bangladesh textiles and clothing sector is facing problems because the country does not produce enough raw materials as compared to its demand entailing its high dependence on imports. The country, therefore, can not earn as much foreign exchange from its textile industry as it should.

Generally, the principal materials for the spinning sub-sector are raw cotton and synthetic fibres, for example, viscose and polyester staple fibres. None of these materials, however, are produced in Bangladesh on a large enough scale to supply a significant part of the demand.[126] Although the cotton produced in Bangladesh is of an acceptable standard, the increased cultivation of cotton in this country is not feasible because the crop requires large amounts of land for a substantial yield. As Bangladesh population size is very large, owing to food demand and farmers choose to grow rice over cotton. Presently, locally grown cotton can afford only 4-5% of the total requirement of this sector. On the other hand, the production of the synthetic/man-made fibres used in the textile industry requires fairly advanced technology and higher investment, which is not feasible at the present condition of the sector. Relatively lower international cotton price encourages the entrepreneurs to go for expanding the capacity. Big textile industries have now taken up programmes to set up forward and backward linkages units geared by favourable government policy to face various economic impacts on this sector due to trade liberalization and MFA phasing out after 2004.[127]

5.9 Characteristics of the Industry

The industry is characterised by the following:

a) labour intensiveness; b) import dependence for raw materials, machineries, design and specification and professionals; c) limited scope of aggressive marketing or using brand name because of making according to buyers' specifications; d) low retained value addition from the sector; e) weak backward integration and linkages; f) concentration of factories mostly in two cities, namely Dhaka and Chittagong; g) preponderance of women employment; h) weak trade unionism; i) easy absorption of technology after a short training on the job; and

---

[126] Azizur Chowdhury, Op. Cit.

[127] "Rejuvenating the textile sector-favourable policy infuses new investment", by Shahriar Karim, The Daily Star Business Page, Volume 3, Number 638, Tuesday, June 19, 2001

j) one of the lowest wage paying sectors in the country, given the huge involvement of female labour.

5.10 Contribution of the Industry and its Growth

The RMG industry is Bangladesh's single-largest foreign exchange earner. The contribution made by the sector over years has grown in two distinct phases pre and post 1990-91. The growth in the first phase has been mainly due to duty-free and quota-free access to the USA, while growth in the latter period has been largely courtesy the duty-free and quota-free access to the EU market. The RMG share in exports increased from a modest 12% in 1984/85 to 50% by 1990/91. The contribution of the sector peaked in 1997/98 with an 83% contribution margin and by 1999/2000 this reached 75.6%. Foreign exchange earnings for the fiscal year 2000-2001 is US $ 4.584 billion. Individual sub-sector wise break-up shows that export earnings for woven RMG between 1992-93 and 2001-2002 were 1240.48 and 3124.82 million US$, and knitwear position on the same years were 204.54 and 1458.93 million US$. In terms of contribution made by the industry to the sectors of the economy, the figure has been very impressive (Table 5.1) The growth dynamics of the sector over the last decade evince two clearly discremible phases: during the initial period it was woven-RMG which dominated the structure of apparel exports, whilst in recent years, which could be termed as a second phase, it is the knit-RMG which has emerged as the better performer and was able to robust growth.

Table 5.1
Year over Year Growth Rate of Woven and Knit Garment Export of Bangladesh
(In million US$)

Year	Woven Garment	Knit Garment
1992-93	1240.48	204.54
1993-94	1291.65	264.14
1994-95	1835.09	393.26
1995-96	1948.81	598.32
1996-97	2237.95	763.30
1997-98	2844.96	937.51
1998-99	2984.96	1035.20
1999-2000	3081.19	1268.51
2000-01	3364.82	1495.51
2001-2002	3124.82	1498.93

Source: BGMEA, 2002

Table 5.2 provides the relative growth rates of knit-and woven RMG over the last decade and half. The growth dynamics presented in the Table 5.2 also demonstrates how jute, the traditional export commodity which contributed three-fourths of Bangladesh's export in the 1970s, was gradually replaced by the ascending RMG sector.

Table 5.2
Trend Growth Rates of Major Export Product Groups of Bangladesh (per cent)

Commodity	1982-98	1982-90	1990-98	1994-98
Jute	-0.81	-0.83	-0.2	3.5
RMG	36.30	59.10	21.5	20.8
Woven-RMG	34.20	59.00	18.5	17.8
Knit-RMG	-	-	42.9	32.0
Total	13.20	10.70	15.7	16.6

Source: Export Promotion Bureau (EPB), 2000

5.10.1 Performance of the Knitwear Sub-sector

The knitwear sector has made tremendous developments to become the world's largest supplier. It is engaged in manufacturing relatively lower value items but is a high-volume business. The reason why more Bangladeshi exporters opt for knitwear garments unit instead of a woven garments is because of the differing sophistication levels required and costs involved (Brook, 1992). The backward linkage industry of Bangladesh has the capacity to cater to 60% of the local exporters' demands. This reduce the cost and the lead-time of the exporters thereby making them more competitive globally. The emergence of this sector has substantially stemmed from 1992 and contributed noticeably in earning the vast quantum of foreign currency. In 1992-93 fiscal year only 9% foreign currency was earned by this sector amid the whole export income. In 2000-2001 fiscal year it earned foreign currency to the amount of 1495.51 million US$ (44.45%)[128] The country exports a large variety of knitwear items but only three items constitute 85% of the total exports to the European Union markets. These are men's and boys' knit shirts, T-shirts/singlets and sweaters/cardigans. Bangladesh has to diversify the concentration of product offering to cater to the maximum number of segments possible. Total contribution by the sub-sector during the FY 2001-2002 was US$ 1458.93 million.. However, this sector suf-

[128] "A Brief Delineation on Bangladesh Knitwear Manufacturers and Exporters Association (BKEMA) with its Problems and Factors to be Integrated for Sustainable Trade Globalization in Post MFA Regime". A paper prepared by the BKEMA President in view of the Asia Pacific Textile and Clothing Forum (ASPAC-6) in Dhaka in August 2001.

fers from shortage of raw materials and working capital[129] as well needs modern facilities for manufacturing quality fabrics.

5.10.2 Performance of Woven Sub-sector

Bangladesh has been making significant strides in moving towards the more high value items. This is evident from the list of buyers that the country now has in her portfolio. But again, in spite of the shift, four woven items exported from the country makes up 86% of the total exports into the EU. These items are men's and boys' woven shirts, women's and girls' blouses, anoraks/parkas, coats and cotton trousers/shorts. Total contribution by the sub-sector during the FY 2001-2002 was US$ 3124.82 million. In total Bangladesh exports approximately 1.5% high value items, 30-40% mid-value items and the remaining 58.5 to 68.5% low value items. Most of the industrialists of our country did not seem to be keen on diversifying into higher value items because of having incur costs to restructure the units. Currently, "only 10% of the demand for woven fabrics are produced locally and price is higher than those of imported ones despite huge incentives by the government."[130] Bangladesh weaving mills constantly fall short of production owing to chain link shortage of yarn/grey fabric production in the spinning sub-sector. As a result, the country has to import 3.15 billion meters grey per year adding tax, transport and other costs making the fabric expensive.

5.11 Industry Structure of RMG

The RMG industry has contributed in more ways than one to the local economy. Upto June 2002, there were in total 3618 RMG industries in operation as per BGMEA data (Figure 5.4). 2810 of those are located in Dhaka, 804 in Chittagong, two in Khulna and two in Barisal. The average capacity utilization by the units is 86.4% whereas total installed capacity is 124,120,000 dozen items. On an average each unit invests approximately seven million taka.

5.12 Condition of Infrastructure Linked to Textile and Clothing Industries of Bangladesh

Bangladesh has two sea-ports namely, Chittagong and Mongla. However frequent labour problems in these ports results in unnecessarily delay in discharging imported goods. RMG industries, being greatly dependent on imported fabrics and often committed to time bound orders from the foreign buyers, has to

---

129 Azizur Chowdhury, Op. Cit.

130 "BGMEA Sees Boon in New GSP Provision", The Daily Star, Business Page, Vol.3, No.339, available at http://www.dailystarnews.com/200008/10/n0081001.htm, downloaded on 29 Sept, 2000.

face serious problems. A proposal is, therefore, underway to establish green channels to facilitate discharge of such goods with almost no customs checking:

"Imports of garments exporters with no bad record in the last five years will be released through the green channel virtually without any customs checking and there will be no checking on way to warehouses. The custom officials at the port will however check five per cent of the goods at a random so that the facility can not be misused."[131]

Figure 5.4
Growth of Readymade Garments Industry of Bangladesh

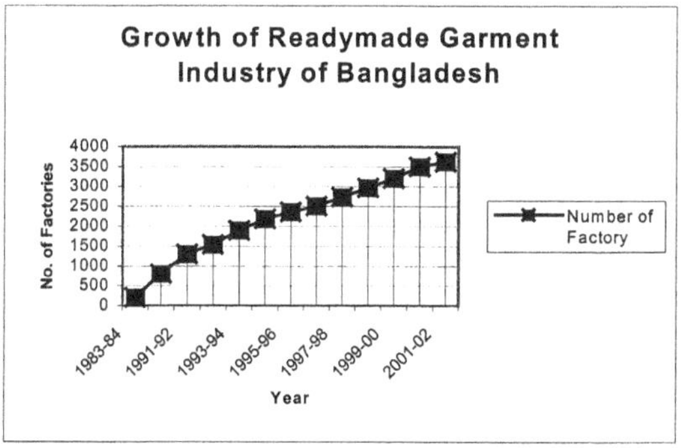

Source: BGMEA, 2002

In the view of frequent strikes, hartals and work abstention by workers and employees, the exporters demanded that these services be declared essential. The effectiveness of the system envisaged would, however, depend on the sincerity from all quarters. Moreover, another proposal to establish a deep-sea port has been mooted, success of which again depends on proper management and commitment to the objective.

Sometimes, industries fell sick due to stock lot problem, which happens mostly due to political disturbances and port problems[132] and many of them had to pull down their shutters being overburdened with indisposed inventories of finished products.[133] Paucity of credit from banks is another major stumbling block in the way of smooth operation of some factories in the RMG industries.

---

[131] "Chittagong Port to Have Green Channel for Garments Exporters", The Daily Star archives, 26 September, 200 issue. Available at http://www.dailystarnews.com, downloaded on 10 October, 2000.

[132] BGMEA News Letter, Vol.10, October 1999 issue 8 available at http://www.bgmea.com/news.htm, Downloaded on 03 January, 2000.

[133] "BGMEA Has a Lot to Do" By Prof. Dr. Nizamuddin Ahmed, BUET, Dhaka, The Daily Star Archive, 20 August, 1997 Issue.

Many factories' production suffers from shortage of working capital.[134] Currency devaluation by some of the neighbouring countries, such as India, Pakistan, Thailand, Sri Lanka, Malaysia is another problem for the garment exporters of Bangladesh because it facilitates foreign buyers to buy goods at a lower price resulting in a shift of the export orders from Bangladesh to other countries. To sustain a stiff competition in garment exports arising out of such devaluation, the BGMEA seeks at least 10 per cent cash incentives against their export earnings.[135] To eliminate such difficulties, BGMEA seeks like quota distribution system by EPB, the representative of the association in the law and order, customs, bank and insurance and port management bodies. The demand seems quite reasonable in view of the problems currently the RMG sector is experiencing.

On the other hand, due to low bank interests of India and Pakistan, the government has been requested, as of May, 1999, to reduce bank loan interests at 10 per cent for project and well as for working capital loans instead of current 16 per cent.[136] Recommendations have also been put forward to make export income of textile products tax-free, waive double insurance systems on imports for export purposes, to make flood insurance optional, to allow duty free import of raw cotton, and dyes and chemicals consumed in the export oriented industries, to introduce a specialised bank for providing loans to export-oriented industries, and to set up some textile parks with similar facilities as in the Export Processing Zones (EPZs).[137] Therefore, the condition and operational status of roads, power, telecommunications, banking, insurance, customs all need to be enhanced since the poor infrastructure facilities increase in the cost of production of the industry. In addition, adequately developed backward linkage industry is a pre-requisite for reducing the lead time in the RMG sector.[138]

5.13 Establishment of an Apparel Board

In view of the competitive global trade in RMG after phase-out of quota restrictions in 2005, the implications of an Apparel Board is far reaching, particularly when it is important to retain a market niche in the international arena. It should

---

[134] Ibidem

[135] Export Promotion Bureau (EPB), Dhaka, Bangladesh, homepage (http://www.epbbd.com/Month22/BGMEA%20for%2010pc.htm, 03 October, 2000

[136] "Working capital hits country's textile sector", The Daily Independent, July 17, 2002, available at http://www.independent–bangladesh.com/22/2207200bs.htm#A1, downloaded on 20 July, 2002.

[137] "Government urged to take steps for development in textile sector", The Daily Star, Business page, Vol.2. No.258, May 12 and more information are of May 1999, available at http://www.dailystarnews.com/199905/12/n9051205.htm#BODY3, downloaded on 29 Sept. 2000.

[138] "BTMA seminar calls for soft loans to textile sector- Move to face post-2004 duty and quota- free regime". The Daily Star, Business page, Vol.3. No.618, May 29, 2001.

be fostered as an institutional structure to act permanently for issuing country of origin certificate, export license, textile visa, GSP certificate etc. Establishment of an Apparel Board has been hanging since last 15 years due to conflict led in-decision among concerned ministries.[139]

5.14 Establishment of an Institute of Fashion Technology

Roughly 20,000 skilled foreign workers are employed in the garment manufacturing industries of Bangladesh for whom entrepreneurs have to spend about 60 billion Taka as their salary and bonus.[140] Due to shortage of local skilled manpower, garment owners are bound to engage foreign experts and their service is required to produce high quality and high value items in the RMG. Bangladesh is, therefore, lagging behind in export of high valued items to the EU and USA. To satisfy the need of efficient manpower in garment industries as well as to attain the expected standard in the quota free global market after 2004, BGMEA has established an Institute of Fashion Technology (IFT) with the financial assistance from the World Bank and the Finance Ministry of the Government of Bangladesh at Uttara, Dhaka. The Institute has already commenced its functioning in the year 2000 to provide Graduate, Diploma & Trade Certificate Courses.

5.15 The Fifth Five Year Plan 1997-2002 and Textile Sector of Bangladesh

The major focus of the textile sector during the Fourth Five Year Plan period was on generation of employment, private investment, export, rationalisation of tariffs, providing monetary and fiscal incentives, product diversification and horizontal market expansion etc.[141]

It also brought together programmes on BMRE[142] of the selected old mills, and private investment was given priority in all segments of the textile and clothing chain. However, the Fifth Plan reads as follows:[143]

"The target set for employment generation in the textile sector was 1.79 million numbers. As against this target, only 0.80 million people were employed. High prices of inputs, stiff external competition in yarn and fabric markets and weak institutional back-up were responsible for the slow response of the textile sector excluding garments. As a result textile sub sector was not able

---

139 The Daily Ittefaq, (Leading Bangla Daily of the country) available at http://www.ittefaq.com/current/special/news5.pdf, downloaded on 22 January, 2001

140 BGMEA News Letter, Op.Cit.

141 "The Fifth Five Year Plan 1997-2002" Planning Commission, Ministry of Planning, Government of the People's Republic of Bangladesh (GOB), Dhaka, March, 1998, p.24.

142 Balancing, modernisation, replacement and expansion

143 GOB, Op.Cit. p.25

to generate the targeted employment." The term institutional back up perhaps indicates the lack of backward linkage support in textile and clothing in the country.

5.16 Environmental Issues in Textile and Clothing

Presently, garments manufacturing plants are dispersed almost all over Dhaka city including the residential areas. Surely, this has repercussions on the basic municipal services such as electricity, road, water, drainage, waste management etc. Moreover, housing for the garment workers (All these matters will be discussed in later chapters in details) who are principally migrants from the villages poses a serious threat to the normal city life. The low-paid female garment workers compelled to live in slums, which lack basic municipal services being attacked by various diseases. Moreover, a vast amount of solid waste including pieces of leftover clothes, plastic materials etc. are extracted from the garments industries.[144] And the situation has been upgraded as these leftover materials are now consumed in the cottage industries to produce toys, dolls, cushions, mattresses etc. The growing textile industries as backward linkage to the garment industries may cause a serious environmental problem.

Waste Water Treatment Plants in the specific Textile Industrial bases of Bangladesh is extremely necessary in view of the pollution by the dyeing industries.[145] But it involves high costs which the entrepreneurs cannot afford. Government should extend assistance to arrange financial support from abroad for the development of social and environmental performance in the RMG and the textile industrial bases of Bangladesh to comply the buyers demand from developed countries. However, these cause many economic and social impacts in our society.

5.17 Duty Structure in the Textile and Clothing Sectors of Bangladesh

Tax structure of the textile and clothing sector can be obtained from the Table 5.3 Apparently it seems that it encourages establishment of backward linkage industry in this sector as import of raw cotton and textile machinery is completely tax-free. Conversely, fabrics import is scheduled to pay the highest tax payment, an indication to use local fabrics. Nevertheless, import of spare parts and dyes and the chemical is cordoned by a fair amount of tax payment which appears unfavourable to entrepreneurs to invest in this sector. Moreover, there is

---

[144] "Sustainable Trade and Environmental Concerns in Bangladesh" by Saleemul Huq, Khandakar Mainuddin and Dawiyan Mallick, The Daily Star, Features, Vol. 3. No. 185, March 01, 2000.

[145] A Paper prepared by BKEMA President, Op. Cit.

an implicit loophole which is not conceivable from the table. Raw cotton is entirely tax free, and very low per cent of tax is tagged to man-made fibre import. On the other hand, import of yarn is pegged with high tax which is apparent from the table. Certainly, government's policy was to encourage value addition through import of cotton, and discourage of import of yarn by imposing tax. But the unscrupulous importers import cotton tax free, makes yarn locally and sell at the same price as the imported yarns. The loophole lies here. On the other hand, there taking advantage of government's tax incentives and harnessing the benefit by levelling off the price with the imported yarn disrupting the growth spinning sector of the country. This is surely an imported yarn disrupting the growth spinning sector of the country. This is surely an impediment to the development of the backward linkage industries of Bangladesh as well as the impact of the trade liberalization. An example would help to understand this loophole. Roughly, 1,500,000 bales of cotton yarn are consumed annually in Bangladesh while 200,000 bales are produced locally. (See Table 5.5). Obviously, to fill the gap of 1,300,000 bales of cotton yarn government has decided to make cotton import tax free to stimulate the local production of cotton yarn. This local production costs say, Tk. 12,000 per bale while the imported yarn costs Tk. 20,000 per bale, counting almost 40% formal and informal tax. Now, these local producers of yarn, using tax-free imported cotton, charge prices equal to the imported yarn i.e. Tk. 20,000, reaping benefit dishonestly of Tk. 8,000 per bale. This instance has been disclosed by an official of the Bangladesh Handloom Board. The figures may vary to some extent but this is replica of the actual field situation. Ultimately, this dishonest practice is impeding seriously the growth of much-talked trade liberalization in this sector and backward linkage industry in the textile and clothing sector of Bangladesh, shrinking employment opportunity for its nationals.

Due to weaver of tax, textile machinery import surged to Tk. 13 billion in FY-2000 from less than Tk 8 billion in FY 99, and in the current fiscal year the import figure is anticipated to be not less than Tk. 12 billion.[146] This capital import is commendable as it augments investment in the sector. The Executive Director of BRAC[147], Abdul Muyeed Chowdhury, has suggested scrapping the bonded warehouse facility for the RMG units and cash subsidy for the export sector as these two facilities create scopes for corruption. Unscrupulous people under the bonded warehouse facility import duty free fabrics and sell them in the open market impeding the growth of local textile industry. He also suggested duty-free import of fabrics because "withdrawal of duty on imported fabrics, it

146 "Rejuvenating in Textile Sector, More Mills are Going for BMRE to Grab the post-MFA Opportunity", by Shahriar Karim, The Daily Star, Business page, Vol.3 No.637, June 18, 2001.

147 Bangladesh Rural Advancement Committee (BRAC), one of the Leading Non-government Organization (NGO) in Bangladesh.

will also save time for the RMG exporters at least by eight to ten days, spent at the customs points."[148] If this is not done, the ultimate victim will be the RMG sector itself as local production of fabrics and accompanying value addition is being disrupted through such practices. Again, duty-free import of fabrics may annoy the local textile producers. To minimize their losses, drastic reduction of bank interest rates and major tax incentives or subsidies may be given to these local producers.

Table 5.3
Duty Structure of the Textile Sector of Bangladesh

Item	Import Duty	Value Added Tax (VAT)	Advanced Income Tax (AIT)	Infrastructure Development Surcharge	Licence Fee	Excise Duty only for Local Sale
Raw Cotton	-	-	-	-	-	-
Man Made Fibre	-	-	3%	2.5%	2.5%	-
Textile Machinery	-	-	-	-	-	-
Spare Parts	5%	-	3%	2.5%	2.5%	-
Yarn	5%	15%	3%	2.5%	2.5%	Tk.1.50 per kg
Fabric	37.5%	15%	3%	2.5%	2.5%	Tk.0.50 per mtr.
Dyes and Chemicals	5 to 25%	15%	3%	2.5%	2.5%	
Starch, Glue & Gum	5%	15%	3%	2.5%	2.5%	

Source: Bangladesh Textiles Mills Association (BTMA), November, 2001

BTMA Chairman theoretically agrees with the duty exemptions proposal on import fabrics if the measure is backed by proper compensation for the local fabric producers. He, however, adds that hand looms, power looms and small textile units will not be able to face the competition by duty-free foreign fabrics and that lower interest rates won't be enough to save these groups. Meanwhile, the customs authorities have decided to simplify customs formalities for the country's garment sector, and already started from October 1, 2001 allowing garments traders to collect only 12 signatures instead of 51 from different officials and various places for their consignments.[149] It is aimed at facilitating import and export trade in the garment sector, saving garment traders from harrassment.

148 "BTMA Seminar calls for soft loans to textile sector- Move to face post-2004 duty and quota- free regime". The Daily Star, Business Page, Vol. 3, No. 618, May 29, 2001.

149 "Garments Sector-Simplified Customs Rules from Oct. 1", The Daily Star, General News, Vo. 3, No. 734, Sept. 24, 2001.

Recently, BGMEA appointed the US based lobbyist firm, Palton Boggs, to lobby for quota and duty-free access of Bangladeshi garments to the US, and a research organisation, the "Trade Partnership World Wide", to conduct a study to assess impact of quota and duty-free import of textiles and clothing from Bangladesh on the US economy. Two separate agreements were signed in this regard in Dhaka on 12 August, 2001.[150]

5.18 Consumption and Requirements of Yarn and Fabrics

The effective demand for fabrics vis-à-vis yarn for export-oriented readymade garments of the country has been worked out for the period 1990-91 through 1998-99 based on the quantum of exports and shown in Table 5.4 There has been spectacular growth in use of both woven and knit fabrics from 1990-91 through 1998-99 for export of RMG.

Table 5.4
Consumption and Requirement of Yarn and Fabrics for Export-oriented RMG of Bangladesh from1990-91 to 1998-99

Year	Woven Garments			Knit Garments			Total		
	Quantity million dozen	Input require-ment		Quantity million dozen	Input require-ments		Quantity million dozen	Input require-ments	
		Fabric million metre	Yarn million kg		Fabric million metre	Yarn million kg		Fabric million metre	Yarn million kg
1990-91	25.49	472.07	78.68	5.08	91.44	15.24	30.57	563.51	93.92
1991-92	34.00	629.68	104.95	6.00	108.00	18.00	40.00	737.68	122.95
1992-93	36.05	667.65	111.27	10.66	191.88	31.98	46.71	859.68	143.25
1993-94	34.35	636.16	106.03	10.82	194.76	32.98	45.17	830.92	138.49
1994-95	47.21	874.33	145.72	15.30	275.40	45.90	62.51	1149.73	191.62
1995-96	48.82	904.15	150.69	23.19	417.42	69.57	72.01	1321.57	220.26
1996-97	53.45	989.89	164.69	27.54	495.72	82.62	80.99	1485.61	274.60
1997-98	65.59	1214.73	202.45	32.60	586.80	97.80	98.19	1801.53	247.60
1998-99	64.79	1199.91	199.99	36.66	659.88	109.98	101.45	1859.79	309.97

Source: Export Promotion Bureau, 2000

Assumptions for deriving input requirements:

1) One dozen of woven garment requires 18.52 metres of woven fabrics.
2) One dozen of knit garment requires 18.00 metre of knit fabrics
3) One kg of yarn produces 6 metre fabrics for knit garment.

---

[150] Bangladesh High Commission, Singapore, News Letter, August 2001, Vol. IV, No.5

There has been spectacular growth in the use of both woven and knit fabrics from 1990-91 through 1998-99 export of RMG. In 1990-91 Bangladesh exported a total of 30.57 million dozen of both woven and knit garments which increased to 101.45 million dozen in 1998-99. The ratio of consumption of fabrics for woven and knit garments in 1990-91 were 84.16 which changes to 64.36 in 1998-99. During 1990-91 to 1998-99 the consumption of woven fabrics grew at the rate of 12% per annum, while the knit fabric consumption grew at a faster rate of 28% per annum. It has also been observed that in the growth rate of export of woven and knit RMG vis-à-vis consumption of woven and knit fabrics gradually showed a declining trend. This decline was caused mainly due to commencement of implementation of phasing out of MFA from 1995. The trend of export growth of woven RMG may further decline if appropriate backward linkage facilities, such as spinning, weaving and dyeing-finishing, can not be developed for production of yarn and fabrics.

5.19 Investment and Bank Loans

The country's textile braces challenge for investment as the quota- free regime for readymade garments industry approaches nearer. In 1999, a study sponsored by the International Finance Corporation (IFC), the private sector lending affiliate of the World Bank, concluded that it would not be cost-effective for Bangladesh to develop backward linkage industries specially in the spinning and weaving sub-sector. However, two years down the lane, the assumption proves to be wrong as the recent investment figures in the textile sector show an upward trend.[151] Investments are flowing into the textile sector both for technological up-gradation and capacity improvement. As mentioned earlier, gaps of 499.9 million kg in yarn and 2395.5 million meter in fabrics between demand and supply exist at present for both export and local markets. Imports of textile machinery and raw materials are also increasing to meet the gap. Although, there are not enough as the demand increases in future. Moreover, there is a growing local demand that should be taken into consideration by the entrepreneurs. A CPD (Centre for Policy Research) paper says that, around US$ 0.5 billion has been invested in the textile sector over the last five years.[152] Four nationalised commercial banks (NCB's) and Pubali Bank alone disbursed over Tk 7000 million as loans among 231 textile units till FY 2000 from FY 1996.[153] Other private banks have also financed many textile projects that will come into production in the near future. According to BTMA, the total investment in the

---

[151] "Garments Sector-Simplified Customs Rules"- The Daily Star, General News, Vol. 3, No. 734, September24, 2001

[152] "Textile Industry Getting Ready to Reap post-MFA Benefits, US $ Half a Billion Invested in Five Years till 2000", The Daily Star, Business Page, Vol.3, No. 621, June 01, 2001

[153] Ibidem

textile sector now stands at Tk. 80 billion. Against the backdrop of the investment records and upward trends, Dr. Debapriya Bhattacharya, Executive Director of CPD, says, "it is an achievable job to get US$ 3 (Tk.16.5 billion) billion investment that the textile sector needs by 2004. Such investments would help meet at least 80 per cent of the country's demand for fabrics both for export and local markets."[154]

BGMEA-ADB row assumed a shape when ADB's Senior Economist Narhari Rao said the country's textile sector did not have comparative advantage for setting up backward linkage industry, while realising the Bank's Quarterly Economic Update on Bangladesh in June 2001.[155] ADB sprang to its conclusion when the Bangladesh Garment Manufacturers and Exporters Association's (BGMEA) demanded for government co-operation in setting up textile villages and special interests rates for textiles plants. BGMEA expressed its concern over the comment and said, "we are deeply concerned when a senior economist of an international organisation like ADB commented before the press on the viability of setting up of backward linkage industries and its overall positive impact on the Bangladesh economy."[156]

On the other hand, the BMRE programme is being carried out in the textile sector in a satisfactory pace. For instance, Prime Textile Spinning Mills Ltd. is now implementing the BMRE programme at a cost of Tk. 300 million to increase its production capacity and efficiency.[157] This is surely a soothing step to turn the future global challenge into opportunities as well as the positive economic impact in the Bangladesh economy, specially in many sub-sectors. Not only the spinning mills, the weaving units have also been investing in a bigger way for capacity expansion. Unicom Textile Mills Ltd.-of Youth Group also raised its production capacity from 9 million meters to 12 million meters. The group has finalised the primary works for setting up a spinning mill with Tk. 1 billion investment. Similarly, Bengal Indigo Ltd. which produces high quality denim fabrics and started production just three and half years back, has also taken up a Tk. 100 million expansion programme to raise its production capacity from 3 million meters to 5 million meters.[158] BTMA says that entrepreneurs are now taking up the BMRE programme to face the challenges in the liberalized economy after 2004.

Again, CPD predicts that demand for yarn both for export and local markets will increase to between 908.9 million kg and 979.1 million kg in 2010

---

[154] Ibidem

[155] "BGMEA for talks with ADB to end controversy over textile sector", The Daily Star, Business Page, Vol. 3, No. 658, July 09, 2001

[156] Ibidem

[157] "Rejuvenating the textile sector, more mills are going for BMRE to grab the post-MFA opportunity" by Shahriar Karim , The Daily Star, Business Page, Vol. 3, No. 637, June 18, 2001

[158] Ibidem

from 649.3 million kg in year 2000.[159] Accompanying demand for fabrics will be between 5463.2 million meter and 5874.7 million meter, up from 3895.3 million meter in 2000 (ibid.). This indicates that the textiles and clothing sector of the country has an enormous potential for investment. It is true that, Bangladesh has an enormous investment potential in textile spinning, weaving and dying-printing-finishing industry[160] in view of the globalization and trade liberalization of the textile and readymade garments sector under the new WTO agreement and eventual phasing-out of the Multi-Fibre Agreement after 2004. The garment industry is import dependent with few domestic linkages (see Table 5.4 and 5.5) . Therefore, the government has put impetus for development of this sector as well other private industries, and speed privatization process in the context of trade liberalization. The above Table (Table 5.5) provides BTMA forecast data for requirement yarn and fabric for export oriented garment industry from 1998/99 to 2009/2010. The table requirement of both yarn and fabric have been shown as declining. An explanation of this declining trend might be the absence of reserved quota for export of RMG after 2004 with accompanying competition from the competitors of Bangladesh in the free trade regime. Existing capacity and efficiency of the textile industry of the country is not enough to compete with the global textile market. A strong base of primary textile i.e. spinning, weaving, and dyeing-printing is essential to continue the growth of garment industry. The Textile Policy 1995 of the government of Bangladesh, however, envisages the establishment of the following number of mills to meet the domestic and export needs of the country for yarn and woven fabric by the beginning of 2005.[161]

i) 246 Spinning mills with 25,000 spindles each,
ii) 481 Weaving mills each with capacity to produce 17 million meters of fabrics,
iii) 481 Dyeing-printing-finishing units each with same capacity to process the above quantity of fabrics.

The Government of Bangladesh has extended following major incentives and facilities for the local and foreign investors to help increase investment in the country for all industrial sectors, including textile and clothing.[162]

i) Five years tax holiday is allowed for Dhaka and Chittagong divisions (Excluding 3 hill districts of Chittagong division),
ii) Seven years of tax holiday is allowed for Rajshahi, Khulna, Sylhet, Barisal and 3 hill districts of Chittagong,

[159] "Rejuvenating the textile sector-favourable policy infuses new investment" by Shahriar Karim, The Daily Star, Business Page, Vol.3, Number 638, June 19, 2001.

[160] "Textiles of Bangladesh, Bangladesh" Textile Mills Association (BTMA) Publication, November 21, 2001 Issue

[161] Ibidem

[162] Ibidem

iii) Tax exemption on royalty, technical know-how fees received by any foreign collaborator, firm, company and expert, interest on foreign loans, income tax upto 3 years of the foreign technicians, income of private sector power generation, capital gains from the transfer of shares of public limited companies listed with stock exchange,
iv) Avoidance of double taxation,
v) No restriction on issuing work permits,
vi) Facilities for full repatriation of invested capital, profit and dividend,
vii) Remittance up to fifty per cent of the salary,
viii) Reinvestment of repairable dividend is treated as new investment,
ix) Working capital loan from commercial banks

Table 5.5
Projected Requirement of the Total Yarn and Fabric for Export Oriented RMG Industry of Bangladesh 1998/99–2009/2010

Year	Readymade Garments		
	Quantity (million dozen)	Input Requirement	
		Fabric (million meter)	Yarn (million kg.)
1998-99	101.45	1859.79	309.97
1999-00	99.83	1829.79	304.96
2000-01	98.25	1800.53	300.09
2001-02	96.71	1772.01	295.33
2002-03	95.21	1744.23	290.70
2003-04	93.71	1717.19	286.20
2004-05	92.32	1690.70	281.78
2005-06	88.62	1622.66	270.44
2006-07	85.08	1557.56	259.59
2007-08	81.70	1495.41	249.24
2008-09	78.46	1434.85	239.31
2009-10	75.37	1379.06	229.84

Source: Bangladesh Textile Mills Association (BTMA). Growth rate assumed 1.25% upto 2004-05 and –3.75% thereafter.

In order to stimulate rapid economic growth of the country, particularly through industrialization, the government has adopted an open door policy to attract foreign investment to Bangladesh. The Bangladesh Export Processing Zone (BEPZ) is entrusted to attract, protect and facilitate foreign investment in the EPZs, with the Board of Investment (BOI) as responsible for all other areas. Two EPZs, one is Chittagong, and the other in Dhaka have been operational for more than 10 years. In the wake of increasing demand of the investors, the

Dhaka EPZ has been expanded. Development work of the EPZ at Mongla, a southern part of Bangladesh is progressing fast. Three other EPZs in Comilla, Syedpur, Nilphamary are in the implementation stage. Some private EPZs have also been allowed to be set up. Moreover, there are some facilities for setting up the industries at EPZs :

i) Land and factory building are available on rental basis
ii) Electricity, telecommunication, gas and water are provided by the zones authority
iii) Import and export permits are issued by EPZ within 24 hours
iv) Work permits are issued by BEPZA
v) The EPZ is a secured and protected area
vi) Recreational facilities are available. Availability of food stuff and beverages on payment on the nominal tax for foreigners working at EPZs.
vii) Tax holiday for 10 years
viii) Duty free import of machines, equipment and raw material and duty free import of goods
ix) GSP facility for export to USA, EU and Japan. Export from Bangladesh to USA enjoys Most Favoured Nation (MFN) status.
x) No ceiling of foreign investment and many other facilities.

BTMA in association with CPD organised the seminar to mark inauguration of a two day local textile and apparel show at Hotel Sheraton on May 28, 2001 in which speakers called for loans at subsidised interest rates for the textile sector and creation of efficient infrastructure facilities to face the challenges of the duty-and quota-free regime after 2004.[163] They also said the government should subsidy the financial institutions so that the backward linkage industries of the RMG sector get soft loans. However, speakers apprehended that lowering bank interest rates might encourage entrepreneurs to go for non-viable capital intensive units and that must impact our economy and asked the policy planners to think twice before going for interest cuts.

5.20 Incentives for the Textile and Clothing Sector

The government has been providing generous cash incentives[164] for exports of fabric manufactured from domestic yarn since 1994. The incentives are given to the fabric exporters, provided no duty bond or duty drawback facility is accessed.[165] This has enabled the yarn and fabric producers to raise their prices considerably over the world prices of similar products. For example, domestic

---

[163] "BTMA seminar calls for soft loans to textile sector-Move to face post-2004 duty and quota free regime", The Daily Star, Business Page, Vol. 3, No. 618, May 29 2001

[164] "Taka 300 Cr. Cash incentives for textile exporters", Business and Finance, The New Nation, available at www.nation-online.com/200210/23/n2102303.htm

[165] The incentive is now substantially above whatever duty fabric or yarn manufacturer might pay.

carded yarn sells for about US$ 3.00 per kg while the Indian price is US$ 2.40. Thus the domestic yarn price is 25 per cent higher than the Indian price. The domestically produced cotton twill costs US$ 1.35 per yard when the Indian price is about one dollar. The Chinese twill is even cheaper. Both yarn and fabric manufacturers, who quoted these prices, freely admitted that it would have been very difficult, if not altogether impossible, for them to survive the overseas competition without the cash incentives.

As per policy of the government huge investments are to be made in the textile sector. Considering the growth potential of the textile sector, some incentives and facilities have been given by the government. The package of the textile sector incentive has been aimed at primarily to boost the exporters. DEDO (Duty Exemption Drawback Organization) is one of them i.e. exporters of manufactured products are entitled to draw back, after the export is effected, the amount of duties and taxes already paid at the time of importing raw materials (Hossain, 1989). Another one is Bonded Warehouse Facility which is allowed for some exporting sectors, including the garments manufacturers and producers of specialised textiles. Exporters are permitted to import inputs worth up to 70 per cent of the value of L/Cs under this facility. Any export oriented units, not enjoying the bonded warehouse facilities can avail duty drawback. At present 25 per cent cash assistance is also available to RMG, hosiery and textile units which are either not covered or refrain from using the facilities provided under bonded warehouse and duty drawback facilities.[166]

Cash assistance is also provided for exporting indigenous handloom Jamdani Sari Lungi and Gamchha[167] instead of Bonded Warehouse or Duty Draw-Back incentive. As per the directives of Bangladesh Bank, a system of paying 25% cash incentive by the government against direct export or supplying to local RMG industries of the indigenous handloom fabrics was already in place. But this generous incentive was grossly misused by a section of fraudulent suppliers and exporters as they provided fabricated materials instead of these items (Chowdhury, 1989) Government of Bangladesh suspended providing this incentive against export or supply to local RMG industries from 18 August 1998 for Jamdani Sari, and from 25 November 1998 for Lungi and Gamchha. In lieu of this, government adopted another policy of paying 10% cash incentive of the Free on Board (FOB) value of these items from 01 July 2000 if not availed the Bonded Warehouse or Duty Draw-back facilities subject to the following conditions:[168]

---

[166] Textiles of Bangladesh, Bangladesh Textile Mills Association (BTMA) Publication, November 21, 2001 Issue

[167] Sari is a traditional women's wear, Lungi is a men's wear as a loose trouser, and Gamchha is a local towel used in Bangladesh

[168] Foreign Exchange Department, Bangladesh Bank Head Office, Dhaka, F.E. Circular No. 8 dated 04 March, 2001.

1. The exporters should be registered with the Handloom Board as producers and Export Promotion Bureau (EPB) as exporters of the commodities.
2. This 10% cash incentive would be paid only against the export L/C.
3. Cash incentives for these items would be paid if export price ceilings were US$ 40.00 for Jamdhani Sari, US$ 3.00 for Lungi, and US$ 0.50 for Gamchha.
4. 10% cash incentive would be paid, the amount of which is minimum in either of the two cases as below:
   (a) FOB export value of these items,
   (b) Total amount as calculated by the ceilings at serial 3.

Government has adopted this step to check fraudulent practice of delivering fabricated materials and reap incentive benefits deceitfully by some exporters of these items. Now, incentive is provided only for export, and not for supplying to local RMG. As may be calculated from the data in Table 5.6, the supply of domestically produced fabrics increased at the rate of 36.02 per cent from 1994-95 to 1998-99, but the cash incentives increased at the rate of 92.71 per cent during the same period, and at the rate 76.43 per cent during the period 1994-95 to 1999-2000. Thus, cash incentives increased at a much faster rate than the increase in the local supply of fabric for RMG.

Table 5.6
Domestic Fabrics for Export-oriented RMG and Cash Subsidy (Bangladesh)

Year	Domestic fabrics used in Export-oriented RMG		Cash Subsidy	
	Million Metres	Growth (%)	Million Taka	Growth (%)
1993-94	45	-	78	-
1994-95	104	131.1	290	271.8
1995-96	169	62.5	488	68.5
1996-97	231	36.7	800	64.0
1997-98	317	37.2	2236	179.5
1998-99	356	12.3	4000	78.9
1999-2000	456	15.9	4958	24.0
2000-2001	555	17.2	5270	27.0

Source: Ministry of Textiles and Bangladesh Bank

This is a barrier to develop backward linkage industries with attending value addition, which would certainly impact many economic activities of the country. Moreover, direct export will also be diminished due to the ceiling of export prices as mentioned. However, this ceiling has blocked the scope of under-invoicing and filching of foreign exchange.

5.21 Value Added Ratio and Contribution of RMG

We have calculated total value added of garments for all the years on the basis of export figures and structure of the RMG by appropriate blowing up. As observable in the Table 5.7 RMG constitutes 30 per cent of Manufacturing Value Added (MVA) of the country in 1998-99 and 20.6 per cent of MVA in 1997-98 increased from 6.5 per cent in 1993-94.

Table 5.7
Value Added (VA) Ratio and Contribution of RMG to MVA of Bangladesh (Million AKA)

Indicators	1981-82	1993-94	1997-98	1982-84	1994-98	1982-98
Output	171	54937	175096			
Input	128.20	44652	133090			
RMG VA	42.80	10285	42006			
VA to Output (%)	25.00	20.00	24.00			
MVA	23447	159215	203626			
Share of RMG VA in	0.18	6.50	20.60			
Growth of RMG VA				58.00	42.20	53.80
Growth of MVA				17.30	6.30	14.40
Elasticity of MVA to				0.298	0.15	0.27

Source: Coded from Dr. N.C. Nath, (External Competitiveness of RMG Industry of Bangladesh: Analysis of Status and Strategies, BIDS, Dhaka, 2001)

Elasticity of MVA to RMG exports leads to an increase of manufactured value added by 3 per cent, growth of value added of RMG has been spectacular in all the periods of the eighties and nineties.

5.22 Backward and Forward Linkages of RMG with other Sectors

The total chain of production and supply in the textile and clothing sector might reasonably be perceived as the backward and forward linkages to the global market of RMG products in the unrestricted quota-free international market in 2005. It might be understood clearly from the flow chart in the figure 5.4. Notably, India has such backward and forward linkage value chain, which is evident from the excerpt below:[169]

"It is only industry, which is self-reliant and complete in value chain from raw material (cotton) to the highest value-added products (garments and made-ups). Consequently, the growth of this industry has a significant bearing on the overall development of the country."

[169] WTO and Textile Industry, by T. S. Vishwanath, Op. Cit.

Similarly, Hong Kong has a strong supply chain, which is not product-driven, rather it is buyer-driven. This is apparent from the following citation.[170] "Hong Kong textile and apparel industry is a leader in managing the supply chain on a world-wide basis. It differs from producer-driven supply chains led by multinational companies. The apparel industry is a buyer driven commodity chain led by a coalition of retailers, contractors, sub-contractors, merchandisers, buyers and suppliers. Each participating entity plays a role in a network of supply chains with span from fibres, to yarn, to fabrics, to accessories, to garments, to trading and marketing,"

Figure 5.5
Backward (B.L) and Forward Linkages (F.L) to RMG Exports of Bangladesh

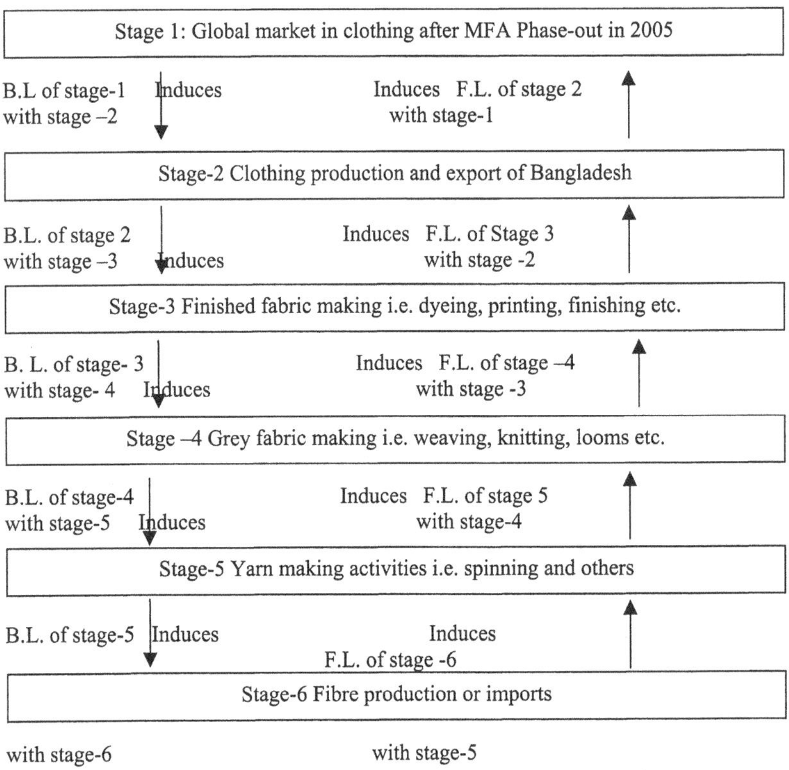

[170] "Information Technology Infrastructure for Textile and Apparel Industry in Hong Kong", by Benjamin P.-C. Yen and C.J. Su (http://www.electronicmarkets.org/netacademy/publications.nsf/all pk/87abstract

Anderson (1992) mentions that Dixit and Grossman (1982) have developed an elegant model of manufactures which are produced via a vertical production structure with many stages. At each stage value is added to an intermediate material to yield a good-in-process for the next stage. The good at stage i + di is produced from one unit of stage i output. All stages produce the final product.[171] Although it is almost similar to that in figure 5.5, a considerable simplification has been made in this model. For example, the manufacturing of carpet, a home textile, does require weaving. However, the backward linkage chain as mentioned in the figure 5.5 certainly involves at every stage, some factors that are linked horizontally to that specific stage.

Table 5.8
Input-Output Ratio in Different Sectors (1993-94)

Input Supplying	Sectors Input-Output Ratio
Mill Cloth	0.59
Yarn	0.004
RMG	0.01
Other Textiles	0.10
Food & Entertainment	0.001
Paper & Board	0.002
Printing & Publishing	0.01
Chemicals	0.0004
Petroleum and its Products	0.002
Fabricated Metals	0.14
Machinery	0.0064
Transport Equipment	0.0006
Miscellaneous Industries	0.005
Urban Building	0.009
Rural Building	0.009
Construction: Electricity & Gas	0.0000002
Electricity	0.0044
Gas	0.000173
Trade Service	0.029
Transport Service	0.016
Health Service	0.000029
Public Administration	0.00081
Banking & Insurance	0.00164
Professionnel Service	0.00115
Communications	0.002
Total Intermediate Input	0.81
Total Output	1.00
Value Added Output	0.19

Source: Coded from Dr. N.C. Nath, (External Competitiveness of RMG Industry of Bangladesh: Analysis of Status and Strategies, BIDS, Dhaka, 2001)

[171] "Structural Adjustment in Australia and New Zealand", by Peter Lloyd In. New Silk Roads, East Asia and World Textile Markets, edited by Kym Anderson, Cambridge, University Press (1992), p. 189

Again, as shown in the Table 5.8, RMG has overwhelmingly high backward linkage with textile sector providing fabrics, yarn and other ancillaries. It has important backward linkage with utilities like electricity, gas etc. It has high backward linkage with machinery and spare parts supplying sectors. It has forward linkage with transport, communication, banking and insurance and trade services. There is a considerable subcontracting linkage within the sector. Thus this tremendous impact in almost all the industrial and manufacturing sector of Bangladesh.

5.23 Developmental Contribution due to RMG Sector

These encouraging factors fuelled the rapid expansion of RMG in Bangladesh. Added to this the international environment was completely favourable to the tremendous growth of this industry. By the mid 70's the already established developed suppliers of apparels in the world markets viz. Hong Kong, South Korea, Singapore, Taiwan, Thailand, Malaysia, Sri Lanka and India were severely constrained by the quota restrictions imposed by their major buyers like.the USA, EU, and Canada. To maintain their business and competitive edge in the world apparel markets, they followed a strategy of reallocation of RMG factories in those countries which were free from quota restrictions, and at the same time had enough trainable cheap labour. Thus, this industry has developed a group of entrepreneurs who have acquired skill in international marketing and organising production to compete in the international market. The role of external as well internal factors have contributed to the development of this sector which are as follows:

5.23.1 Role of External Factors

The fast development of RMG has been due to external factors as well as domestic initiatives which were undertaken since late 1970s. The rapid growth of the RMG industry in Bangladesh has been facilitated by the Agreement on Textile and Clothing (ATC), Multi-Fibre Agreement (MFA) and Generalised System of Preferences (GSP) as discussed below:

As I have discussed about the explanation of Agreement on Textiles and Clothing in the previous chapter, here I will concentrate on the other main issues of external factors like the Multi-fibre Arrangement (MFA) and Generalized System of Preferences (GSP).

5.23.1.1 Multi-Fibre Arrangement (MFA)

The Agreement on Textiles and Clothing (ATC) made under the auspices of the Uruguay Round of the agreements stipulates phasing out of MFA by the year 2005. The ATC sets out provisions to be applied by members during a transition period for the integration of the textiles and clothing sector into GATT 1994. The ATC cannot be extended.

Table 5.9
RMG Industry in Bangladesh

Year	RMG export (million US$)	Share of knitwear in RMG export (%)	RMG share in total exports (%)	Employment	No. of RMG factories
1983-84	31.57		3.89	n.a	134
1984-85	116.2		12.44	n.a	384
1985-86	131.48		16.05	0.198	594
1986-87	298.67		27.74	0.283	629
1987-88	433.92		35.24	0.306	685
1988-89	471.09		36.47	0.317	725
1989-90	624.16		32.45	0.335	759
1990-91	866.82	15.13	50.47	0.402	834
1991-92	1182.57	10.03	59.31	0.582	1163
1992-93	1445.02	14.15	60.64	0.804	1537
1993-94	1555.79	16.98	61.40	0.827	1839
1994-95	2228.35	17.65	64.17	1.200	2182
1995-96	2547.13	23.49	65.61	1.290	2353
1996-97	3001.25	25.43	67.93	1.300	2503
1997-98	3781.94	24.79	73.28	1.500	2726

Note: n.a stands for not available
Source: BGMEA

Initially Bangladesh was given "quota free" status because its RMG industry was underdeveloped. The number of garment factories grew rapidly after 1983/84. (Table 5.9), following the relocation to Bangladesh of quota-limited sourcing from the Republic of Korea and also from Sri Lanka.

After January 1985, a number of countries imposed quota on imports of garments from Bangladesh under the Multi-Fibre Arrangement. The MFA commenced its drive in 1974. From 1985 Bangladesh emerged as a good regular supplier of apparels. The competitive strength of the RMG sector was due to the availability of cheap female labour. There are as many as 31 categories of apparels exported from Bangladesh to the USA which are subject to quota restrictions and 14 categories in Canada. This meant that even if Bangladesh agreed to supply these categories on better terms or at lower prices, it could not exceed the quota limit. Quotas were not binding for Bangladesh as utilization rates were usually less than 100 per cent. But quota provided a guaranteed market for

Bangladeshi garments in the USA and Canada without facing any competition, as buyers were looking for locations where quotas were available.

5.23.1.2 Generalized System of Preferences

As I have discussed earlier, the market access conditions of the EU for RMG products from Bangladesh is determined by the EU regulation on the Generalised System of Preferences (GSP) since 1992. The bilateral agreement initiated on 29 December 1994 was an important step for the textile and garment trade policy between the EU and Bangladesh. The categories were 4 (T-shirts and undervest), 6 (trousers) and 8 (men's and boys woven shirts). Export licences were to be issued by the Export Promotion Bureau.Virtually no quantitative restrictions apply for these categories. This bilateral agreement is expected to expire on 31 December, 2004. In this context, I will discuss in about the General principle of GSP, and European Union and Bangladesh concern.

5.23.1.3 Introduction of the GSP by the European Union

The Generalized Tariff Preference (GTP) was first conceived and mooted in the First UNCTAD Conference held in Geneva in 1964, and the Second UNCTAD Conference held-in New Delhi in 1968-established the key principles of the Generalized System of Preference (GSP). The Conference resolution embodied its application to all developing countries, non-reciprocity of concessions and internal non-discrimination.

Later on, for the first time, the European Union (EU) introduced a scheme to implement GSP. But as the system deviates from the normal GATT Rules, relating to Most Favoured Nation (MFN) clause, treating virtually everyone equally, its implementation was subject to prior approval from the GATT in the form of a formal derogation decision, which is commonly known as enabling clause, initially adopted on the 25th June, 1971 and renewed for an indefinite period on 28 November, 1979. Switzerland and Norway had introduced the GSP Scheme on March 1st, 1972, while Japan had introduced the same on August, 1, 1971.

5.23.1.4 The European Union and Bangladesh

As stated in the chapter four, EU countries provide duty-free and quota free access to garment exports from Bangladesh under the Generalised System of Preference. These concessions are a major factor in increasing the RMG exports to EU countries. One of the requirements for availing GSP is that the fabric used in apparels exported to the EU must be manufactured locally. This has facilitated the growth of a substantial market for the fabric manufacturers of the country.

Table 5.10
RMG Export to European Union
(million US $)

Year	Exported to EU	% of total export
1991-92	548.90	46.42
1992-93	660.21	45.69
1993-94	862.41	55.43
1994-95	1100.02	49.36
1995-96	1405.23	55.17
1996-97	1624.10	54.11
1997-98	1934.73	51.16
1998-99	2105.60	52.38

Source: Export Promotion Bureau of Bangladesh, 2001

EU countries are the largest garment importers from Bangladesh. At present, 52 per cent of the total garment exporters to the EU. Belgium, Denmark, France, Germany, Italy, the Netherlands, Spain, U.K. are the major importers of Bangladeshi garments.

Since July 1971, Bangladesh had the preferential market access to EU countries under the EC-GSP scheme. Preferential treatment under the EC-GSP scheme allows EU importers to claim duty draw back on imports of apparel from Bangladesh. The rules of GSP have changed many times since its introduction. From January 1, 1999 the EU has relaxed rules of origin for textiles and apparel. The new GSP is now based on a two-stage derogation for knitwear manufacturers, and one-stage derogation for woven garments, instead of a three-stage and two-stage respectively. Knitwear manufacturers in Bangladesh can therefore buy yarns abroad and woven garment makers can buy fabrics produced with foreign yarns. The new GSP are likely to increase Bangladeshi garment exports to the EU. However, the new rules would have adverse effects on Bangladeshi yarn manufacturers. Also since 1999, a two-stage transformation requirement, i.e. yarn to fabric and fabric to garment, is in place for both knit and woven garments. Recently, EU has permitted a derogation of the rules of origin under the GSP scheme.

The basic rule of the present GSP was that of 1995, where duty free access were provided to Bangladesh if accompanied by Certificate of Origin as a Least Developed Country (LDC). Since November 1997, Bangladesh has obtained permission to apply derogation from the rules of origin conferring preferential tariff treatment for RMG products imported into the EU. RMG products manufactured in Bangladesh on the basis of imported woven fabrics or yarns originating from ASEAN countries (excluding Myanmar) or SAARC[172] coun-

[172] South Asian Association of Regional Cooperation, a regional Body established in 1982.

tries were to be considered as products of Bangladesh preferential origin, subject to specific quantitative annual ceilings.

5.23.2 Role of Internal Factors

Domestic initiatives have been playing a very important role for the growth of this sector which we have discussed earlier. Here we will give emphasis on a few points:

5.23.2.1 Role of Private Sector

The growth of the industry resulted from external factors, role of a catalyst as well as conducive government policies. The competitive strength of the RMG sector was due to the availability of cheap supply of female labour. Before employment in RMG women in Bangladesh were confined to the precinct of the household (Zohir, 2000). The role of a catalyst was important to bring these women out of their home as well to create mid-level managers. The most critical factors in the success of garment industry in Bangladesh was the on-the-job training and the back-to-back letter of credit under the special bonded warehouse facility. Moreover, the government provided various export promotion measures since 1978 as discussed below.

5.23.2.2 Continuity in Policies in Successive Government

The government has played the role of facilitating the private sector by taking conducive policies. The continuity of policies pursued towards industrialisation has been a key factor in the growth of the RMG industry. The validity of the export and import policy were subsequently increased from six months to one year, and then to two years. Finally it is now for five years (Islam, 2002). This will create confidence that policy reversal will not take place in the short run. Some of the policies which benefited the RMG industry were:

i) Decontrol of the reserved sectors;
ii) Ceiling on private investment was abolished;
iii) Incentive for export oriented industries were published in the newspapers and implemented through the guide to investment of 9th September, 1978;
iv) Export Credit Guarantee Scheme (1978);
v) Garment in the Free Sector (no permission needed) 1983;
vi) Back-to-back L/C and bonded warehouse facilities;
vii) Successive industrial policies including Structural Adjustment Policies (1985/86-1992/93) continued support for the RMG industry.

The shift towards private sector-led and export-ed growth started since late 1970s. The New Industrial Incentive Package (NIIP) was not, however formally published as a policy at that time, although its provisions were announced in the press. So it has been ignored by the researchers in assessing impact of policy. The NIIP 1978 was published as New Industrial Policy (NIP) 1982 which has been widely acclaimed for being a corner stone in policy shift. The choice of the shift year has made a great difference in impact analysis.

Although the IFC (1999) report suggests that the back-to-back letter of credit formula which worked in Sri Lanka was lifted and applied to Bangladesh, but the report notes that:

"Bangladesh's export oriented RMG sector does not benefit from any public incentives and subsidies." But on the contrary another World Bank[173] Report notes that:

"Without any improvement in the domestic financial sector, and without making any changes to Bangladesh's then high tariff walls, the sector grew because of the external financing through back-to-back letters of credit and the provision of special bonded warehouses to access inputs at international prices." (World Bank, 1994)

5.24 Concluding Remarks

The discussions made in this chapter clearly show that many factors are affecting the growth and development of readymade garments industry in Bangladesh which are intensively associated with present government role and international regulations regarding textiles and clothing sector. All these regulations and policies from both the internal and external perspectives affect the Bangladesh economy as well trade liberalization process in the country. In this context, the chapter six would also analyse in detail the review of world production of textile and clothing and Bangladesh performance.

[173] World Bank and IMF are the major Development Partners of Bangladesh

CHAPTER SIX
REVIEW OF WORLD PRODUCTION AND BANGLADESH PERFORMANCE

6.1 Introduction

Bangladesh is one of the few developing countries which have emerged as significant exporters of garments within a short-period of time. Yet, in recent years, concerns have been raised about the viability of the clothing sector of Bangladesh. Because of heavy dependence of imported inputs, the contribution of the clothing sector in total manufacturing value added is far from spectacular in Bangladesh. The share of manufacturing value added in GDP increased only from 9.8 per cent in 1980 to 10.3 per cent in 1995. Given the current structure of government incentives, a new dualism has emerged in Bangladesh, with export-oriented sectors such as clothing, having little linkages with domestic market oriented sectors. It has been argued that Bangladesh may lose its competitive position relative to other South Asian and East Asian countries in a liberalized trade environment because the clothing sector of Bangladesh lacks backward linkages (UNCTAD, 1998). Promotion of industrial linkages is one of the major features of export, industrial, trade and textile policies of the government of Bangladesh. The textile and garment manufacturers and the exporters association of Bangladesh also support the policy of promoting industrial linkages. As discussed earlier, during the last decade or so, Bangladesh has substantially liberalized its trade regime, moving away from costly protectionst policy toward a more export-friendly trade regime. The current industrial policy (1999) and export policy (1997-2002) have identified the textile and clothing sector as one of the "thrust" sectors of Bangladesh (Islam, 2001). The patterns of comparative advantage and hence the structure of exports and imports involving textiles and clothing, as stated before, depend on the stages of economic development in Bangladesh and other countries. However, this chapter attempts to evaluate the competitive position of Bangladesh, scrutinise the global market, market access of Bangladesh RMG in the world market and Bangladesh position in the above context.

6.2 Global Market Analysis

Analysis of global markets in textiles and clothing exhibits a number of perceptible changes. One such change is the increasing share of clothing compared to textiles in the world trade. For instance, the share of yarn declined to 9% in 1993; fabrics decreased 32% from 1980 to 30% in 1993, while share of clothing increased to 60% in 1993 from 55% in 1980. Another important aspect of global textile trade is the projection of the GATT Secretariat about the textiles and clothing in view of the effects of liberalization measures on the world economy. According to the three versions of the model, the annual compound growth rate for textiles and clothing upto 2005 (using 1992 as base year) will be 1.2% and 4.1% for version- 1, 1.3% and 4.9% for version-2, and 4.3% and 8.6 for version-3 respectively. However, of these three versions, the annual growth rates implied by the third version were found realistic by analysis carried out by a recent study (Ministry of Commerce, 1996). In this stage, as mentioned earlier, Bangladesh needs to find a "market niche" in the global market for its clothing exports after the phasing out of MFA quota restrictions in 2005. Because, in an increasingly globalized economy, industries will have to be more market-driven than ever before. Any strategy formulated to run into this objective "will have to start with the markets and work with its various type of impact in the local economy."[174] Bangladesh textile and clothing sector needs, therefore, to work backward to cater satisfactorily to the quantity, quality and price requirements of both domestic and international markets, keeping in view the industry's potential for employment through the expansion of the backward linkage industries which will automatically impact the various other sectors of the country. At present, the EU and the US provide the lion's share of markets for RMG exports of Bangladesh, which indicates that the international market for RMG products is not diversified. Therefore, identification of markets and products for each market is crucial, particularly in view of the impending quota free global trade in textile and clothing.

6.2.1 Leading Textile and Clothing Exporters

With the updated data upto 1997 for textiles exports, it is observed that (Table 6.1) in 1997, three East Asian countries i.e. Hong Kong, China, and South Korea occupied the top three slots among the leading textile exporters of the world, although positions of Taiwan, Japan appear later. These five countries altogether account for 39.5% of the World's total exports in textiles.

174 "Importance of Textile Sector in Tamil Nadu" (http://www.focustamilnadu.com/tamilnadu/textile_policy.htm, downloaded on 22 October, 2000.

Table 6.1
Leading Textile Exporters (million US $)

Country	1994		1995		1996		1997
	Value	Share (%)	Value	Share (%)	Value	Share (%)	Value
Hong Kong	12574.0	9.7	13185.0	9.2	14146.0	9.4	14602.0
China	11818.0	9.1	13918.0	9.3	12112.0	8.0	12828.0
South Korea	10693.0	8.2	12313.0	8.2	12718.0	8.4	13346.0
Germany	12654.0	9.7	14389.0	9.6	13787.0	9.2	13053.0
Italy	10861.0	8.3	12797.0	8.5	13206.0	8.8	12901.0
Taiwan	10260.0	7.9	11882.0	7.9	12048.0	8.0	12731.0
U.S.A.	6592.0	5.1	7372.0	4.9	8009.0	5.3	9193.0
France	6224.0	4.8	7468.0	5.0	7303.0	4.9	7214.0
Bel-Lux	6797.0	5.2	7880.0	5.2	7438.0	4.9	7010.0
Japan	6780.0	5.2	7178.0	4.8	6927.0	4.6	6750.0
U.K.	4492.0	3.5	5163.0	3.4	5398.0	3.6	5618.0
Pakistan	3985.0	3.1	4256.0	2.8	4919.0	3.3	4594.0
Turkey	2194.0	1.7	2527.0	1.7	2722.0	1.8	3352.0
Netherlands	2694.0	2.1	3526.0	2.4	3240.0	2.2	3010.0
Spain	1947.0	1.5	2595.0	1.7	2886.0	1.9	2784.0
Indonesia	2498.0	1.9	2719.0	1.8	2835.0	1.9	2255.0
Thailand	1647.0	1.3	1937.0	1.3	1830.0	1.2	1925.0
Austria	1843.0	1.4	1989.0	1.3	2005.0	1.3	1911.0
Switzerland	2112.0	1.6	2267.0	1.5	2010.0	1.3	1795.0
Portugal	1344.0	1.0	1627.0	1.1	1610.0	1.1	1629.0
Others	10211.0	7.8	12648.0	8.4	13501.0	9.0	15779.0
WORLD	130220.0	100.0	150260.0	100.0	150650.0	100.0	155280.0

Source: World Trade Organization (WTO)[175]

Again in the similar list with regard to the clothing exports in Table 6.2, China and Hong Kong secured the top two positions in 1997 among the leading clothing exporters of the world. China, Hong Kong, South Korea and Taiwan-these four countries altogether account for 35.4% of the world's total export of RMG. Unfortunately, Bangladesh has no position in the list of top twenty exporters upto 1997, but in the year 2001, Bangladesh's position in the world export market of RMG is 18th.

[175] Downloaded and edited from Thailand textile institute website: http://www.thaitextile.org/

Table 6.2
Leading Clothing Exporters (million US$)

Country	1994		1995		1996		1997
	Value	Share (%)	Value	Share (%)	Value	Share (%)	Value
China	23731.0	16.9	24949.0	15.3	25034.0	15.1	31803.0
Hong Kong	21404.0	15.2	21297.0	13.5	21976.0	13.3	23107.0
Italy	12525.0	8.9	14175.0	9.0	16172.0	9.8	14851.0
USA	5616.0	4.0	6651.0	4.2	7511.0	4.5	8672.0
Germany	6669.0	4.8	7500.0	4.8	7579.0	4.6	7289.0
Turkey	4582.0	3.3	6119.0	3.9	6067.0	3.7	6697.0
France	4974.0	3.5	5621.0	3.6	5529.0	3.3	5345.0
U.K.	4116.0	2.9	4648.0	3.0	5184.0	3.1	5281.0
South Korea	5653.0	4.0	4957.0	3.2	4221.0	2.5	4192.0
Thailand	4508.0	3.2	5008.0	3.2	3845.0	2.3	3770.0
Netherlands	2622.0	1.9	2771.0	1.8	3053.0	1.8	3655.0
Taiwan	3445.0	2.5	3251.0	2.1	3207.0	1.9	3410.0
Portugal	3287.0	2.3	3805.0	2.4	3591.0	2.2	3303.0
Bel--Lux	2161.0	1.5	2723.0	1.7	3017.0	1.8	3007.0
Indonesia	3206.0	2.3	3376.0	2.1	3591.0	2.2	2904.0
Malaysia	2071.0	1.5	2266.0	1.4	2376.0	1.4	2329.0
Philippines	2185.0	1.6	2420.0	1.5	2389.0	1.4	2315.0
Tunisia	1840.0	1.3	2322.0	1.5	2396.0	1.4	2299.0
Poland	1847.0	1.3	2304.0	1.5	2373.0	1.4	2217.0
Pakistan	1578.0	1.1	1611.0	1.0	1872.0	1.1	1805.0
Others	22400.0	16.0	30546.0	19.4	34887.0	21.0	38359.0
WORLD	140420.0	100.0	157420.0	100.0	165870.0	100.0	176610.0

Source: World Trade Organization (WTO)[176]

East Asian countries, therefore, enjoy a vibrant position in world trade for both textiles and clothing.

6.2.2 Input Requirements for Textile and Clothing: An International Comparison

In recent years, in Bangladesh, as stated earlier, import intensiveness of textile and clothing sectors has received a great deal of attention. Any policy of import substitution of inputs requires a careful analysis of the cost or input structure of the relevant sectors. In order to assess the import-intensity of inputs for textiles and clothing sectors, the following section provides data based on several indicators. Table 6.3 shows values of Import Similarity Index (ISI) for Bangladesh and selected countries for 1990, 1996 and 1997. Bangladesh has the highest

[176] Downloaded and edited from: Thailand textile institute: http://www.thaitextile.org/

similarity index with Sri Lanka while the lowest with Pakistan. The index with India is low compared to that with most countries. Furthermore, the ISI with several countries such as Indonesia, Pakistan, South Korea, Thailand and Taiwan, was lower in 1997 than in 1990, suggesting that the structure of textile imports of Bangladesh has become more dissimilar compared to these countries.

Table 6.3
Import Similarity Index for Bangladesh in Textile Products

Countries	1980	1990	1996	1997
Sri Lanka	.60	.83	.82	.82
India	.36	.45	.50	.40
Pakistan	.37	.33	.31	.31
Indonesia	.68	.71	.65	.65
China	.49	.75	.68	.55
Hong Kong	.58	.75	.70	.57
Malaysia	.53	.82	.72	.57
South Korea	.53	.62	.46	.45
Singapore	.55	.72	.66	.53
Thailand	.46	.72	.59	.55
Taiwan	.48	.74	.53	.46
Vietnam	.76	.63	.65	.62
Philippines	.59	.75	.77	.67
Mexico	.48	.63	.61	.53
Dominican Republic	.53	.80	.71	.55
Jamaica	.53	.78	.69	.67
Turkey	.30	.66	.53	.51

Note: Textile products include yarns and fabrics
Source: The World Trade Analyser.

This is likely due to the fact that other developing countries are less dependent on imported fabrics than Bangladesh.

6.2.3 Cost Structure of Textiles and Clothing Sector

The cost structure of textiles may differ from that of clothing because of differences in input requirements. The cost structure of textiles or clothing may differ across countries because of differences in the composition of products and differences in factor prices. Analysis of the structure of these sectors should be useful on identifying major input supplying industries for these industries. Table 6.4 represents the cost structure of textile industries for selected countries/ regions. Several points from this Table can be highlighted.

Table 6.4
Cost Structure of Textile Industry (%), 1995

Component	India	Sri Lanka	Rest of S. Asia	China	Taiwan	South Korea	Indo	Sing	Vietn	Ho. Ko	USA
Skilled Labour	2.6	1.6	2.2	0.8	3.6	1.7	2.6	7.2	2.0	3.2	3.8
Unskilled Labour	16.7	10.2	14.5	5.1	11.3	8.8	14.0	24.7	12.5	7.4	17.6
Capital	10.6	28.4	9.2	8.9	9.0	9.8	19.0	9.0	4.5	8.8	11.2
Fibres	1.9	0.1	2.0	10.4	1.7	2.3	1.1	0	2.6	0.1	4.3
Textiles	22.2	24.2	26.3	41.1	28.5	36.2	21.2	0	44.8	1.3	29.0
Chemicals	5.4	8.1	7.4	9.6	23.8	21.8	27.0	14.1	7.5	13.3	16.9
Electricity	7.3	6.7	6.1	1.9	2.7	2.5	1.3	4.9	8.1	5.3	1.4
Trade & Transport	9.6	15.3	9.0	8.7	4.4	2.3	6.3	13.6	1.5	43.5	6.2
Financial Services	0.4	0	0.4	3.0	4.4	3.8	2.2	13.1	1.1	8.5	4.0
Others	23.9	5.4	22.9	10.5	10.6	10.8	5.3	13.4	15.4	8.6	5.6
Total	100	100	100	100	100	100	100	100	100	100	100

Source: The Global Trade Analysis Project (GTAP) Version 4.

First, textiles constitute the major input in the textiles sector itself in most of the countries. Textile yarn, for instance, is used to produce textile fabrics. The proportion of textile inputs in total costs varies substantially across countries because of differences in the composition of textile products being produced. Second, the shares of skilled and unskilled labour in textiles are lowest in China and highest in Singapore. Third, the share of labour including skilled and unskilled labour in the textiles sector of the Rest of South Asia which includes Bangladesh is higher than in most of the countries.

Fourth, chemicals constitute a major component in most countries, especially in Taiwan, South Korea and Indonesia. The share of chemicals is relatively low in the rest of Asia, India, and Sri Lanka. Finally, the share of electricity in textiles is higher in Asian countries/regions than in most countries.

Table 6.5 reports data on the cost structure of the apparel sector in selected countries. It is clearly evident that textiles constitute the major input in the apparel sector in all countries. The share of textiles in total costs ranges from 22.2 per cent in India to 55.9 per cent in Singapore. The table also shows that the share of labour including skilled and unskilled labour is lowest in China. The share of labour appears to be lower in South Asian countries/regions than in most other countries. But the comparable data for Bangladesh are not available.

Table 6.5
Cost Structure of the Clothing Industry (In %), 1995

Component	India	Sri Lanka	Rest of S.Asia	China	Taiwan	South Korea	Indo	Sing	Vietn	Ho. Ko	USA
Skilled Labour	1.3	1.4	1.1	0.9	3.6	2.0	1.7	1.8	2.2	5.7	5.9
Unskilled Labour	9.1	9.8	7.9	6.4	21.73	10.6	12.3	8.2	15.7	16.1	21.3
Capital	19.6	23.8	17.0	9.0	5.4	5.3	18.1	4.4	5.7	9.1	14.4
Apparel	3.0	3.2	3.0	0.6	5.3	1.3	17.0	11.5	12.3	7.5	18.9
Textile	22.2	51.2	26.3	53.2	35.2	54.7	30.6	55.9	50.9	41.0	22.9
Leather	0	0.8	0	0.8	0.2	6.8	2.4	0.1	0.6	.0	0.6
Electricity	7.3	0.9	6.1	0.2	1.1	1.3	0.6	0.3	3.0	0.3	0.6
Trade & Transport	9.6	6.3	9.0	10.9	7.6	4.6	5.2	2.8	1.2	9.1	4.7
Financial Services	0.4	0	0.4	2.4	5.0	3.5	1.6	3.9	1.3	2.6	4.3
Chemicals	5.4	1.9	7.3	4.2	8.4	1.7	6.1	2.4	1.9	2.3	3.5
Others	22.1	0.7	21.9	11.4	6.5	8.2	4.4	8.7	5.2	6.3	-
Total	100	100	100	100	100	100	100	100	100	100	100

Source: The Global Trade Analysis Project (GTAP)[177] Version 4 (four)[178].

6.2.4 Dynamics of Trade Balance in Clothing and Textiles: An International Comparison

The level of industrial development differs across countries. Accordingly, different countries are at different stages of the textile cycle. Trade balances in different components of the textile sector should highlight the positions of different countries. Table 6.6 shows trade balances in fibres, yarn, fabrics, clothing, textile machinery, and chemicals.

Countries such as Bangladesh, Sri Lanka, Vietnam, the Philippines, the Dominican Republic, and Mexico apparently belong to the same stage with a substantial trade surplus in only clothing, while these are deficits in other components.[179]

177 The GTAP model adopts the Armington approach to import demand, differentiating products by origin. The approach assumes that similar products originating from different countries are imperfect substitutes.

178 Version 4, covers 50 sectors and 45 regions/countries and contains the benchmark data for the year 1995.

179 For Bangladesh the deficit in textile machinery is associated with a downward trend in the level of production. The index of production has declined from 100 in 1988-89 to only 16.1 in 1997-98 (Statistical Bulletin, Bangladesh Bureau of Statistics, February, 1999, Table 5.31).

Table 6.6
Trade Balances in Textiles Cluster (millions of US $), 1997

Countries	Fibres	Yarn	Fabrics	Clothing	Textile Machinery	Chemicals
India	-60.3	1,510.3	1,013.3	4,533.2	-535.0	256.0
Bangladesh	-72.7	0.2	-757.8	3,376.3	-31.8	-43.1
Sri Lanka	2.9	-9.6	-462.8	2,095.0	-58.7	- 25.6
Vietnam	-47.1	-54.4	-359.4	1,068.4	-86.8	-6 1.1
Philippines	-205.5	-108.6	-723.9	1,119.4	-99.1	-166.3
Dominica	-6.0	-44.9	-200.3	1,157.4	-48.5	-15.9
Mexico	-47.9	-77.3	-937.0	2,577.3	-834.2	-404.4
Pakistan	-64.5	1,441.1	1,967.3	1,908.8	-192.7	-128.6
Thailand	-433.4	413.8	152.4	3,560.2	-316.9	-327.0
Indonesia	-907.8	489.2	-23.4	4,655.6	-753.2	-462.4
Malaysia	-252.7	369.4	-590.9	2,093.4	-327.6	-235.3
China	-3,464.0	-2,480.7	-5,475.5	30,348.3	-1,971.7	-522.3
Korea, Rep	311.6	451.1	5,442.1	2,169.5	-84.9	-264.7
Taiwan	301.6	1,403.9	7,159.9	2,537.3	224.6	-79.0
Singapore	-36.6	67.6	-264.8	357.0	-10.4	72.4
Hong Kong	-344.6	-660.8	-560.5	10,164.2	-150.1	-209.3
Japan	-76.3	-731.8	3,060.8	-15,708.9	3,379.1	900.6
USA	3,549.4	183.7	-1,482.5	-35,739.6	-957.3	888.0
Italy	-2073.6	-211.8	6,554.6	9,870.2	2,026.7	-357.8
Turkey	-771.2	-97.0	175.2	6,786.9	-1,868.4	-600.2

Source: Global Trade Analysis Project (GTAP)

During the 1980-96 period, Bangladesh had a deficit in yarns. For instance, in 1996, Bangladesh had a trade deficit of $ 321.2 million in yarns. However, in 1997, as reported in Table 6.6, Bangladesh had a small surplus of .2 million in yarns, with exports of $82.7 million and imports of $82.5 million. It appears that the figure for 1997 is an anomaly. Pakistan, India, Thailand, Indonesia, and Malaysia had surpluses in two or more components. China and Hong Kong have trade surpluses in clothing only.

However, the deficits of China and Hong Kong in fabrics may be the result of a deliberate policy of greater emphasis on exporting clothing. Taiwan and South Korea apparently belong to a similar stage given the fact that both countries have huge trade surpluses in fabrics. However, Taiwan has trade surpluses in all components except chemicals.[180]

[180] The data on chemicals in Table 6.6 refers to chemicals for dyeing, tanning, and colouring covered by SITC code, 53

Table 6.7
Dynamics of Trade Balances in Textiles

Countries/ Regions	Trade Balance in 1965	Peak Year of Deficit	Beginning of Surplus	Peak Year of Surplus	Trade Balance in 1995
Sri Lanka	Deficit	1994	-	-	Deficit
India	Surplus	-	-	-	Surplus
Russia	Surplus	-	-	-	Surplus
Indonesia	Deficit	1981	1987	1992	Surplus
Thailand	Deficit	1967	1976	-	Surplus
Malaysia	Deficit	1994	-	-	Deficit
Philippines	Deficit	1991	-	-	Deficit
Korea, South	Deficit	1970	1974	-	Surplus
Vietnam	Deficit	-	-	-	Deficit
Singapore	Deficit	1992	-	-	Deficit
Taiwan	Deficit	-	1969	-	Surplus
Hong Kong	Deficit	-	-	-	Deficit
China	Surplus	-	-	1992	Deficit
Mexico	Deficit	1994	-	-	Surplus
Central Ame.	Deficit	-	-	-	Deficit
Turkey	Deficit	1974	1978	-	Surplus
Rest of EU	Surplus	-	-	-	Surplus
Japan	Surplus	-	-	1983	Surplus
UK	Surplus	-	-	1970	Deficit
USA	Surplus	-	-	1980	Deficit
Argentina	Deficit	1980, 1992	-	-	Deficit
Brazil	0	1974	1976	1992	Deficit

Source: Global Trade Analysis Project (GTAP)

Advanced countries, such as the USA and Japan, have huge trade deficits in clothing but trade surpluses in chemicals. Japan, however, maintains a trade surplus in textile machinery and fabrics. Italy, although an industrial country, has huge trade surpluses in fabrics, clothing and textile machinery.

Table 6.7 and 6.8 show the dynamics of trade balances in textile and clothing since 1965 for selected countries. In clothing, the selected countries can be placed into several groups. First, some countries such as Sri Lanka, Indonesia, Thailand, and Mexico had trade deficits in 1965 but achieved trade surpluses later. The trade surpluses for these countries however, have not yet peaked. The second group includes countries such as China, and India which have surpluses since 1965 but surpluses have not peaked. The third group includes Taiwan, Hong Kong and South Korea which have surpluses since 1965 but the surpluses have already peaked. The fourth group includes industrially advanced countries such as Japan, USA and UK which have trade deficits in clothing.

Table 6.8
Dynamics of Trade Balances in Clothing

Countries/ Regions	Trade Balance in 1965	Beginning of Surplus	Peak Year of Surplus	Beginning of Deficit	Trade Balance in 1995
Sri Lanka	Deficit	1974	Not Yet	-	Surplus
India	Surplus	-	Not Yet	-	Surplus
Russia	0	1966	Not Yet	-	Surplus
Indonesia	Deficit	1977	Not Yet	-	Surplus
Thailand	Deficit	1972	Not Yet	-	Surplus
Malaysia	Deficit	1972	1993	-	Surplus
Philippines	Surplus	-	Not Yet	-	Surplus
Korea, South	Surplus	-	1988	-	Surplus
Vietnam	0	1979	Not Yet	-	Surplus
Singapore	Deficit	1970	1989	1994	Deficit
Taiwan	Surplus	-	1987	-	Surplus
Hong Kong	Surplus	-	1991	-	Surplus
China	Surplus	-	Not Yet	-	Surplus
Mexico	Deficit	1973, 1983	Not Yet	-	Surplus
Central Ame.	Deficit	1982	Not Yet	-	Surplus
Turkey	0	1971	Not Yet	-	Surplus
Rest of EU	Surplus	-	1986	1992	Deficit
Japan	Surplus	-	1969	1973	Deficit
UK	Surplus	-	-	1966	Deficit
USA	Deficit	-	-	-	Deficit
Argentina	0	1967	1978, 1989	1979, 1991	Deficit
Brazil	0	1971	1993	1995	Deficit

Note: "-" indicates the information is not applicable
Source: Global Trade Analysis Project (GTAP)

Table 6.7 shows the dynamics of trade of balances in textiles for selected countries during 1965-1995. The first group of countries include Sri Lanka, Malaysia, the Philippines, Hong Kong, and Vietnam which always had deficits in textiles. In Hong Kong and Malaysia however, trade surpluses in clothing have peaked, as observed in the previous table.

The second group of countries include Indonesia, Thailand, Taiwan and South Korea which had deficits in textiles in 1965 but achieved surpluses later. However, for both Taiwan and South Korea, as seen in the previous table, surpluses in clothing have already peaked. Thus these two countries are at a higher stage of "textile cycles". It is instructive to note that for Indonesia it took only six years to achieve a trade surplus in 1987 from the peak year (1981) of deficit of textiles. For Thailand and South Korea, the time periods were 9 and 4 years respectively. India and China present contrasting cases with India having trade surpluses in textiles but China trade deficits by the year 1995. The advanced countries such as USA and UK have deficits in textiles as well as clothing.

Three points deserve to be mentioned. First, as the experiences of South Korea and Indonesia show, a country can achieve trade surpluses in textiles from the peak year of deficits through a policy of import substitution within a short period of time. Second, textiles and clothing cycles are not existing. For instance, Indonesia witnessed a trade surplus in clothing in 1977 (Table 6.8) while a surplus in textiles in 1987, with a lag of 10 years. For Thailand, the time lag was only 4 years. Finally, for some countries, such as Singapore and Malaysia, textiles and clothing cycles appear to be short with trade deficits in textiles. Apparently, these countries have shifted away from textiles and clothing toward other industries.

6.2.5 Productivity in Textiles and Clothing

International competitive advantage in a product group is ultimately maintained and improved through continuous increases in productivity (Porter, 1990). The performance of Bangladesh in this regard has been far from impressive. Table 6.9, 6.10 and 6.11 report data on wages, productivity, and related variables for the apparel, knitting mills and spinning, weaving and finishing industries of Bangladesh for the 1990-2001 period.

Table 6.9
Productivity and Wages in Apparel (In US $) in Bangladesh

Year	Annual Wages	Labour Productivity	Average Size	Share of Wages	Share of Value Added (%)
1990	305.7	778.8	25	39.3	35.0
1991	308.5	788.7	123	39.1	31.7
1992	344.4	803.1	163	42.9	28.3
1993	329.6	810.4	234	40.7	25.4
1994	350.0	806.2	206	43.3	30.9
1995	338.3	638.0	252	53.0	27.1
1996	344.4	692.8	205	49.7	26.0
1997	299.5	869.3	244	34.5	25.8
1998	345.5	989.4	239	34.9	27.4
1999	352.2	965.1	245	36.5	28.0
2000	334.7	951.1	288	35.2	26.6
2001	340.9	890.1	315	38.3	24.7

Notes: 1. Average size refers to the average number of employees per establishment
2. The share of wages to the share of wages in value added
3. The share of value added refers to the share of value added in output

Source: United Nations Industrial Development Organization (UNIDO)

The information from these tables can be summarised as follows. First productivity growth in the three groups of industries has been quite small. In apparel industries, for instance, labour productivity increased from $ 778.8 in 1990 to only $ 890.1 in 2001. In spinning, weaving and finishing industries, productivity appears to have declined. Labour productivity is higher in knitting mills, compared to that in the other two groups of industries. Second, the average wage appears to be higher in spinning and weaving industries, compared to that in apparel and knitting mills. The average wage in apparel industries has increased from $ 305.7 in 1990 to $ 340.9 in 2001.

Table 6.10
Productivity and Wages in Knitting Industries of Bangladesh

Year	Annual Wages (US $)	Labour Productivity (US $)	Average Size	Share of Wages	Share of Value Added (%)
1990	300.1	961.5	9	31.2	21.1
1991	242.2	991.9	10	24.4	20.7
1992	259.3	1072.9	10	24.2	18.1
1993	268.1	1112.4	9	24.1	15.4
1994	253.6	824.0	9	30.8	12.6
1995	156.9	1263.2	9	20.3	18.2
1996	315.5	1178.0	9	26.8	17.7
1997	330.3	974.5	11	33.9	18.2
1998	320.1	868.3	10	36.9	15.5
1999	329.4	815.7	10	40.4	15.8
2000	306.6	961.8	8	31.9	18.8
2001	378.2	1043.3	9	36.3	22.4

Source: UNIDO

Third, the share of wages in value added and the share of value added in out put in apparel industries have declined over the 1990-2001 period. The share of wages in value added is higher in spinning and weaving than in apparel and knitting industries. Finally, the average size of the establishment is lower in knitting industries, compared to that of the other two groups of industries.[181]

[181] The average size of establishment in terms of employees in garment industries of Bangladesh increased to 550 in 1997/98, according to the Bangladesh Bureau of Statistics (BBS).

Table 6.11
Productivity and Wages in Spinning, Weaving and Finishing Industries: Bangladesh

Year	Annual Wages (US$)	Labour Productivity (US $)	Average Size	Share of Wages	Share of Value Added (%)
1990	615.6	986.3	1591	62.4	45.0
1991	499.8	784.4	1501	66.8	40.7
1992	462.5	892.9	1377	51.8	43.5
1993	532.3	892.4	1333	59.6	39.1
1994	536.2	807.6	1287	66.4	31.2
1995	613.8	1189.0	1376	51.6	49.8
1996	684.3	1216.4	1342	56.3	51.7
1997	664.5	1160.8	142	57.2	45.4
1998	623.9	1936.6	53	60.2	39.5
1999	747.6	847.8	52	88.2	37.2
2000	638.7	775.9	48	82.3	34.8
2001	590.5	742.5	49	79.5	32.3

Source: UNIDO

6.2.6 Indicators of Competitiveness

In a highly competitive international market, it is the price and quality which determine the competitive position of a supplier. Bangladesh can beat its competitors on account of price which is low labour costs. That Bangladesh has a comparative advantage in hourly wages can be seen from table 6.12. The unit labour cost is also the lowest for Bangladesh. Productivity per worker for shirts is higher than that of Sri Lanka, and almost the same as in India.

Table 6.12
Unit Labour Cost in South Asia 1998

Countries	Unit Labour Cost ($/shirt)	Wages ($/ Year)	Productivity (Shirt/Worker)
Bangladesh	0.11	290	2536
India	0.26	668	2592
Pakistan	0.43	1343	3100
Sri Lanka	0.79	570	719

Source: World Bank (1999)

Table 6.13 shows that the average prices for Bangladeshi products are generally the lowest among the major suppliers to the USA in their respective categories. The prices are 21% and 42% lower than the average USA import price, for knitted men's cotton shirts and women's sweaters. The price of products from China is almost double of that from Bangladesh. For woven men's shirts, China's price is around 60% more, while that of India is about 30% more per piece. Bangladesh is also the most inexpensive source for trousers amongst the major suppliers. The average prices are 26% lower than the total USA imports. At present China is competing for the products of the same price range as imported from Indonesia and the Philippines. Of these four products, India is exporting only men's woven shirts. This suggests that India has diversified to other products. Although at present neither India nor China are competing with Bangladesh in low end products imported by USA, but may change their strategies after 2004.

Table 6.13
Average Prices of Imported Apparel in the USA by Major Importers (1998)
(in US $)

Country	Men's Knitted Shirts	Women's Sweater	Men's Woven Shirts	Men's Trousers & Cotton Breeches
World	6.14	7.84	6.77	8.94
Bangladesh	4.12	4.48	5.07	6.55
China	9.35	9.36	8.20	9.49
Costa Rica	5.71	-	-	8.13
Dominica	-	-	-	8.95
El Salvador	4.23	-	-	-
Gautemala	4.79	-	7.55	8.79
Honduras	4.67	-	5.44	8.99
Hong Kong	10.99	9.65	8.52	10.24
India	-	-	6.52	-
Indonesia	8.18	6.60	8.00	9.20
Italy	-	33.92	28.37	28.15
Macao	-	10.06	-	-
Malaysia	9.03	-	9.74	-
Mexico	4.80	-	6.44	8.79
Pakistan	5.30	-	-	-
Peru	8.26	-	-	-
Philippines	8.10	6.94	8.24	9.12
South Korea	-	6.14	6.76	-
Sri Lanka	8.10	-	5.57	-
Taiwan	-	8.77	8.68	-
Thailand	8.28	6.06	-	-
Turkey	5.83	-	-	-

Source: International Finance Corporation (IFC), 1999

It is highly likely that production may shift to China when quotas are eliminated. For example, in 1991 Sweden eliminated all quotas on textiles and clothing products, and a massive shift took place towards China, whereas countries in Southeast and South Asia hardly profited. Also when Canada unilaterally removed quotas on shirts/blouses, there was again a massive shift towards China and particularly a large shift away from Bangladesh. Table 6.13 further shows that El Salvador and Honduras are close competitors for Bangladesh in the USA market for men's knitted shirts. Mexico also competes with Bangladesh for men's woven shirt and trousers.

6.2.7 Growth of Clothing Export to the USA: Selected Countries

Table 6.14 provides data on the rate of change of clothing exports from selected countries to the US market during 1997/98 and 1998/99. The East Asian countries that clearly experienced increases in export of knitted as well as non-knitted clothing during 1997-98 are Thailand, the Philippines, Singapore, South Korea, Taiwan and Malaysia. However, Indonesia's export increased for non-knitted clothing but declined for knitted clothing. For Taiwan and Hong Kong, exports of knitted as well as non-knitted clothing declined during 1998/99.

Table 6.14
Growth of Clothing Exports to the USA: Selected Countries

Countries	Apparel Knitted (HS 61)		Apparel Non-Knitted (HS 62)	
	% change in (1997-98)	% change in (1998-99)	% change in (1997-98)	% change in (1998-99)
Bangladesh	7.7	10.3	14.6	-2.0
China	2.3	8.9	-8.4	-1.5
Hong Kong	10.8	-3.3	13.0	4.5
India	16.3	-2.6	8.8	3.3
Indonesia	-5.0	-8.2	6.1	5.3
Malaysia	19.4	4.9	4.2	3.1
Mexico	30.2	17.5	26.1	14.0
Pakistan	14.6	11.4	0.3	3.4
Philippines	10.9	5.1	8.9	1.1
Singapore	7.5	2.7	2.9	22.4
South Korea	34.7	9.6	13.0	11.3
Sri Lanka	7.6	-1.0	8.5	-3.6
Taiwan	3.5	-1.0	2.6	15.2
Thailand	27.9	-4.0	2.3	9.1

Source: International Trade Commission, USA

It is also evident from the table that non-knitted clothing exports declined for Bangladesh and Sri Lanka during 1998/99. For knitted clothing, the performance of Bangladesh was better, during 1998/99, compared to that of Sri Lanka and India.

6.2.8 Network of World Trade in Clothing

Table 6.15 presents data on the network of trade in clothing for selected years. It is clearly evident that developing countries are increasingly relying on developed countries for exporting clothing. In 1980, about 78% of developing countries clothing exports were destined for developed countries. The figure increased to 82% and 79.16% in 1990 and 1997, respectively.

Table 6.15
Network of World Trade in Clothin (millions of US$ and in %)

From /To Countries	Developing Countries	Developed Countries	All Countries
A. 1980			= 100%
Developing Countries	4,424.2	15,720.6	20,144.8
Developing Countries (in %)	21.96	78.04	100
Developed Countries	2,568.0	49,830.7	52,398.7
Developed Countries (in %)	4.9	94.1	100
All Countries	6,992.2	65,551.3	72,543.5
All Countries (%)	9.64	90.36	100
B.1990			
Developing Countries	11,746.0	53,869.1	65,633.1
Developing Countries (%)	17.92	82.08	100
Developed Countries	4,959.6	40,011.1	44,970.7
Develpoed Countries (%)	11.03	88.97	100
All Countries	16,723.6	93,880.7	110,603.8
All Countries (%)	15.12	84.88	100
C. 1997			
Developing Countries	26,323.0	99,991.7	126,314.7
Developing Countries (%)	20.84	79.16	100
Developed Countries	15,704.0	53,915.3	69,619.3
Developed Countries (%)	22.56	77.44	100
All Countries	42,027.0	153,907.0	195,934.0
All Countries (%)	21.45	78.55	100

Source: The World Trade Analyser, 1999

It is also apparent from Table 6.15 that inter-developed country trade in clothing decreased during 1980-1997. In 1980, about 94% of developed countries' clothing exports were destined for developed countries. By 1997, the figure declined to 77.44%. In 1980, developing countries accounted for only 4.9% of developed countries' clothing exports. By 1997, the figure went up to about 22.56%.

6.3 Market Access of Bangladesh RMG and the World

In the light of the Marrakesh Declaration as well as the Singapore, Geneva and Doha Ministerial Declaration of the WTO, developed countries should be urged to give greater market access for goods coming from the LDCs, specially the RMG products. In this context, the owners of Bangladesh's leading apparel groups, all directors, past and future presidents of BGMEA will proudly point the country's steadily increasing export volumes which today comprise 76% of the country's total exports.

6.3.1 Bangladesh RMG Export

Within a short period of time, it has attained high importance in terms of its contribution to GDP, foreign exchange earning and social changes. Both international and national environment favoured the rapid growth of this industry in Bangladesh. Fetching only US $ 31.57 million in 1983-84 (Table 6.16), garments sector of the country has now become a nearly US$ 5 billion foreign exchange earner, enjoying the status top ten garment exporter to the US and the European Union, and largest shirt and T-shirt exporter to the EU.

Buyers already here represent a who's who of the world's major volume retailers: Wal-Mart, The Gap, K-mart, Sears, JC Penney, Levi Strauss from the U.S., C&A, H&M, Marks & Spencer, and a host of smaller brands from the EU. Some of these brands were not in Bangladesh even five years ago.

6.3.2 RMG Exports to Major Markets and Trend of Export to the EU and US

Presently the Bangladeshi garments are being exported to 90 countries. United States is the single largest buyer of Bangladeshi garments (Table 6.17). The countries that rank to the USA are Germany, UK, France, Italy, the Netherlands and Belgium. The garments export from Bangladesh comprises both woven items and knit items. Again the woven items are shirts, trousers, jackets etc, while the knit items are T-shirts, polo shirts, blouses, jackets etc. while the knit items are T-shirts, polo shirts, sweaters etc. On the other hand Table 6.18 shows the indication that export share from 1991-92 to 2000-2001 concentrated only in two large markets, USA and EU.

Table 6.16
Contribution of RMG Export in the National Export Earnings

Year	Total RMG Export (Million US $)	Total National Export (Million US $)	% Share of RMG in National Export
1983-84	31.57	811.00	3.89
1984-85	116.20	934.43	12.44
1985-86	131.48	819.21	16.05
1986-87	298.67	1076.61	27.74
1987-88	433.92	1231.20	35.24
1988-89	471.09	1291.56	36.47
1989-90	624.16	1923.70	32.45
1990-91	866.82	1717.55	50.47
1991-92	1182.57	1993.90	59.31
1992-93	1445.02	2382.89	60.64
1993-94	1555.79	2533.90	61.40
1994-95	2228.35	3472.56	64.17
1995-96	2547.13	3882.42	65.61
1996-97	3001.25	4418.28	67.93
1997-98	3781.94	5161.20	73.28
1998-99	4019.98	5312.86	75.67
1999-2000	4349.41	5752.20	75.61
2000-2001	4859.83	6467.30	75.17
2001-2002	4583.75	5986.09	76.57

Source: Export Promotion Bureau and BGMEA, 2002

Because of larger quotas granted by the USA and GSP privileges provided by EU, more than 95% of our garments are exported to these two markets. Canada as a single country buys about 2.3% of our total export. The above table shows the export share to the USA is 45.24% in 2000-2001, which is 3.74% less than that of the year 1991-1992, however, the 0corresponding share to the EU has experienced an increase of 4.09% over the year 1991-92.

Table 6.17
Garment Export to Major Markets in 2000-2001 (Value in min. US$)

Countries	Woven	Knit	Total	% of Total
Austria	5.93	3.83	9.76	0.20
Belgium	89.35	90.85	180.20	3.71
Denmark	23.52	39.25	62.77	1.29
Finland	10.63	11.08	21.71	0.45
France	169.72	167.04	336.76	6.93
Germany	442.43	287.54	729.97	15.02
Greece	1.77	0.58	2.35	0.05
Ireland	15.61	4.67	20.28	0.42
Italy	127.96	77.47	205.43	4.29
Netherlands	155.00	114.45	269.45	5.54
Portugal	2.52	1.50	4.02	0.08
Spain	45.99	36.03	82.02	1.69
Sweden	47.28	41.78	89.06	1.83
UK	267.49	172.26	439.75	9.05
Total EU	1405.20	1048.33	2453.53	50.49
Canada	74.06	35.31	109.37	2.25
USA	1825.36	373.05	2198.41	45.24
Others	59.70	38.82	98.52	2.03
Grand Total	3364.32	1495.51	4859.83	100.00

Source: Export Promotion Bureau (EPB)

Thus the increment in the EU share has simply replaced the declining share in the USA market, which suggests that instead of diversification, the Bangladesh export market has still remained concentrated in these two areas over the past decade. The combined market share of the USA and EU has thus decreased from 95.56% to 95.73% between the 1991-92 and 2000-2001. Recently Japan and Canada have provided duty and quota free access of garments of Bangladesh to the Japanese and Canadian markets. Bangladesh should try to expand her market share to Japan and Canada, which is now only 4-5%. Russia and Australia are also two major importers of apparel. Bangladesh should also try to capture these two markets with all her efforts.

Table 6.18
Trend of RMG Export to the US and EU

Year	Exports to the USA as a % of Total Export	Exports to the EU as a % of Total Export	Combined Share of the US and EU Export (%)
1991-92	49.14	46.42	95.56
1992-93	48.72	45.69	94.41
1993-94	38.08	55.43	93.51
1994-95	45.15	49.36	94.51
1995.96	39.33	55.17	94.50
1996-97	41.49	54.11	95.60
1997-98	44.23	51.14	95.35
1998-99	43.24	52.38	95.62
1999-2000	45.83	49.93	95.76
2000-2001	45.24	50.49	95.73

Source: Export Promotion Bureau and BGMEA

6.3.3 Main RMG Items Exported from Bangladesh

Figure 6.1
Main RMG Items Exported from Bangladesh

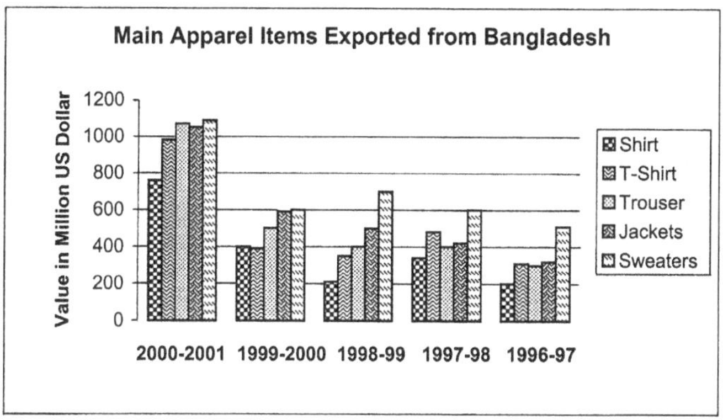

The garments export from Bangladesh comprises both woven items and knit items. Again the woven items are shirts, trousers, jackets etc. while the knit items are T-shirts, polo shirts, blouses, jackets etc. It is evident from the figure 6.1 that Bangladesh's main exportable apparel items are sweaters, T-shirts are from the knit groups and trousers, jackets, shirts are from the woven category.

Again, Bangladesh is the largest shirt and T-shirt exporter to the European Union which has more than two times increased from 1996-97 through 2001-2002. The export of sweater, trousers and jackets increased tremendously from the 1996-97 through 2001-2002.

6.4 Concluding Remarks

From the above discussions, it is clear that Bangladesh is now enjoying quota facilities for RMG exports predominantly in the US market and from the EU under GSP facilities. These are assured market facilities as member of Least Developed Countries. But this advantage will linger no more from 1 January 2005. At that time, Bangladesh RMG exports will face stiff competition from other countries for example China, India, Pakistan, Thailand and so on. The countries which, which do not enjoy quota facilities, now are capable of exporting readymade garments by their own supply chain, using mostly indigenous materials, for instance China and India. On the other hand exports of apparel from Bangladesh are more concentrated in terms of categories and markets, compared to for example, China and India. Bangladesh would diversify its exports toward products such as women's apparel and other high value added items. Sustained efforts should be made to increase exports to non-quota markets like Japan.[182] The study by the International Trade Centre also suggests that potential exports from Bangladesh to Japan are significantly higher than the current export.[183] So it is high time for Bangladesh to penetrate new markets like Japan, Australia, Russia and also to restructure and modernise the textile and other related sectors to serve first the growing of RMG industries.[184] There is no room for complacency with the existing secure and assured quotas and GSP oriented markets in the USA, Canada and European Union. It must search and expand in the new areas to face the challenge of global competition and trade liberalization during the post 2004 era. Now, with the economic experiences of trade liberalization concerning RMG industry in Bangladesh, we can move to the social aspects of readymade garments industry and its possible impact on Bangladesh society.

---

[182] For instance, India's new quota system introduced in November, 1999 contains provisions- to promote exports to non-quota countries and to increase exports of high value added products.

[183] The Trade Performance of Bangladesh examined by the International Trade Centre is available at www.intracen.org

[184] "MFA phases out after 2004: Critical challenges await the economy's thrust sector" available at www.independent-bangladesh.com/news/may15/15052003.pd.htm

CHAPTER SEVEN
SOCIAL ASPECTS AND BANGLADESH GARMENTS INDUSTRY

7.1 Introduction

Industrialization and urbanisation brought a great change of women's lives and attitudes towards their position in the family and society. Bangladesh as a developing country of the third world tries to develop its super-and infrastructure participating by its population both men and women in every field of productive and development activities.

According to the International Labour Organization (ILO), employment covers any work, be it for wage or salary, profit or family gain, including production for own consumption (ILO, 1996) It defines the category of employment, and considers employment in the labour force as a paid employment, i.e. persons who perform work for wage or salary, in cash or kind. The rapid growth of the RMG industry in Bangladesh since the mid 1980s has generated considerable female employment in the formal export-oriented manufacturing sector. This has made women visible in statistics and brought a social change in Bangladesh.

Women, specially in the third world like Bangladesh, are forced to confirm not only the roles of wife, but also to bear the additional burdens and restrictions on their freedom of movement and association, within both home and society. There is a marked sexual division of labour, and a strict normative gender role system such that women often have little power to exercise choice over their lifestyles. Scholarly interest in the study of women in Bangladesh was expanded and diversified mainly during the 1970s. During the 1950s and 1960s the studies on women did not attempt to raise any particular issue, but they mostly described the prevailing situation of women's activities in the country. As I have mentioned in the previous chapter, there are small scale qualitative studies on women garments workers in Bangladesh based on in-depth interviews analysing intra-household power relations. Others have used the questionnaire survey to look into intra-household relations (Zohir and Paul-Majumder 1996). But none of these studies relate systematically to male-female differences over a time period to see how the intra-household relations have changed. The minimum legal age of admission to employment in Bangladesh has been variously defined as between the age of 12 to 16 years under different labour laws. According to Bangladesh labour law, the economically active population is defined as persons aged 10 years and above who are working at least one hour or more per day for wage or profit, or are performing work without wage in a family farm or enterprise, or are performing work for profit or salary, are in the category of employed, and those who are looking for employment in the past two months or willing to work are in the category of unemployed. But to facilitate international comparisons, analysis in this chapter will refer to persons aged 15 years and above, however, many impacts are going on the social life of RMG workers in Bangladesh.

7.2 Data Analysis

With a view to collect and know the information and data about the social aspects of garments workers in Bangladesh, I have collected a sample of 226 male and 356 female workers in 1995; 190 male and 470 female workers working in garment industries located outside Export Processing Zones (EPZ) in 2000, and 27 male and 92 female workers working in garment industries located within EPZ also in 2000. For both the surveys a list of garment industries were collected from Bangladesh Garment Manufacturers and Exporters Association (BGMEA) and the firms were randomly drawn from the list. In 1995, 32 industries were surveyed, while 34 industries were surveyed outside EPZ and 5 were surveyed within EPZ in the year 2000. Two structured questionnaires were administered one for the management and another for the workers in these surveys. But the timing was different for the surveys: the 1995 survey was conducted during October-December 1995, while the 2000 survey was conducted during June-October 2000. In addition to the above survey, a few secondary sources of information were incorporated for the development of the study.

7.3 A Review of Factors Affecting Working Conditions

Since various studies argued that several changes took place such as the establishment of Export Processing Zones (EPZs) at Dhaka and Chittagong, globalization of the economy, NGO[185] initiatives, BGMEA initiatives and social labelling, the effects of these factors seem to be mixed.

7.3.1 Positive Effect on the Working Conditions

There are many positive effects on the working conditions of RMG workers in Bangladesh which are discussed below:

7.3.1.1 Establishment of Export Processing Zone (EPZ[186]) at Dhaka and Chittagong

There are two[187] EPZ operating at Chittagong and Dhaka, which were established in 1983 and 1993 respectively.[188] Table 7.1 shows that the working con-

---

185 In Bangladesh about 12,000 organisations are registered as Non-government Organisations (NGOs), mostly of these organisations are funded from Western countries.

186 EPZ are "special areas where potential investors would find a congenial investment climate".

ditions and wages are better in the garment factories located in the EPZ at Dhaka, which has created not only alternative job opportunities for women but also provided better working conditions, state of social security.[189] But EPZs are exempted from certain articles of the Employment of Labour (Standing Orders) Act (1965), the Industrial Relations Ordinance (1969) and the Factories Act 1965 relating to the organisation of workers for the purpose of collective bargaining. This constitutes a violation of their fundamental rights. Recently, there is a pressure from USA to withdraw this restriction.

7.3.1.2 Refixation of Minimum Wage

The government declared the minimum wage rates for the various categories of workers employed in the garment industries in Bangladesh in 1985.

The minimum wage for the unskilled workers was fixed at Taka[190] 627 per month. There was no mention of minimum wage[191] for apprentices. The minimum wage was revised in July 1994 for the garment industry. It was fixed at Tk 930 per month. The wage for apprentice/trainee was fixed at Tk 500 per month. It is noted that of the sectoral minimum wages, the garment sector had the lowest wage both in 1985 and 1994. Even Biddies, which had the same minimum wage as the garments industry in 1985 (Tk 627), had a revised wage of Tk. 1450 in 1995. It appears that there may be male bias in the setting of minimum wages. The price of labour is lower than that of neighbouring countries as well as some other garment producing countries in Southeast Asia and East Europe.[192]

---

[187] At present there are six EPZs in Bangladesh.

[188] A study on Chittagong Export Processing Zone (BIDS, 1994) which covers a range of industries, a few of which are garments, suggests that female share of employment in the Chittagong EPZ was 75% of the employees in fully foreign owned industries, 52% in the joint ventures and 49% in the locally owned enterprises.

[189] "Readymade Garments Industry Facing the Challenge" by Kazi Alauddin Ahmed. The Daily Star Homepage (http://www.dailystarnews.com/19911/03/n9110309htm, Downloaded on 30 Sept. 2000, Feature Page, Vol.3, no. 72.

[190] Taka is Bangladesh currency and 1 US$ is about 60 Taka.

[191] At present the minimum wages in Bangladesh is 1500 Taka per month.

[192] Bangladesh Garments Manufacturers and Exporters Association, Dhaka, Press Conference, http://www.bgmea.com/ban.htm.,Downloaded on 03 October, 2000.

Table 7.1
Nature of Working Conditions by Location of Factories

Working Condition	Location			
	Factories within the city centres	Factories outside the city centre	Factories within DEPZ	All
Very good ventilation	76 (13.0)	54 (52.4)	89 (73.6)	219 (27.1)
Moderately good ventilation	315 (53.9)	32 (31.1)	26 (21.5)	373 (46.2)
Bad/very bad ventilation	193 (33.1)	17 (16.5)	6 (5.0)	216 (26.7)
Not congested	81 (13.9)	83 (80.6)	105 (86.8)	269 (33.3)
Moderately congested	219 (37.5)	13 (12.6)	10 (8.3)	242 (29.9)
Very congested	284 (48.6)	7 (6.8)	6 (4.9)	297 (36.8)
Very clean	31 (5.3)	63 (61.2)	90 (74.4)	184 (22.8)
Moderately clean	246 (42.1)	11 (10.7)	31 (25.6)	288 (35.6)
Not clean	307 (52.6)	29 (28.2)	- -	336 (41.6)
No. workers having smell from toilet	304 (52.1)	43 (41.7)	14 (11.6)	361 (44.7)
Mean of work hour (in hours)	12.0	11.9	9.9	11.8
Wage rate of female	1280	1320	1504	1321
Wage rate of male	2202	2514	2299	2258
Female share in male earnings	58.0%	53%	65%	58.5%
Factory size in terms of employment	512	832	1767	713
Share of female workers (%)	55.7%	53%	65%	58.5%
No. of weekly holidays per factory	0.5	1.0	3.0	1.4
Share of paid leave in total leave (%)	23.1	63.0	60.3	24.1
% of workers having transport	0.0	0.0	93.0	13.9
Facilities provided by factory of workers having lunch room	28.8	49.5	93.4	41.0
% of workers having restroom	34.7	67.0	100.0	49.3
% of workers having access to doctor	7.8	37.0	89.0	17.0
No. of factories having plan to introduce two shifts of work	3	1	-	4
% of workers having indenty/ attendance card	90	95	100	92
Total No. of workers	584	103	121	808

Note: Figures in parentheses are % of the total workers in each location.

Source: Quoted from: Pau-Majumder 1998, "Health and Status of Garments Workers in Bangladesh: Findings from a Survey of Employers and Employees", BIDS, Dhaka.

7.3.1.3 NGO Initiatives in Providing Housing

Social status of the workers depends to a large extent on safe and secure housing. Initiatives have been taken by the NGO groups in providing housing for women working in the garments industry, such as by Nari Uddog Kendro (NUK) since 1991. By 2001, there were four hostels accommodating about 600 women garment workers. Women can overcome one of their genuine practical needs if the government, entrepreneurs in the industry and NGOs replicate such innovative initiatives.

7.3.1.4 Establishment of Health Care Service and Training Centre

Another notable initiative taken during the last decades has been the establishment of training and health care centres.[193] The training project started in July 1991, organised by the Bureau of Manpower Employment and Training (Ministry of Labour and Manpower), and BGMEA, financed by UNDP and ILO. About 1654 workers were trained by 1995. This project ended in February 1995. It is strongly felt that such training needs to be continued and expanded further. BGMEA has finally taken note of the fact that the health of the workers needs to be taken care of in order to increase productivity. Since, July 1994, BGMEA started a hospital-cum-school for the garment workers at Malibough Chowdhury Para in Dhaka city. Health care services are available during two shifts a day: 9 a.m. to 2 p.m. and 2 p.m. to 6 p.m. Such initiatives need to be undertaken in other areas where there is concentration of firms. It would be useful to include childcare programmes, so that more married female workers can work in the garments industry. Studies have shown that primary health care services are also provided by Gonosasthya Kendro, a healthcare based national NGO and Dhaka Community Hospital. Supply of health facilities at the doorsteps of the factories are provided by various NGOs such as Unity through Population service (UTPS), NUK, Radda Burmen, Marie Stopes etc.

7.3.1.5 Non-formal Education Programme

Under the component of the Child Labour Elimination Project, 8,219 students were enrolled in 336 schools run by the two local NGOs namely, Bangladesh Rural Advancement Committee (BRAC) and Gono Shahajya Sangstha (GSS). Upto now, 29 schools are giving education to remaining students of the target group.

---

[193] For details, see BGMEA various years News Letter.

7.3.1.6 Earn and Learn Programme

A new concept of "Earn and Learn" has received considerable attention of all the parties, and they are in the process of developing a system to help the children continue education under some special arrangements while they would be earning a livelihood. Under this component, BGMEA has given on the job training to 900 MOU students through local NGOs. ILO and UNICEF are also providing skills training on tailoring, embroidery, garments machine maintenance, manufacturing and wool knitting to 200 more students. In future more students will get these facilities.

7.3.1.7 Support for Income Loss

A monthly compensation at the rate of US dollar 7 is being provided to each student, who was retrenched from the sector as child labourers and now covered by the child labour elimination project. BGMEA provides 50% of the fund.

7.3.1.8 BGMEA- ILO Extended Projects

With the support of BGMEA the ILO Dhaka office, has undertaken two projects for the former child labour students of the BGMEA-ILO-UNICEF project. Under the Projects, over 1400 students will be given skill training, and their 100 elder members of 100 families would be provided micro credit ranging from Taka 2,000 to 10,000 for income generation. The Underprivileged Children Education Programme (UCEP) and SUROVI, two reputed local NGOs along with Singer Bangladesh (a multinational company), have been providing skill training to the students. Starting from July 16, 2000 a total of 1,194 students have already received skill training and 56 families have got the micro credit.

7.3.2 Negative Effects on Working Conditions

The negative effects on the working conditions are discussed below:

7.3.2.1 International Pressure to Improve Working Conditions

Linking of labour standards to international trade policy has led the developed countries to social labelling of their imports, and such initiatives threaten the existence of our RMG industry. Among these initiatives, legislation to eliminate the use of child labour and clean cloth campaign are important.

7.3.2.2 Issue of Child Labour: Harkin Bill

Senator Tom Harkin placed a bill entitled, "The Child Labour Deterrence Act of 1993", in the US Senate. The Harkin Bill had significant impetus in promoting the case for prohibiting child labour, which had led to the elimination of child labour in the export-oriented manufacturing and mining industries. Before the Harkin Bill, the government estimated that there were 60,000-70,000 children in the garments industry. They were removed from the factories a fine achievement.[194] Many garments industries retrenched child workers from their factories. These retrenched children ended up in more strenuous and less remunerative jobs, or turned to begging in the street and/or selling flowers. The Bangladesh RMG sector has set a unique example by collective efforts that eventually led to the development of safety net programmes for the child labourers. After several meetings, the revised Memorandum of Understanding (MOU) was signed by BGMEA, UNICEF and ILO on August 4. 1995. Many of the retrenched child workers have been placed in a school, and are receiving a monthly stipend. Also a qualified family member of the under-aged worker has been provided with employment. Following the tremendous success of the MOU-I, BGMEA member industries are now completely child labour free. The success of the project has been acclaimed globally which has brightened Bangladesh's international image. The soccer ball manufacturing industry of Pakistan has followed the BGMEA Model of Child Labour Elimination. The US Embassy in Dhaka has played a significant role in the successful implementation of the project. The role of the Government of Bangladesh (GOB) is also remarkable.

7.3.2.3 Issue of Clean Cloth Campaign by a Netherlands-based NGO

In the absence of demonstrated improvement in wages and working conditions, thousands of workers may lose jobs if the campaign in the European countries gain momentum, and this is likely to pose a threat to exports of RMG from Bangladesh. In November, 1995, two Dutch representatives visited Bangladesh to review the wage structure and the working conditions of the garments workers. A Fair Trade Charter was developed, based on the ILO conventions and it includes such pre-requisites as reasonable wage, the freedom of organisation, and collective bargaining, no forced overtime, no discrimination, no child labour, and safe and healthy working conditions. This issue needs to be taken seriously like the child labour issue.

7.3.2.4 Garment units Becoming Sick

According to the various reports,[195] between 800 to 1000 industries became sick during 2001-2002. Hence, thousands of workers lost their jobs. As mentioned earlier, garments industry expanded substantially during 1990-2000. This ex-

---

194 "Child Labour - Thank you, Mr. Harkin" downloaded from http://www.newint.org/issue292/thank.htmhttp://www.newint.org/issue292/thank.htm

195 For more details, please visit www.independent-bangladesh.com/news/may15/15052002pd.htm and nation.ittefaq.com/artman/publish/article_1258.shtml and also www.nation-online.com/200211/14/n2111409.htm

pansion has led to price under-cutting among the enterprises due to competition. To overcome the problem the government could restrict the entry of new firms in this sector (for a specified period) as it has done in 1984-85. Moreover, the unstable political situation and frequent hartals (strikes) as well as the unstable international economic and political environment due to September 11 terrorist attacks and the Iraq war have also adversely affected the garment industry, as many buyers have cancelled orders.

7.3.2.5 Phasing out of MFA

As mentioned earlier, after January 2005, textile and clothing trade will be fully integrated into General Agreement on Tariffs and Trade (GATT). Hence the challenge that Bangladesh will face beyond 2005 is that Bangladesh will have to compete on equal terms with a large number of established suppliers for markets in USA and Canada. Countries having cheap labour along with backward linkage such as India, Pakistan and China are likely to be major competitors.

7.4 Changing Characteristics of the Labour Force

Before discussing the intra-household relations, it is important to know whether there had been changes in the characteristics of the workers in the garments industry. Studies in South Asian countries have shown that export-oriented industries such as the garment industry tend to employ relatively young, unmarried when with some education (Elson and Pearson 1981a, 1981b; ILO 1985; Joekes and Moayadi 1987; Lim 1990; Baden and Joekes 1993).

7.4.1 Age Distribution

Table 7.2 shows the age distribution, education and marital status of the garment workers. The mean age of the workers suggests that there has not been much change between last decade. The mean age of the workers has increased from 19 years to 19.5 years for the female, while that of male workers decreased from 24 years to 23.5 years. For the EPZ, the mean age was found to be much higher. 21 years for female and 25 for male. Female workers on the whole tended to be younger than their male counterpart.

But there has been a change in the structure for female workers. Hossain's *et al.* (1990) study, based on a small sample survey, reported that 18% of the female workers were under 20 years of age in 1984. During 1995-2000, the proportion of workers under 20 years of age increased for females from 47.6% to 54%, while that of men remained almost unchanged (20% in 1995 and 20.5% in 2000). The difference was larger in the EPZ: 40.2% female and 7.4% male under 20 years of age.

7.4.2 Education Level

The level of education has changed significantly over the last decade in Dhaka city and gender gap persists. There has been an increase in the proportion of female workers with primary level education from 32% to 40% and a decline in female workers with education above secondary level to from 10% to 2%. The proportion of workers with no education and those with secondary education remained unchanged. On the other hand for male workers the increase in secondary level education has been from 42% to 61% and those with primary level education from 11 to 19%, while decline was noted for those with no education above secondary level. In the EPZ the education level of the workers is significantly higher than the non-EPZ area for both men and women This is because the firms in the EPZ are producing products, which are of relatively higher value added, and hence require skilled workers.

Table 7.2
Characteristics of Garment Workers by Gender in Dhaka City

Characteristics	Non- EPZ				EPZ	
	1995		2000		2000	
	Male	Female	Male	Female	Male	Female
Age Group						
15-19	19.9	47.6	20.5	54.0	7.4	40.2
20-24	36.3	28.7	31.6	23.4	44.4	41.3
25-29	23.9	12.1	30.5	13.6	33.3	13.0
30-34	13.7	7.3	13.7	6.0	7.4	2.2
35-39	4.0	3.9	1.6	2.3	7.4	3.3
40+	2.2	0.3	2.1	0.6	-	-
Education						
None	7.1	26.2	3.2	27.2	-	-
Primary	11.1	32.1	18.9	40.4	-	18.5
Secondary	42.5	31.5	61.1	30.4	63.0	72.8
Above Secondary	39.4	10.1	16.8	1.9	37.0	8.7
Marital Status						
Unmarried	45.9	62.8	58.4	50.2	59.3	47.8
Currently married	45.1	36.3	40.5	38.7	40.7	47.8
Widow/Separated/ Divorced	9.0	0.9	1.1	11.1	-	4.3
No. of Workers	226.0	356.0	190.0	470.0	27.0	92.0

Source: Own Survey

7.4.3 Marital Status

Marital status also significant changes has been noted in Table 7.2. While for male workers the tendency for workers being unmarried has increased (45% to 58 %), but the opposite was true for female workers (63% to 52%). The preference for ever-married female workers has increased during the last decade in non-EPZ firms of Dhaka city. A higher proportion of the female workers in the EPZ was found to be currently married (48%) than the non-EPZ areas (39%). This may be because women who live near EPZ have family support to look after their children while they are away at work, or they have their children in their home village.

7.5 Intra-Household Gender Relation

Workers aged 15 years and above will be analysed in this section to see the impact of paid worker's well being. Intra-household gender relations will be analysed by discussion of decisions on access to and control over income, participation in household decision-making and conflicts within households.

7.5.1 Access to Income

Employment in garment industry has provided direct access to cash income for the first time to many women. Prior to entering the garment industry, about 50% of the female workers and 15% of the male workers were doing unpaid household-based work in 1995. The 2000 survey showed that for 96% of the male and female workers in the non-EPZ the proportions were 88% and 82% respectively. Hence, for the first time a large number of women were getting regular wages each month. In 1995 a women aged 15 years and above in the garment industry was earning an average of Tk. 968 as monthly pay while a male worker earned Tk.1403. By 2000, the earning of women increased by 36% to Tk.1316 and that of men increased by 62% to Tk. 2,267. Hence, female-male wage gap has increased and female earned only 58% of male workers' income in 2000 while it was 69% in the 1995. This is likely to be due to piece rate payment for knitwear to male workers. In the EPZ wages were Tk. 1521 for females and Tk. 2299 for males. The wage gap between EPZ and non-EPZ was found to be only 2% for men but 16% for the women. Of the workers aged 15 years and above, the 1995 survey noted that about 32.9% of the female workers and 12.8% of male workers earned less than the minimum wage of Tk 627. In the 2000 survey these figures were found to have declined more for men than women: 30.2% for women and 5.3% for men. In the EPZ these proportions in 2000 were 26.1 for female and 3.7 for male workers.[196]

[196] These were below the minimum wages of Tk. 930 set in 1994 and Tk. 1500 per month in 1998 new pay scale.

Besides that fact, excerpts from women workers narratives (Absar, 2001), Piyara, a married garment worker said:

"I like working in the factory because it feels good to get money in my hand: I don't have to adjust to the moods of a family in a private house. I like my work because of the money. Money is everything". Why does Piyara think money is everything? Piyara answered with a meaningful smile: "Without money, this world is nothing."

7.5.2 Income Contribution to Their Families

Both male and female workers contribute a substantial proportion of their earnings to their families. The 1995 survey findings showed that the contribution to family income per month was 44% of their earnings for female and 64% for male workers, aged 15 years and above. Their contribution to family income almost remained the same in 2000: 43% for male workers and 65% for female workers. The workers in the EPZ contributed slightly higher towards their family income: 47% for female and 75.5% for male. The overtime payment, which they usually received in the third week, greatly helped many families to have a cash flow at the end of the month. The migrant women also have now taken the responsibility of remitting some money to the rural areas. On average women workers remitted Tk. 669 and the male workers remitted Tk. 1569 yearly in 1995. Not only women contributing to their family income but some have also become the bread-winner of their family. Of the workers aged 15 years and over, about 33% of the female workers and 69% of the male workers were primary earners[197] of the family. In 2000 it declined slightly for women and increased for men: 31% for female workers and 78% for male workers were primary earners. The figures for EPZ were 34 and 63% respectively.

It is sometimes said that when women gain employment in the garment industry, they spend on conspicuous consumption. But on the contrary, the 1995 survey showed that the gender difference was minimal: the female workers spent 14%, while the male workers spent 12%, of their monthly pay for own expenses like clothing, cosmetics, shoes, etc. These expenses have declined to 12.5% and 11.4% respectively in 2000 for workers in the non-EPZ areas. The EPZ workers, however, spend slightly higher on conspicuous consumption: 19.7% of female pay and 17.8% of male pay.

Moreover, in 1995, same percentage of male and female workers aged 15 years and over, had bank accounts: 21%. Slightly less proportion of workers had a bank account in 2000: 15.7 per cent and 19.5% of female and male workers had bank accounts. A higher proportion of workers had bank accounts in the EPZ (25.9% for female and 33.7% for the males). Also interestingly, the average savings of the non-EPZ workers was the same in 1995: Tk.74. Findings showed that, women are on average better savers as they save 7.6% out of their

[197] Primary earner was defined as the member whose earning was the highest in the family.

smaller income, while men save 5.3%. In 2000 the amount saved increased substantially for both men and women: Tk 145 for women and Tk 230 for men implying that workers are saving about 10% of their monthly pay. Workers in the EPZ saved slightly higher amounts Tk. 167 by women and Tk. 304 by male workers.

Also during the 1995 garment workers survey, it was noted that women are now taking up the roles of paying house rent and schooling expenses for their brother and sisters. Despite the fact that they get lower incomes, the female garment workers of age 15 years and over, were spending the same amount as the male workers on the studies of younger brothers and sisters at home. On average Tk. 68 were spent by female workers and Tk. 65 by male workers in 1995. Their contribution has declined in 2000 to Tk. 37 by female and Tk. 53 by male workers. Those working in the EPZ contributed a higher amount: Tk. 55 by female and Tk. 74 by male workers. It seems that other family members or government programmes are now financing their education, as enrolment at the primary level has significantly increased at the national level.

The 1995 survey further showed that female workers were able to spend their own earnings on their own marriage: about 2% of the male and female workers had used their own savings for marriage expenses. Moreover, about 5% of the female workers and 3% of the male workers were found to be savings for their own future. Information on how they spent their savings on buying assets. This included land, house, business or ornaments.

7.5.3 Control over Income and Participation in Decision Making

Control over their earnings and a greater role in household decision making are important measures of economic empowerment of female workers. In Bangladesh, women's role in household decision-making is usually much more limited than men's. On the other hand, it expounds by stating that they are playing an important role in decision making in their house-holds and are being able to do things more independently outside home.The 1995 and 2000 garment workers survey findings showed that their employment had given just over a third (37% in 1995 and 37.7% in 2000) of the women scope to participate in household decision making with full control over expenditure of their earnings. For about one-fourth (25% in 1995 and 24% in 2000) it gave a joint decision making role over expenditure of their earnings. However, for the rest (38%), had no role in decision making about the spending of their earnings and to completely hand over their income. Similar finding was for EPZ for full control over their income but joint decision making was a bit higher (33%). On the other hand, only 16-18% of the male workers had no control over their income.

7.5.4 Indicators of Social Changes in Garments Workers' Life

Table 7.3 shows that women were taking household decision alone, going out alone, buying according to their own choice, and could go to market alone. These were roles, which were traditionally closed to women. That is they are wearing lipstick (purchasing lipstick), and going to cinemas (purchasing tickets), and some of the things often cited to indicate that they are adopting modern ways of life. Table 7.3 further suggests that still women had to carry on their traditional role of cooking and housework. A citation regarding such income spending by garment factory helper Mrs. Hurmuti is given below: (ibid., p. 4).

"Recently I bought a cotton sari for Tk. 250 (US$ 4.5). The price is little bit high. Do not you think? My monthly pay is Tk 900 (US$ 15). I could not bargain very well for the sari. Reduced ten taka only. I bought it from a ferriwala. It was difficult for me to pay so much. I have bought this because it is needed for work in a garment factory. If I wear torn and dirty clothes, people will think badly of me."

The narratives indicate that women are becoming so called "modern" to meet city life requirements. The extent of improvement in women's position varied with the level of income of the worker. Those who were earners were more empowered within their households. It was also noted that the variables in the Table 7.3 were highly correlated. Hence, decomposition of gender sub-ordination has taken place.

Table 7.3
Indicators of Social Changes in Garment Workers' Life

Indicator	Male		Female	
	Before	After	Before	After
Takes decisions alone	62.8	77.0	26.4	43.3
Goes out alone	90.3	92.0	19.9	47.5
Buys alone	71.7	85.0	23.3	44.4
Goes to the market	84.5	77.0	11.5	21.3
Does cooking	9.3	13.3	59.8	60.1
Do not do housework	37.6	48.9	3.4	14.7

Source: Own Survey

But there has been loss of social status as the female workers reported both in 1995 and 2000 that their relatives and neighbours do not think that working in the garment factories is good. The female workers themselves feel that it is a good job, but are looked down by the society.

7.5.5 Household Conflicts and Cooperation

The concept of co-operation and household conflicts can be used for understanding the intricacies of intra-household relations and decision making in case of the garment workers. Wage employment had a positive impact on some married women's relation with their husband in 1995. The 1995 survey suggests that about 34% of married women reported that there has been an improvement in marital relations, while 6% reported that marital relations had deteriorated after joining the garment industry. In 2000, these proportions were 47 and 10% respectively in the non-EPZ areas and 4.5% in the EPZ areas. For most of the married women, the marital relationship remained unchanged. The cases where the marital relationship deteriorated were mostly for those who had been working for 7-12 months. Earlier it was noted that the social status of the workers had been lowered to some extent in the eyes of relatives and society. But the economic gain from employment in garment industry had offset the negative social impact, and the conjugal relationship had improved. The relationship with the husband had improved, and most for those who had worked for only 8 hours a day.

7.5.6 Marital Relationship

Another indicator of improved marital relationship is that though in Bangladesh, threat of divorce and physical assault on the wife is very common for low income families, about 87% of married garment women had not faced threat of divorce. Those who had been working for 4-6 years in the garment industry faced the highest threat of divorce. Thus, employment in garment industry had not adversely affected the marital life of most of the women. Many of the married women had more "co-operation" from their husbands. About 52% of married garment women reported that their husbands help them with domestic work in 1995, and this reporting increased to 73% in 2000. But there has been a decline in the average hour the husband spent on household work a day: from 2 hours to 1.4 hours. Moreover, the longer the women worked in the factory, the more the husband shared household work. But, the husband shared household work more when women's earnings were the lowest in 1995, and it reversed in 2000 especially for those working in the EPZ (Table 7.4).

Also for unmarried women it was observed that the more she earned, brighter became the chance of her getting married. In 1995, only 3% of the unmarried workers have reported that their possibilities of getting married have been reduced because of employment in the garment industry, but in the 2000 survey this proportion rose to 22%. About 31% of the married female workers got married after entering the garment industry in 1995.

Table 7.4
Household Work Done by Husband of Garment Workers (hours per day)

Variables	Non-EPZ		EPZ
	1995	2000	2000
Women's outside work (Hour)			
Upto 8 hour	2.2	1.4	1.6
9-10	1.4	1.6	2.1
11-12	1.9	1.4	3.5
13-14	2.4	1.3	1.2
15 and above	4.0	2.4	-
Women's earning (Tk)			
Upto 500	2.7	1.2	-
501-1000	1.5	1.3	1.1
1001-1500	2.1	1.5	1.2
1501-2000	0.5	1.2	2.5
2000 and above	2.1	1.6	2.6
All Women	1.9	1.4	1.9

Note: Table based on 160 married women in 1995 and 182 married women in non-EPZ areas and 44 married women in EPZ areas in 2000.
Source: Own Survey

Also there has been some change in the attitude of unmarried women: they felt they were too young to get married even at the age of 20 years. Thus, the unmarried workers can have more say on their own marriages, and may have refused to marry rural men. About 16% of the unmarried women were unwilling to marry as they were responsible for family maintenance, and about 8% workers had not married as they preferred to live alone. On the other hand it was noted during the survey, that in many instances, men working in the garment industry would marry a rural woman, as they think the garment factory women were too smart for them.

Wage employment would seem to have made women conscious about fertility control and family size. It was noted in the 1995 survey that of the married workers 38% did not have any children, while 31% had one child. Over the 1995-2000 period, more married women with no children were getting employment in the garment industry as about 52% of the married women had no children and 22% had only one child. On the other hand in the EPZ there were more with one child (50%) than those with no children (30%).

7.6 Cost of Working in the Garment Industry

Wage work at the garment industry has empowered women and increased their status by making possible re-negotiation of implicit intra-household gender contracts and allowed greater spending on personal and family needs, but these had to be done at some cost. These were in-terms of their health and increased risk of harassment.

7.6.1 Health Cost of Work in the Garment Industry

It was noted that although women have gained access to paid work, their income is very small. The problems women face, in terms of low wages, discrimination at the work place, long hours of work, no job security and gender subordination have already been discussed in various studies. Also the burden on women in terms of time have to be emphasized. These are likely to affect the health of female worker.

The working conditions of the factories are important factors for the health conditions of the workers. The working hours for the garments workers were about 12 hours a day in 1995 and it remained unchanged in 2000, with only half hour to one hour lunch break. These long working hours with a short lunch break are exhausting the work force. Other facilities such as lack of leave provisions. Lack of transport facilities, lack of proper sanitation and occupational safety may affect workers' health adversely.

It is important to know the specific impact of paid manufacturing work on women's health because (a) physiological factors, such as, differences in physical strength and women's ability to become pregnant, which may result in different health outcomes for men and women: (b) men and women hold different jobs and consequently are exposed to different types of hazards; and (c) men and women differ in the amount of control they have over their own jobs. To measure the impact of wage employment on worker's health, this section will look into the incidence of illness, provision for leave and mode of transport of the garment workers.

7.6.2 Incidence of Illness

Almost all the workers reported that they were in good health before joining the garment industry. The survey noted that about 5% of the women workers had fainted during the months of June-July. These are the hottest months in summer. The management complained that this was due to the malnutrition of the women workers. This reflects the traditional pattern that disadvantaged women are last and least to eat in the household.

Work in the garment industry does not affect health of the male and female workers in a similar way. The survey results showed (Table 7.5) that the incidence of illness was higher for female workers than male workers for almost all types of illness both in 1995 and 2000. The most frequent illness was cough and cold, followed by physical weakness and headache in 1995. Work related illness like physical weakness and headache remained high even in 2000. Table 7.5 further shows that there has been a significant decline in the incidence of illness, which is related to work. The incidence of work related illness as much lower for EPZ male than in non-EPZ areas but that of female were similar.

Of these illnesses, cough, cold and fever are seasonal illnesses, while stomach upset and jaundice are water borne diseases. Eye trouble, headache, physical weakness and urine trouble are the result of stress at the work place, and time constraints faced by women workers who have to balance productive and reproductive work. It was observed that during the survey in October- December in 1995 that workers suffered from cough and colds as they mostly walked to work early in the morning and went to home late at night. So they were very prone to catching cold. They came to work even though they were ill, as it was the peak season for the garment industry[198], so the illness spread among other workers easily. Coughs and colds were found to be more prevalent among operators and sewing helpers. However, in 2000, incidence of coughs and colds was found to be much lower as the survey was conducted during June-October.

The second common illness was weakness and headache (Table 7.5). These are likely to result from the long hours of work, lack of leave facilities, lack of sleep, walking long distances, lack of proper ventilation and light at work place, and the low quality of food they take. Workers whose occupations are cutting helper and iron man suffered relatively more from headaches, while iron man and finishing helper suffered relatively more from weakness. The gender difference was found to be wide in case of eye trouble and urine infection (workers have to seek permission to use toilets) in 1995, but gender difference declined for urine infection in 2000. Eye trouble was found mostly among the operators and finishing helpers. Sewing puts strain on the eyes, especially for operators. Leave is usually not granted for jaundice and stomach upsets, so these illnesses spread easily at work place. There was almost no gender difference for water borne diseases. Majumder (1995) reported that the air in the factories is full of dust, and the textiles contain several chemicals. Due to that and their other working conditions the workers complain about eye-problems, headache, illness and general weakness.

Most of the incidences of illness occurs at a lower age for female than for male workers. The most vulnerable age for illness found to be 20-22 for women and 23-25 years for men. The length of service also affects workers' health. Usually workers who had worked for a year as operators had eye trouble. On average the male workers had worked for 3 years while the female workers had worked for 3 years and 4 months. By this time a worker usually had a work-

[198] The peak season for quota items is from November to January.

related illness. Low pay is also responsible for much of illnesses. Workers earning lower than the average pay were more prone to cold and fever as well as work related illness like eye trouble, headache and weakness. Due to lack of transport facilities most of the workers, especially females, walk to work. Those who commute by walking to work are more prone to illness, as they get physically exhausted. The long hours of work are (12 hours a day), along with reproductive work and travelling time, limits the time available for sleep and leisure.

Table 7.5
Incidence of Illness by Gender in the Bangladesh Garment Industry

Incidence of Illness	Non-EPZ				EPZ	
	1995		2000		2000	
	Male	Female	Male	Female	Male	Female
Work Related						
Eye Trouble	43.8	54.2	18.9	30.2	11.1	33.7
Headache	61.9	76.7	56.8	69.6	33.3	72.8
Weakness	65.9	75.0	52.6	63.2	37.0	65.2
Urine Infection	18.1	28.1	18.4	15.1	18.5	19.6
Seasonal						
Cold and Fever	73.5	81.7	46.8	45.5	14.8	38.0
Water Borne						
Jaundice	23.9	23.6	n.a.	n.a.	n.a.	n.a.
Stomach Upset	23.3	32.6	28.4	28.7	29.6	25.0
Other Diseases	11.9	28.1	17.4	22.1	25.9	30.4
No. of Workers	226.0	356.0	190.0	470.0	27.0	92.0

Note: "n.a." indicates not available
Source: Own Survey

Additionally, the health constitution of the women workers differs from the health of their male colleagues since the women grew up since their childhood with poor health care and nutrition (Scott & Carr, 1985).[199]

On average workers slept for 6.6 hours a day (both in 1995 and 2000), while before joining the garment industry they used to sleep for about 9 hours a day. Although the sleeping time is the same for men and women, the women had lower leisure time: 2.7 hours for women and 3.4 hours for men a day in 2000.

[199] For more details concerning the workers' health situation see UTPS, 1999.

7.6.3 Reasons for Taking Leave

The extent of garment workers illness can also be measured from the reason for taking leave. About 55% of the workers, aged 15 years and above, worked without taking any leave in the month preceding the survey: 55.3% for female and 56.4% for male. This suggests that the rate of absenteeism was not higher for female than for males in 1995. But in 2000, women abstaining from work has increased and that of male declined as 47.7 and 61.6 % of female and male workers respectively worked without taking any leave. The incidence of abstaining from work was less in the EPZ: 57.6 and 25.9% of the female and male workers worked without taking any leave. The most important reasons for taking leave was own illness and more women took leave for their own illness (61% in 1995 and 62% in 2000) than men (52% in 1995 and 44% in 2000). The second important reason for leave was to go to the village in 1995, but in 2000 other reasons, which included other family members being sick, was the second important reason. Women workers have additional responsibility of looking after sick members of the family, which male workers do not have to do. As most workers are migrants from rural areas, they have to go to the village to maintain link with their families (Table 7.6). Leave taken due to own illness was found to be more prevalent among the sewing helpers, reflecting the fact that these workers earn very low incomes and are malnourished. In any case, granting of leave is minimal in the garment industry. During the peak season, the workers have to work not only overtime but also on weekly holidays. Although workers are paid for overtime work holidays, no alternative holidays are given. This is a violation of the Factories Act 1965, which provides for a weekly holiday, and stipulated that no worker is to work without a holiday more than 10 days consecutively. During the peak season, the workers have to come to work even if they are sick. The workers wanted at least two holidays a month in 1995. But the union leaders never raise this.

Table 7.6
Reasons for Taking Leave in the Bangladesh Garment Industry

Reasons	Non-EPZ				EPZ	
	1995		2000		2000	
	Male	Female	Male	Female	Male	Female
Own illness	52.0	61.0	43.8	62.2	42.8	53.8
Household work	11.2	6.3	6.8	9.3	57.1	12.8
Went to village	25.5	15.7	20.5	10.9	-	10.2
Other reasons	11.2	28.1	28.8	17.5	-	23.1
No. workers	98.0	159.0	73.0	246.0	7.0	39.0

Source: Own Survey

7.6.4 Mode of Commuting

The nature of commuting is also exhausting the work force. Most of the workers walk to work in groups, both in 1995 and 2000: the proportion of female workers walking has increased more than that of male workers (Table 7.7). On an average a worker has to commute about 4 kilometres every day, spending about 40-45 minutes in 1995. In 2000 the workers were found to be living closer to their work place: they commuted about 2 kilometres every day. Traditionally, women were confined to the precinct of the household, and their presence in the street was very rare. Hence wage work at the garment industry has increased mobility of women but still neither the employers nor the government have provided transport for them. Only in the EPZ workers commute by factory bus.

The different health conditions of the male and female workers are also due to the social division of labour in the household. Studies based on the Labour Force Survey 1991 have shown that the entry of women in the garment industry has not reduced their reproductive (household) work in the household.

Table 7.7
Bangladesh Garments Workers' Mode of Commuting

Commuting Mode	Non-EPZ				EPZ	
	1995		2000		2000	
	Male	Female	Male	Female	Male	Female
Walk to work	54.0	57.3	57.9	68.9	7.4	7.6
Walk and Rickshaw	1.8	0.6	3.7	7.0	3.7	3.3
Walk and Bus	8.0	15.7	21.6	15.5	3.7	3.3
Bus/Tempo	24.8	18.8	4.2	2.1	3.7	2.2
Factory Bus	4.0	2.5	0.5	-	77.8	79.3
Rickshaw	4.4	4.8	6.3	2.8	-	2.2
Others	3.1	0.3	5.8	3.7	3.7	2.1
No. of Workers	226.0	356.0	190.0	470.0	27.0	92.0

Source: Own Survey

On an average a female garment worker spents about 4 hours a day on reproductive (household) work, while a male worker spends only 1.4 hours. About two-third of women's reproductive time is spent on cooking and cleaning. Hence, work in the garment industry has increased hours of paid work for women without reducing their time spent in reproductive work. The sexual division of labour which designates reproductive work as a female task has not been changed. It is taken for granted that women can stretch their time. But our discussion shows that the breaking point is being reached for some women as suggested by Brydon and Chant (1989). This will have costs not only for the women but also for their households and the society as well.

7.6.5 Increased Vulnerability: Risk of Harassment

The increased participation of women in the garment industry have made them exposed to risk of harassment which can take place at the factory or in the street. It is very likely that the workers will under report such incidents. Table 6.8 shows that in general there has been a decline in the incidence of harassment over the period 1995-2000 for both men and women employed in the garment industry. In 1995 as well as in 2000, the most frequent incident reported by female workers for themselves and their female colleagues was "harassment in the street" while men reported "attack by *masthans*"[200] (Table 7.8).

Table 7.8
Distribution of Workers by Type of Harassment

Types of Harassment	Non-EPZ								EPZ			
	1995				2000				2000			
	Self		Colleagues		Self		Colleagues		Self		Colleagues	
	Ma.	Fe.	Ma.	Fe.	Ma.	Fe.	Ma.	Fe.	Ma.	Fe.	Ma.	Fe.
Factory												
Beating in the Factory	2.2	4.4	7.1	4.2	2.6	1.9	1.1	2.6	-	14.1	-	13.0
Fear of Dismissal	8.8	17.1	6.2	14.3	2.6	6.2	2.1	6.6	11.1	5.4	25.9	2.2
Rape in the Factory	-	0.3	1.3	2.2	-	-	-	-	-	-	-	-
Street												
Attacked by Muggers	10.2	4.5	12.8	9.8	3.2	4.0	4.2	4.9	3.7	1.1	3.7	2.2
Got Afraid in the Street	7.1	14.6	5.8	7.6	0.5	13.6	-	3.6	3.7	12.0	-	2.2
Harassed by Police	2.2	1.1	2.2	2.1	1.6	0.8	1.6	0.8	-	-	-	-
Harassed in the Street	6.2	19.4	-	21.5	1.6	34.9	4.7	31.0	-	21.7	-	9.8
Raped in the Street	-	-	3.5	3.9	-	-	1.1	0.2	-	-	-	-

Note: The figures show the proportion of workers reporting experience of different types of harassment
Source: Own Survey

200 Bengali expressions for street gangster, often engaged on behalf of persons or organisations to assert their interests by force.

This is because, due to lack of transport facilities women have to walk to work in groups. The incidence of being "harassed in the street" has declined for male workers in 2000 but has increased for female workers.

On the other hand there has been a marked decline in the proportion of those reporting "afraid in the street" in 2000. Hence, women are learning to cope with vulnerability while commuting and have gained self-confidence. Most of them now confirm to the practice to covering their head while walking. This "purdah" has now given them respect. It may also be observed that over the period 1995-2000 there has been improvement in street lighting and hence women feel secured while walking. More of unmarried female workers were scared while commuting. Female workers have reported even harassment by police but this incidence has declined over time.

"Mugged" while commuting was more prevalent for men than women in 1995, but it has reversed in 2000. Although the law and order situation has deteriorated over time, the reported incidence of mugging has declined over the period 1995-2000. The incidence of rape in the street was higher than in the factory in 1995. In 2000 none reported rape at the factory, but one female and two male workers reported rape in the street for their colleagues.

Within the factory, a larger proportion of women workers than men reported the fear of being dismissed, although the incidence has declined in 2000. There has been a decline in beating in the factory. The incidence of harassment was lower in the EPZ than non-EPZ in general. But Table 7.8 shows that more female reported beating in the factory in the EPZ than in the non-EPZ factories.

7.7 Implementing Labour Law

The fact that labour laws are not implemented in the garments industry has been mentioned in several studies. Moreover, in the 1995 survey, most entrepreneurs opined that the laws are outdated and need to be changed (Table 7.9). Much of the working conditions of the workers would improve if the Labour Law Reform Report 1994 is approved and enforced. These changes include: appointment letter to be made compulsory; maternity leave to be provided for two surviving children; workers need to give 60 day's notice to leave jobs; working hours for women will be from 6 a. m. to 10 p.m.; provision for one day weekly leave; equal wage to be paid to men and women for equal work; fine for not paying the minimum wages; group of establishment at the same location can form one union; unions cannot be affiliated with political parties; and trade unions to provide training on labour laws. These provisions will certainly help improve the wage and working conditions of the RMG sector if they are properly enforced. Moreover, NGOs and trade unions need to create more awareness about labour laws and monitor implementations. Unless efforts are made to improve these aspects, trade related employment will continue these aspects; trade related employment will continue to provide dead-end, low-skill jobs with poor conditions, intensifying traditional segregation.

Table 7.9
Labour Laws and Suggested Changes by Entrepreneurs

The List of Labour Laws which are Applicable for the Garment Industry are Given Below. The Entrepreneurs were Asked to Give Their Opinion on Them

Existing Labour Laws	Entrepreneur's Opinions
1. An employer has the right to terminate a worker's service by serving a 90-day notice or wages in lieu of the notice.	1. a. It should be one months notice or wage in lieu of the notice. b. It should not be applicable if the worker has to be terminated for stealing. c. Usually the workers are not terminated; they leave on their own. d. As most of the workers are not permanent/confirmed, so this is not applicable.
2. There should be one latrine per 25 females and one per 25 males. Where there are more than 100 male/female workers, it is sufficient if after the first 4 latrines are provided, further latrines are provided at the rate of one for every 50 workers.	2. If the factory building is rented, it may not be possible.
3. Adequate washing facilities are to be provided for each sex, and will have to be conveniently accessible and clean.	3. If the factory building is rented, it may not be possible.
4. First aid boxes are to be kept on the premises; one box for every 150 workers and where more than 500 are employed, there should be an ambulance and a room provided with a qualified medical practitioner in charge, assisted by at least one qualified nurse.	4. a. A qualified medical practitioner does not want to work for the garment industry. b. Nearby nursing home can provide emergency medical facilities.

5. If a factory employs more than 250 workers, canteen facilities should be provided, and where there are more than 100 workers, there should be suitable lunch room.	5. a. Space is a problem in a rented premise. b. All factories should have a lunch room c. Canteen facilities are not needed where there are nearby shops/ hotels.
6. If more than 50 female workers are ordinarily employed, they shall be provided a suitable room or rooms for the use by children aged less than six years.	6. a. Workers should be free to work and keep their family problems at home. b. Due to the space problem, it cannot be implemented. c. So far, there was no demand for it. d. Such provision will hamper work. e. This facility is not needed as women do not bring in children along with them. f. This provision should be abolished.
7. In general, the factory workers are not required to work more than 48 hours a week, or 9 hours a day.	7. a. The garment industry is highly time-constrained for timely production. So, this law should not be practised for garments. b. There should not be a work-hour limit, if workers are working willingly.
8. No workers should be required to work more than 60 hours a week.	8. This provision is not suitable for the garment industry during the peak season.
9. No workers are to be made to work for 6 hours at a stretch without an hour break or two half a hour break.	9. This provision needs clarification.
10. Women are only allowed to work in a factory between 7 a.m. and 8 p.m.	10. a. Not feasible for the garment industry. b. This provision is discriminatory. c. This provision should be extended till 11 p.m.

11. There is a provision for a weekly holiday, i. e. Friday, and no workers are to work more than 10 days consecutively without a holiday.	11. Workers demand two holidays per month.
12. An employee must have been employed by the employer from whom she claims maternity benefit for a period not less than nine months immediately preceding the day of delivery.	12. a. Should work for at least 12 months to claim maternity leave and than should not get pregnant in 5 years. b. The permanent workers should get this benefit.
13. A women is entitled to benefit for six weeks preceding and including the day of her delivery, and for six weeks immediately following that day.	13. a. It should be two weeks prior and eight weeks after the day of delivery. b. Should be without pay.
14. Employees are entitled to enjoy the following leave every year: (i)10 to 20 days-casual leave. (ii) 14 days annual leave. (iii) Sick and medical leave	14. Should be provided to those confirmed, i.e. after one year of service.
15. Wages in a factory or other establishments employing less than one thousand persons are to be paid within seven days after the expiry of the wage period and within 10 days employing one thousand or more persons.	15. a. It should be within 10 days for pay, and within 21 days for overtime. b. Should be implemented immediately.
16. Any employees who sustains a personal injury by an accident arising out of or in the course of his/her employment is entitled to workmen's compensation at the specific rates.	16. a. Usually no major accident is possible in the garment factory. b. Workmen compensation is to be linked to the length of service.

Source: Zohir and Paul-Majumder 1996.

BGMEA started a "earn and learn" programme from July 1998 for the above 14 age group, who have completed their schooling under the MOU but now wants to continue their studies. While the strategy towards the progressive elimination of child labour is a worthwhile initiative, poverty-driven search for employment by under-aged population in Bangladesh is a reality. One way to accommodate this concern in the face of social labelling of Bangladesh exports could be through ratification of the ILO convention No. 138 on minimum age of labour as referred in the Harkin Bill. The provision allows for lower minimum age (12 years) for light work in case of countries where the economy and educational facilities are insufficiently developed. The Tripartite Consultative Committee, therefore, needs seriously to consider ratification of the ILO Convention No. 138 by Bangladesh. BGMEA could extent its 'earn and learn' programme for children of age 12 and above.

Moreover, providing maternity leave may be linked with trade in future. Although laws for providing such leave exists, but the ILO convention on maternity leave has not been signed by Bangladesh yet. Maternity leave can be provided in a way that does not penalise enterprises, which employ a lot of women and does not make it more expensive to employ women, if it is funded by the state. Bangladesh will create a unique example if the tax-at-source from the exporters could be used for paying maternity leave to the garment workers.

7.8 Concluding Remarks

The discussions made in this chapter clearly show that employment in the garment industry has definitely empowered women, increased their mobility and expanded their individual choice. But this they have achieved at the cost of their health and increased risk of harassment. It is important to emphasize that those who are working in the garment industries in 1995, were the first generation of women wage workers. They did not have a "role model" to follow, as they have not seen an older generation of women working in such jobs. The analysis of this chapter suggests that on the whole there has been improvement in worker's well-being over the last decade. Women's access to income-earning opportunities had many implications for their position in intra-household relationships. In 1995, entrepreneurs as well as the workers were the first generation of entrepreneurs and workers respectively. They have now set a "role model" for the next generation. The improvement in the worker's well being will be sustained in future if proper policy supports are extended to the garment industry. The next chapter is, therefore, aimed at the female labour migration and urban adaptation.

CHAPTER EIGHT
MIGRATING TO WORK

8.1 Introduction

Migration has been an important livelihood strategy for the people of Bangladesh. Whenever the population rose to such an extent that people could no longer secure a livelihood, they migrated elsewhere. The country side of Bangladesh is no longer confined to food production but now a source of labour for urban areas (Toufique and Turton, 2002). Their adjustment is heavily influenced by two basic tasks: obtaining a suitable job and finding accommodation. Considering the fact that many migrants had few or no economic resources for establishing themselves in the new factory and urban environment, it is important to focus on their adjustment process. More so because RMG factories started purely with profit motive in Bangladesh and Dhaka city[201] remained largely ill-equipped to house female migrants and respond to their needs. Cornell et.al. (1982) claimed that in the mid-1970s, women were pushed to the factories due to poverty. But on the contrary, studies based on interviews show that better-off women are also entering the garment industry in the 1990s. Kabeer (1995, 1997) has distinguished several reasons as to why women are joining the garment industry. Some had to earn cash out of necessity in order to survive; for some better-off married women, factory work offered an acceptable way to earn cash to improve the living standards of their families; and for some better-off unmarried women, factory work provided a way to save for their dowry. This chapter, therefore, attempts to establish the context in which female labour migration takes place to Dhaka city to understand the migration process and to examine the adaptation process of female migrants and their impact on the social life as well.

8.2 Data Set

This chapter of the study is based on two data sets generated by myself in 1998-99 and 1999-2000 for both male and female labours working in the formal manufacturing sector by employing multiple methods of data collection and multistage sampling.

8.2.1 Data Set I

Using a quota sampling technique, 213 workers were drawn from a list of 530 workers from five garment and three other manufacturing industries (pharmaceuticals, electronics and food processing) in Dhaka city. Table 8.1 presents the

[201] In Dhaka city more than 80 per cent of the RMG industries are located.

sample workers selected for the study by gender, category of work and industry type. The number of male and female workers were 107 and 106, respectively, selected to facilitate comparison and to identify appropriate policy measures. Because the RMG industries have generated considerable female employment since the 1980s, a larger sample of 153 was drawn from garment industry, compared to 60 workers from other manufacturing industries. The workers were interviewed both in their workplace and home. The sample garment industries were established between 1984 to 1994 and expecting the pharmaceutical industry (CIBA Geigy Ltd.) which was founded in 1984, the remaining two (food processing and electronics) were established in the 1960s.

Table 8.1
Total Number of Male and Female Workers of the Sample Industries and the Sample Drawn for the Present Study

Name of the Industry	Total No. of Workers			Sample listed Using Quota Sampling Method			Final Sample Derived		
Garment	**Male**	**Female**	**Total**	**Male**	**Female**	**Total**	**Male**	**Female**	**Total**
Applique Fashion Ltd	115	164	279	27	25	52	15	15	30
Bari Apparels Ltd	235	340	575	33	50	83	16	17	33
Florate Pvt. Ltd	80	170	250	30	43	73	15	15	30
Jeakon Garment Ltd.	300	1200	1500	33	45	78	15	15	30
Sparrow Apparels Ltd.	1100	1400	2500	35	53	88	15	15	30
All Garments	1830	3274	5104	158	216	374	76	77	153
Other Manufacturing									
CIBA Geigy Ltd.	43	28	73	18	20	38	10	10	20
Haque Brothers Ltd.	250	300	550	28	44	72	10	10	20
Mehar Industries Ltd.	67	55	122	25	21	46	10	10	20
All other Manufacturing Industries Ltd.	360	383	743	71	85	156	30	30	60

Source: Own Survey, 2000

The size of the sample industries varied between 250 and 2500 employees. The other sample manufacturing units have nearly 100 employees. However, the food processing industry employs 530 workers. The share of women workers is almost double that of men in the sample garment industries, while in the other manufacturing industries, excepting pharmaceutical (in which men are over presented), there is almost equal representation of male and female workers.

The broader sample of workers drawn through quota sampling revealed that more than 90 per cent of workers of garment factories are migrants. On the other hand, migrants constitute nearly half of the total respondents in other manufacturing industries. Almost no divergence is found along the gender lines in this regard. It should be noted that migrant is defined using both geographic and temporal criteria. A person, who was not born in Dhaka and migrated there between 1980 and 1999, is defined as a migrant. Further, those who migrated in the last five years (between 1994 and 1999), taking the year of survey as the reference period are defined as recent migrants, whereas others (that is, who migrated between 1980 and 1995 are long term migrants. It is assumed that 15 years is sufficient to adjust to the urban environment. Hence, those who came before 1980, were treated as non-migrants.

8.2.2 Data Set II

Unity through Population Services (UTPS), a non-government organisation (NGO) was approached to get a list of workers disaggrgated by gender and occupational category. This is because it covers the largest number of RMG industries in Dhaka city and adjacent areas through its health programmes. According to BGMEA more than 2800 RMG industries are working in Dhaka and UTPS was working with 93 industries in 1999. Since the Action-Aid Bangladesh[202] who also supports a part of UTPS activities, it was easier for me to approach UPTS.[203]

In this study, I have covered at least four types of samples viz. RMG industries, workers, employers of the selected RMG industries and relatives and or neighbours of workers, a multi-stage random sampling procedure was adopted. It allowed me to select the samples in sequential order and adopt judicious combination of quantitative and qualitative methods to generate more useful data than either method taken alone. It was decided to cover at least 15 per cent of the total respondents drawn from the sample industries in the second stage for the same reason as stated above. As a result, out of the total 5182 workers of 14 sample industries, 784 were drawn randomly representing 15 per cent of the total. Out of 784 workers, 595 or nearly three-quarters are female and the remaining 189 or nearly a quarter are male workers roughly corresponding proportional gender composition in each industry. Two-thirds of

[202] An U.K. based funding Non Government Organization (NGO) working in Bangladesh after her independence in 1971.

[203] Formal sources such as Census of Manufacturing Industry (CMI) published by Bangladesh Bureau of Statistics (BBS) or the list of RMG industries published by the BGMEA do not provide such information.

skilled machine operators and nearly 30 per cent of unskilled production workers, who are called “helpers” were covered through the survey technique. Within each of these categories, however, the proportion of male and female workers drawn as “operators” and “helpers” is roughly proportionate to the total number of male and female workers covered under the study. In this process, whilst female workers make nearly two-thirds of operators and a third of helpers, the corresponding figures for their male counterparts are nearly three-fifths and a quarter respectively. Nearly a fifth of the total male respondents also represent other categories such as Quality Control Inspector, Technicians, etc. mentioned above. Of the respondents, 508 (72.8%) were surveyed with the help of structured questionnaire and the remaining 276 or 27.8 per cent were covered by FGD.[204] Each of the FGD consisted of ten to eleven participants, one moderator and one note taker and the discussions lasted approximately two hours. The composition of each group was homogeneous with respect to gender and age category. A total of 26 group discussions were conducted altogether. Generally one group-discussion was conducted from each sample industry and FGDs were evenly divided between male and female groups. In this process 14 FGDs were held, seven with male and seven with female groups from each of the sample industries. In addition, in two big industries, there were more than 700 workers, two more discussions were held to have greater representations from both male and female groups. Further, based on concentration of workers (with a minimum of ten workers), ten FGDs were conducted with relatives and neighbours of respondents in their community of residence. A uniform set of FGD guidelines was used for all sessions. In depth interviews were conducted with management personnel of 14 sample industries, focusing mainly on their perception with regard to the performance of the male and female workers, difficulties they face in running RMG industries, the role of NGOs in the treatment of workers and raising the productivity of the factory, and their attitudes towards sick workers.

8.3 The Context of Female Labour Migration in Bangladesh

Migration is one of the major contributors to urban growth in Bangladesh. A study on the internal migration clearly demonstrated that greater job opportunities in the cities and metropolitan areas “pulled” migrants from rural areas. Rural areas are still home to most of the total population. Migrant accounts for about two-third of the urban growth seen in Bangladesh since independence. The proportion of people living in urban areas rose from 6.2% in 1965 to 9.9% in 1975 and reached 25% in 2000 (UN, 2002). It is widely believed that in the Indian Sub-Continent including Bangladesh, women’s autonomous migration

[204] It was not possible to draw equal number of samples for male and female workers from each and every type of existing positions they are holding, simply because they are not equally represented in all categories.

from rural to urban areas is low, compared to Sri Lanka and South East Asian countries, largely due to low economic growth and rigid norms of Purdah. Notwithstanding such a negative image, with the emergence of the RMG sector, there has been a boost in independent migration by young women in Bangladesh. This is reflected in the urban sex-ratio and specially that of metropolitan cities, which became more balanced in 1994 (Mitra et.al.1994) from being male dominated in the previous census years 1991 and 1981 (Afsar, 1995). For example, the sex ratio of the Dhaka city dwellers declined from 150 to 105 between 1961 and 1993-94. Particularly, the sex ratio obtained for the 15-34 age group in the urban poor agglomerations, where the large majority of the garment factory workers live has gone more in favour of women, from 103 to 65 between 1991 and 1996. While describing restrictive role of Purdah in Bangladesh, Cain et. al. (1979) observed that Purdah restrictions on the movement of outside home excluded them from access to such economic opportunities as paid agricultural work and petty trading. However, empirical studies done in 1980s and 1990s (Rothschild and Mahmud, 1989; Kabeer, 1991) suggest class differences in women's participation as wage labourers.

8.3.1 Motives for Female Migration

Migrants are predominantly young adults from low income families. The workers interviewed in the study stress the economic motives for migration. Nearly three-quarters of men and women migrant came to Dhaka for work related reasons. Three quarters of recent female migrants as opposed to nearly a third of their long-term migrant counterparts came to Dhaka for employment related reasons (Table 8.2). Nearly half of the long-term female migrants came for settlement either with family or their husband. Elsewhere, it was found that those who came for employment, a half of them came for the present job in the case of female workers but declined to two-fifths for their colleagues. Nearly half of the total respondents were directly recruited by the employer's agent from the villages of origin to work in Dhaka. Although migration for employment related reasons has always been high among male migrants, but it too has increased significantly in the last five years. All these tend to suggest that job opportunities for women migrant in RMG industry has increased faster in the last five years than between 1981 and 1991 and also faster than for their male counterparts. The study of Afsar (2000) demonstrated that nearly 90% of women workers in the garment industry had acquaintances in Dhaka prior to migration. This is not unexpected given that the RMG sectors composed predominantly of youth labour force. Four in every five male workers are currently unmarried, as opposed to 43% of their male colleagues. Currently unmarried women also constitute more than 40%, and the remaining one-eighth are either widows, separated or divorced. The average age of the respondents is 20.6 years and this is almost the same for both male and female workers.

Given the fact that poor migrants that can hardly afford to remain unemployed, one must go far beyond unemployment data to examine impact on poverty. However, for those who live on the edge of extreme poverty in rural areas, migration to nearby towns may give them temporary relief from unemployment.

Table 8.2
Distribution of Respondents by Gender and Migration Status and Reasons for Migration: 1999-2000

Migration Status	Reasons for Migration						
	Poverty	Employ-ment	Associati-onal	Educat-ion	Others	All	
	%	%	%	%	%	No.	%
Long -term Migrant							
Male	16.0	68.0	12.3	-	4.0	25	34.7
Female	11.0	35.6	38.1	2.5	12.7	118	30.2
Recent Mi-grant							
Male	4.2	89.4	4.3	-	2.1	47	65.3
Female	2.6	76.1	10.7	1.1	9.5	272	69.8
All Migrant							
Male	8.3	81.9	7.0	-	2.8	72	100.0
Female	5.1	63.9	19.0	1.5	10.5	390	100.0

Source: Own Survey, 2000

Nearly three-quarters of the total respondents fall in the age group 15 and 24 years, and again a half of them are under 20. Population under 20 constitutes nearly half of the total population both for the sample garment industries and in slum and squatter settlements of Dhaka city. Predominance of young and adult men and women in the RMG industries has far-reaching implications in terms of women's urban adaptation and quality of life of the industry workers.

8.3.2 Socio-economic Background of RMG Workers Prior to Migration

Studies on internal migration clearly demonstrated that greater job opportunities in the cities and metropolitan areas pulled migrants from rural areas. With regard to the economic background, it can be said that RMG industry workers, more particularly women workers come from poorer socio-economic background than their male colleagues from the size of landholdings and level of education prior to migration, because these are highly correlated with income. Three-quarters of women migrants belonged to a functionally landless household, and on an average had 0.5 acres of cultivable land. A half of the male migrants also came from the functionally landless families but slightly better economic background than women migrants (Table 8.3). They have 0.8 acres of land on an average in the origin, and also have a higher educational attainment, compared to female workers. However, for those who live on the edge of extreme poverty in the rural areas, migration to nearby towns may give them temporary relief from unemployment.[205] With regard to education, nearly two-fifths of female RMG workers are illiterate and only a handful had secondary level education, compared respectively to a tenth and a third of their male colleagues. Nonetheless, the level of education of a female worker is higher than either her age cohort in rural areas and in slum and squatter settlements.[206] Studies conducted in urban poor agglomerations showed that women have do not more than one year of schooling on an average. By way of contrast, female RMG worker had 2.5 years of schooling prior to migration while the figure was 3.3 for female worker from other manufacturing industries (Table 8.3). Similarly, median years of schooling of a female RMG industry worker is four years as opposed to zero in the case of her age cohort in rural areas. It suggests that, work opportunity in RMG industry adds incentive for female education, as women with primary level of education had greater likelihood to be absorbed in RMG industry than their illiterate counterparts. With heavy concentration of the working age population and unmarried workers, dependency ratio is very low in the families at destination of the migrant workers. Paradoxically, with the migration of young and active adult members from villages, dependency ratio is very high, 76% of those households in rural areas. It suggests that migration is adopted as a family strategy for income diversification, where young and adult working men and women are sent to the areas of economic opportunities. Network support of family members, relatives, friends, neighbours, and acquaintances from same districts facilitate migration of both men and women, prior to and after migration by increasing individual's coping capacity, through the availability of aid and assistance in relocation at an alternative place of residence, for those who live on the edge of extreme poverty.

---

205 For an interesting insight on extremely poor migrant's stories please refers to Hossain et al 2003a.

206 In Bangladesh, education is positively correlated with the income of the households. Seven out of ten female workers from landless households either had no education, or incomplete primary level. Whereas nearly three out of every five female workers from other industries had secondary and above level of education and they belong to small and landholding families.

8.4 Adaptation of Female Migrant Labour to Work and Urban Environment

The migrants' choice of strategy depends on a number of factors viz. their own resources and their access to others, and their cultural tradition and personal experience. In the migration literature Kin, peers and self are considered to be major resources for fall back (Graves and Graves 1987; Graves, 1994; Jong & Richter, 1996). In the absence of impersonal agencies and institutional support that would have strengthened migrant women's self-reliant efforts, female migrant largely use kin and peer reliant adaptive strategy or combine the both. In this section, women's access to material resources and economic dimension of female adaptation has been examined first. This is followed by an analysis of women's political and social adaptation.

Table 8.3
Distribution of Sample Migrant Workers by Some of the Pre-Migrant Characteristics

Pre-Migrant Characteristics	Garment Industries				Other Manufacturing Industries			
	Male		Female		Male		Female	
	No.	%	No.	%	No.	%	No.	%
Level of Education[207]								
No Education	12	16.4	21	29.2	1	5.9	3	21.4
Primary	24	32.9	23	31.9	1	5.9	4	28.6
Secondary	13	17.8	10	13.9	1	5.9	-	-
High School +	24	32.9	18	25.0	14	82.3	7	50.0
Average Education	73	3.0	72	2.5	17	3.9	14	3.3
Land Holding								
No Land	19	26.0	33	45.8	5	29.4	6	42.9
< 1 Acre	20	27.4	24	33.3	4	23.5	3	21.4
1-2.5	20	27.4	13	18.1	3	17.6	2	14.3
2.5-5.00	10	13.7	1	1.4	3	17.6	1	7.1
5.01+	4	5.5	1	1.4	2	11.8	2	14.3

Source: Data Set I

8.4.1 Poverty and Economic Dimension of Adaptation

A skilled and unskilled female worker earn respectively 95% and 73% on an average of what her male colleagues earn. Average monthly take home income

[207] The term "level of education" primary level means 5 years of schooling, secondary level is up to 8 years and high school is 10 years of schooling.

is $ 35 and $ 40 (approximately) for the female and male RMG industry workers respectively. Whilst no gender based disparity is found in the overtime earned by her male counterparts (Table 8.4). After adjusting for the increase in cost of living for the low income households in Dhaka for 1997-98, the cost of food was estimated at Tk 19.87. On the basis of the information that urban households migrant spent 60% of their incomes on food (BBS, 1998), they estimated poverty line at Tk. 11, 905 (per annually) or around Tk. 992 (per capita per month). A RMG sector worker who earns below the level has been identified as moderately poor. The threshold income for extreme poverty (that provides a kilo calorie of 1805 per capita per day) was estimated at Taka 8164 per year or Taka 680.30 per month. A worker whose monthly income is below this level was identified as hardcore poor. As the study was conducted around the same period, it adopted the same poverty line income to estimate the headcount index to determine the magnitude of poverty among workers of the RMG sector. In this context, excerpts from Uchatius (2003) explain what is exactly going on in the readymade garment industry of Bangladesh. He wrote about the worker as she is poor and living in a slum. She has income, bank account of her own, she earns one dollar or 1.20 dollar a day which is about Taka 1,900 per month, but some times no payment from the industry. Table 8.6 shows that 18% of the workers earn below the poverty level income but it increases significantly by gender and nature of the job. Those who earn below poverty level income is more than double in the case of women than their male colleagues, and majority of unskilled production workers fall below the poverty line. For example, 19% women as opposed to 9% men workers are estimated to earn below the poverty level income and the magnitude increases to nearly 60% in the case of female unskilled production workers. The recent estimate on urban poverty by Hossain, Afsar and Bose (1999) shows that 19% of the household in Dhaka city live below the absolute poverty line income, and 49% of the households in slums as opposed to a fraction 2.3% of their non-slum counterparts are moderately poor. On the other hand, Hossain *et al.* (2003) estimated that landless and land-poor farmers have left the agricultural labour market for tenancies, wage labour in trade and business enterprises, rickshaw pulling and other manual non-agricultural activities. Members of medium and large land-owning household with correspondingly larger endowments of human and physical capital-switched from cultivating their own farms to service and business. As a result, the proportion of poor people dropped to 43% in 2000 from 59% in 1988, a reduction of 1.2% per year. There is no direct estimate of the contribution of remittances to poverty alleviation but, indirectly, some conjecture can be made in this regard. The same estimate suggests that of the 9 percent of the urban households living in extreme poverty, 23 percent are located in slum and squatter settlements.

It is also estimated that among unskilled production helpers, who predominantly live in slum, nearly half earn below the poverty line income and about a fifth of them can be described as hardcore poor. Zohir and Paul-

Majumder (1996) show that there are variations in residence types according to job categories. The sewing and finishing helpers live mostly with family members or with relatives. Of their sample, only 14 per cent of the total workers live in slums, the rest live outside slums (16 percent). Although only a fraction of the machine operators can be described as moderately poor, but they have very little scope for upward mobility, especially in the case of women. Men on the other hand, have greater opportunities to augment their income through acquiring higher skills or managing part-time jobs because of their greater scope for mobility and lesser burden of household chores than women. Moreover, lion's share of women's income (52%) is spent on housing, whereas their male colleagues spent around a third for the same.

Table 8.4
Distribution by Various Characteristics

Current designation & Gender	Average Hours of Work		Average Overtime Hours		Average Salary Earned		Average Overtime Earned		Average Gross Take Home Income	
	No.	Hrs.	No.	Hrs.	No.	Tk.	No.	Tk.	No.	Tk.
Operator						(0.95)		(1.00)		(1.03)
Male	43	7.42	37	78.92	45	1507.0	23	476.26	45	1810.5
Female	208	9.56	234	70.43	291	1433.5	219	476.68	291	1860.7
Helper						(0.73)		(0.66)		(0.75)
Male	16	10.59	13	106.38	18	933.33	13	448.77	18	1289.0
Female	100	10.44	112	81.87	133	681.28	109	296.56	133	964.8
Iron man						(1.22)		(1.08)		(1.12)
Male	2	12.00	2	97.50	3	1183.3	3	425.00	3	1701.7
Female	2	10.25	2	96.00	2	1450.0	2	460.00	2	1988.4
Electrician										
Male	1	3.00	2	75.00	2	2150.0	1	250.00	2	2312.5
Quality Inspect										
Male	6	11.25	9	110.56	11	1350.0	8	727.00	11	1933.4
Packer						(0.5)		(0.98)		(0.65)
Male	-	-	1	102.00	1	1400.0	1	612.00	1	2070.3
Female	1	12.00	1	245.00	1	700.0	1	600.00	1	1345.0
Mechanics										
Male	1	13.00	-	-	1	6500.0	-	-	1	6500.0
All						(0.84)		(0.83)		(0.89)
Male	69	8.64	64	89.77	81	1422.4	49	505.04	81	1780.9
Female	311	9.86	349	74.74	427	1197.6	331	417.76	427	1581.1

Note: Figures in parenthesis are the ratio female's earning to male's earning
Source: Data Set II

In addition health expenditure along with clothing, sandals, toiletries, transport and tiffin consumed nearly a quarter of their income. As a result, women workers often resorted to borrowing from friends, colleagues and relatives to meet both ends.

Table 8.5
Gross Monthly Income of Workers by Gender and Occupational Categories, 1999-2000

Income Groups (Tk)	Unskilled Production Workers		Skilled Machine Operators		Quality Control Inspectors	Others		All	
	Male	Female	Male	Female	Male	Male	Female	Male	Female
<500	-	0.8	2.2	-	-	-	-	1.2	0.2
500-991	33.3	50.6	-	1.0	-	-	-	7.4	19.0
992-1491	27.8	36.2	24.4	18.6	18.2	-	66.7	22.2	24.4
1492-1991	33.3	0.8	35.6	46.0	45.4	42.9	-	40.7	31.6
1992+	5.6	3.8	31.1	34.4	36.4	57.1	33.3	28.5	24.8
All(%)	100.0	100.0	100.0	100.0	100.0	100.0	100.0	100.0	100.0
(No.)	18.0	133.0	45.0	291.0	11.0	7.0	3.0	81.0	427.0

Source: Data Set II

8.4.1.1 Strategies Women Industry Workers Adopt to Overcome Poverty

RMG industry provided an opportunity to the young women from rural landless families to work in the formal sector which has hitherto restricted to a few educated women. Earning cash income is the major motive for female labour migration. From almost no cash income 27% female RMG sector worker earns between US $ 42-50 per month. Proportions of the male workers and RMG and both male and female workers other manufacturing industries, who earn the same amount were much higher (one-third and a half respectively). Had they not migrated, they would have remained either unemployed or under-employed or involved in expenditure saving or income earning activities, mostly home based and few might have been working as wage labourers.[208] The latest labour force survey data reveal that whilst 62% of the rural women as opposed to 44% of urban women in salaried services get less than Taka 250 per week and those who get more than Taka 500 per week constitute 26 and 15 % of the urban and rural women respectively. Similarly average wage rates for a female day labourer in

[208] In rural areas, 83% of the employed women aged 15 plus years, compared to 15% of men, belonging to the same age are engaged as unpaid family helpers. Expecting only 4% , who work as employees, the remaining 13% are self-employed (7%) and day labourers (5.6%). Not only rural women have highly limited options for paid employment, the wage/salary they receive is far below the urban average.

urban areas is Taka 36 per day, which is higher by Taka 11 from a rural women's daily wage (BBS, 1995). Existing micro-studies indicate that female workers in the rural and informal sectors earn between a third and a half of male wages. The situation in the urban formal sector appears to be much better, with the ratio of female to male wages ranging between 72% and 97%, depending on skills level (World Bank, 1996).

Despite all these, they face tremendous hardship to cope with poverty and a highly irregulated formal manufacturing sector. Low rate of payment along with irregular schedule of payment lead them from extreme poverty into debt. In this context the Bachmann (2002) study provides the following insights: A leaflet of Bangladesh garments workers union stated: "Although there are exceptions to the rule, the working conditions in the majority of our garments factories still have much room for improvement." (BIGWUF[209], 1999). In particular, the workers themselves named as their main problems three complexes concerning the salaries, their health situation and the working times. Primarily, the workers interviewed in his study complained about the low wages and the irregularities in payment. Organised workers said:

> "We work for 12 hours, even 14 hours a day. But the wage is low. Mostly, they keep the overtime money. Actually we have the possibility to go to the management and complain to them. But everything happens is to say: work or go! This is the only answer all the time."

After three months working in a garment industry every worker is entitled to a minimum wage of Taka 930, now it is raised to Taka 1500. Nevertheless, many workers get less than this amount each month. According to the study of Paul-Majumder and Zohir (1994) one third of the workers in the garment sector earn below the minimum wage. Not every worker has knowledge about the minimum wage law[210], and labour law relating to leave and working hours.[211] Even some of the factory owners are probably not aware of this issue. But some entrepreneurs deliberately evade the minimum wage bill as the quotation of a worker makes it clear: "We have to sign that we get a particular wage but in fact we get less."

---

209 "The Bangladesh Independent Garment Workers Union Federation (BIGWUF) is looking for the better working condition in the factory.

210 That is why many NGOs and the trade unions organise meetings to inform about workers' rights and legal aid. One example is the "930 Campaign Coalition", constituted by 11 unions and federations and 17 concerned NGOs to inform the workers about the minimum wages and also to support the workers who do not get the full amount. In a leaflet the coalition offers a hotline where workers can report to if they get less than the fixed minimum wage.

211 According to existing labour laws factory employee is entitled to have i) an hour's break or two half hour breaks after working for 6 hours at a stretch; ii) 10 to 20 days casual leave; iii) 14 days annual leave, and iv) sick and medical leave. Such laws also stipulates that any factory/establishment employing fewer than 1000 persons must pay wages within 7 days after the expiry of the wage period.

Since the workers have no knowledge about their minimum wage the overtime money is calculated to small. According to the Factory Act of 1965 a basic day of work has 8 hours, every hour this limitation has to be paid as overtime, which is twice the basic salary. Over the empirical data of Wichterich (1998) show that the workers mostly get only half of their overtime wage. Wage reduction is not only one problem, but the salaries were often paid late which has several consequences for the female workers. The workers interviewed by Bachmann (2002, p.21) reported that they have to pay the food traders monthly. So if the wage payment is one or two weeks late they cannot provide themselves and their families. Additionally, the workers face problems because they are not able to pay the rent in time (FE,1999; UTPS 1999). The interviewed workers told, "No money so you cannot pay the vegetableman. And finally, you have no vegetables. So what should I do?"

Workers face also the threat of forceful eviction, family problems and tension affecting both their physical and mental health, particularly, of women workers, and compel them to resort to variety of ways to earn cash income which are likely to increase their vulnerability to health hazards. They adopt the following strategies to overcome poverty and an unfavourable industry situation.

i) Learning machine operation informally with the help of relatives or co-workers and friends to upgrade skills which enable them to be absorbed as skilled workers in the same or other industry and raise their salary twice compared to their current salary. The survey revealed that 84% and 70% of female and male workers who are currently working as skilled operators acquired their skills through such informal training. They have been able to acquire their skills, information and establish strong network connections to stake a claim in the labour market. Thus, for example female worker who have been working for a long time in the RMG sector earn nearly 2.5 times her recent migrant counterpart. Moreover, the gap between male and female wage narrows down from one-third to one-fifth when the length of their stay in the city exceeds five years.
ii) Marriage between co-workers is not rare; rather it is commonly adopted as a means to raise family income.
iii) Resort to more overtime work despite long working hours and the burden of domestic chores. Overtime work is estimated to contribute a third and a quarter to the gross income of unskilled and skilled workers respectively. They work as long as their male colleagues (11 hours per day including overtime), and also work at night without any transportation facility. Bachmann's (2002) study also showed that, half of the firms pay the overtime wage between two to four months later. Besides that delay, some workers never get anything of their overtime wages.
iv) Focus group also gave instances where some unskilled female helpers were involved in pre and extra-marital sex with co-workers or those who are

placed slightly up in the hierarchy for small gifts of cash or upward mobility. Often those workers have a desire for developing steadily relationship with their sex partners. Some cases were cited where lack of desired outcomes from sexual relationship has resulted in change of industry or change of partners. Only in two community based FGD, some participants cited a few cases where some of those unskilled workers who failed to establish steady relationship with their desired partners turned to sex trade.

v) Generate savings to remit to their parents or meet the crisis of the unforeseen future. The proportions of female workers, who save more than male workers and saving of a female worker as a proportion of her urban income, is also higher than male colleagues. Two out of every five female workers from RMG and other manufacturing industries respectively save 8% and 14% of urban incomes (Table 8.6). By way of contrast, one-third of their male counterparts from RMG and other manufacturing industries respectively reported to save 6 and 10% of their urban income. Similarly, a non-migrant worker saves nearly one per cent of his/her urban income, as opposed to 8% and 6% percent of long- term male and female migrants of the RMG sector.

Propensity to save appears to increase with the increasing age of the worker. Thus, workers belonging to the 30 and 39 year age group save nearly one-fifth of their urban income, as opposed to nearly 3% of their youngest counterparts (between 10 and 19 years) in RMG industries. This holds equally for both male and female workers.[212] It should be noted that the monetary wage of a RMG industry worker also appears to increase with their age, which is not the case for the workers of other manufacturing industries. Subsequently, no-such clear and systematic pattern could be observed in this case. Hence, while the study suggests influence of income in enhancing the saving capacity, one has to go beyond this and examine rigorously the impact of other factors in determining saving the capacity of the workers.

Remittances from internal migration are difficult to estimate due to the importance of in kind transfer. In addition to the standard problems of measurement, it is also difficult to separate the contribution of internal migration from international migration since a sending household often has different types of migrant members.[213]

212 However, there are only a few respondents belonging to the 30-39 years age group, since majority of the workers are younger in garment industry, compared to other manufacturing industries. Notwithstanding the smaller number of samples belonging to 30-39 years, one can still observe a positive correlation between age and ability to save in the case of garment industry workers (Table 8.6).

213 Such as recall bias and the tendency to under-report income.

Table 8.6
Average Savings of Respondents Migration Status and Age, 1998-99

Respondents	Average Savings from the Total Income (Tk)		Savings as a Proportion of Income (%)		Total (No.)	
Garment Industry	**Male**	**Female**	**Male**	**Female**	**Male**	**Female**
Non- Migrant	66.70	20.00	1.40	0.40	3	5
Long-term Migrant	261.40	144.10	8.60	6.20	35	37
Recent Migrant	43.40	46.90	2.70	4.10	38	35
All	144.70	145.10	6.4.0	8.00	76	77
Age Group						
10-19	27.30	32.60	2.20	2.90	33	33
20-29	145.70	136.70	5.20	6.70	35	38
30-39	625.00	816.70	14.60	20.70	8	6
Other Industries						
Non- Migrant	584.60	493.80	6.00	5.60	13	16
Long- Term Migrant	383.30	550.00	7.90	15.80	12	14
Recent Migrant	-	-	-	-	5	-
All	406.70	520.00	9.90	14.20	30	30
Age Group						
10-19	-	-	-	-	-	2
20-29	321.40	800.00	7.10	16.60	14	12
30-39	616.70	280.00	14.90	8.80	12	10
40+	75.00	533.30	3.20	17.80	4	6

Note: Income here refers to average monthly wage and overtime income.
Source: Own Survey

However, nearly two-fifths of migrant workers are able to send remittances to their families of origin. An analysis on remittances shows that the average size of the remittances as proportion of the monthly urban income is higher for workers of the RMG sector than those of other manufacturing industries. On an average, a migrant male and female worker of this sector send nearly two-fifths and one-third of their urban income per month (Table 8.7). The corresponding figures for their counterparts in other manufacturing industries is higher respectively were 35% and 11% respectively. The proportion of remitters out of total workers from other manufacturing industries is higher (38%) than those of RMG industries (32%). In both cases, men remitters outnumber their women counterparts.

In Bangladesh, like many other developing countries, migrant households in rural areas use remittances predominantly for consumption, where half of the rural households live below the poverty line. Priorities on consumption expenditure can be viewed as consonant with the "basic needs" approach to development; without this the situation of families of migrants would have been worse off. It is also argued that increased consumption expenditure by migrant households can trigger investment by other households or firms to meet this demand, which may create income multipliers in migrant-source economics (Taylor, 1999).

Younger migrants from RMG industries (aged between 10 and 19) remitted higher proportions of their urban income than their older colleagues. Whereas, the former group sent 45% of their urban income, the proportion declines to 25% for the other categories. Thus, unlike savings which is largely determined by the size of income among others, remittances primarily depends on the intensity of social ties and responsibilities respondents bear at the place of destination and origin. For example, a quarter of female respondents had single parents or siblings at the origin who they need to support. Thus, a majority of remitters (more than 90%) sent money for family maintenance and education of siblings. Expecting female workers of other manufacturing industries, purposes for sending remittances holds alike and both male for female workers. Total for all is not the same for different categories of migrants and different age groups as these are large number of non-migrants in the case of respondents from other manufacturing industries. There were 12 respondents who belonged to 10-19 and 40+ age group because they did not remit last year, were not represented in this table.

A large number of studies from Bangladesh, India, Indonesia and Africa demonstrated that consumption expenditure alone constituted between 80% and 90% of poorer migrants' remittances (Hugo, 1978; Cornell et. al.1982; Prakash, 1988; Afsar, 1995;). In a country like Bangladesh, where half of the rural households fall below the poverty line, priorities on consumption expenditure can be viewed as consonant with the "basic needs" approach to development without which the situation of families of migrants would have been worse off. Existing estimates from panel data on rural households (Hossain *et al*, 2000) suggest that remittances contributed 12.8% to the household income and that a 10% increase in income would lead to 6.5% increase in the demand for food items. These include mainly vegetables, fruits, fisheries, and livestock, indicating stronger potential for the expansion of market for rural processing, storage, trade and transportation activities, a probable multiplier effect of remittances that needs to be confirmed through further research.[214]

[214] Agricultural productivity itself might have stimulated the rural non-farm sector through linkage effects (Mellor, 1976; Haggblade *et al.* 2002). Drawing on data from selected Asian Countries, Haggblade *et al.* (2002) found that for each dollar increase in agriculture value added, an addition $ 0.50 to $ 1.0 income is generated in the non-farm sector. Given that there is growing scarcity of labour and the spread of powe-operated threshers in rural farms in Bangladesh, one may be tempted to link migration and agricultural productivity.

Table 8.7
Average Size Remittances Sent by Respondents and Magnitude of Remitters by Migration Status and Age

Garment Industry	Average Remittances (Tk)		Remitters (%)		Remitters as % of Income		Total (No.)	
	Male	Female	Male	Female	Male	Female	Male	Female
Long-term Migrant	1033.30	600.00	51.40	33.4	34.1	25.8	35	37
Recent Migrant	625.00	457.10	36.80	20.0	39.3	39.6	38	35
All	874.20	535.00	43.80	26.4	38.5	29.6	73	72
Age Group								
10-19	462.50	525.00	12.90	12.5	38.6	45.4	31	32
20-29	880.00	507.10	73.50	40.0	31.4	24.7	34	35
30-39	1250.0	750.00	50.00	40.0	29.3	21.1	8	5
Other Industry								
Long Term Migrant	1450.00	214.00	83.30	50.0	29.9	11.0	12	14
Recent Migrant	1200.00	-	40.00	-	-	-	5	-
All Migrant	1411.10	214.00	70.60	50.0	34.6	11.0	17	14
20-29	1450.00	250.00	42.80	25.0	32.1	8.3	14	12
30-39	1357.00	167.00	50.00	40.0	46.5	13.2	12	10
All Age Group	1411.10	214.00	46.20	31.8	34.6	11.0	26	22

Notes: Income here refers to average wage and overtime
Source: Own Survey

Remittances sent by sample respondents for both family maintenance and education is surely a step forward to achieve sustainable development through investment in human resources. It suggests that labour migration which is adopted as a strategy for income maximization, also helps to strengthen the human resources of the sending families.

8.5 Working Conditions and Political Dimension of Women's Adaptation

Women workers are perceived as docile, hard working, ready to work long hours and have less contacts, exposure and bargaining power than their male counterparts by the employers of the industries surveyed. Findings of the present study do not confirm this, particularly in the RMG sector. Hence it is important to cite other studies (Kabeer, 1991; Kibria, 1995; Markovic and Manderson 2000; Absar, 2000; Bachmann, 2002 and Zohir-Majumder, 1996) based on narratives of women and these studies consist of more than 100 interviewees. In these interviews, the researchers tried to explore the living and working conditions of the RMG workers, specially located in Dhaka city.

8.5.1 Women's Attempt to Change Their Working Conditions

Women workers were found to be active and vocal with regard to their entitlements like their male colleagues which is somewhat contrary to the stereo-type of female docility. Half of the sample women workers of the RMG sector demanded paid leaves and nearly three-fifths bargained for higher wages (Table 8.8). The proportion of men who made similar demands, is slightly higher than of women (63% and 62% respectively). Sample women on the other hand, outnumber their male counterparts only marginally in their demand to change their night duty. The magnitude of both male and female workers of the RMG sector, who demanded to change night duty were much lower (30% and 27%), than those who demanded paid leaves and higher wages.

Women workers from other manufacturing units mainly asked for paid leaves and here they outnumbered their male counterparts. It should be noted, that unlike the RMG sector, which remain open even on weekly and public holidays for longer hours, other manufacturing industries do not have such strong aberrations from normal working hours. Yet more women bargained for paid leaves because of their dual responsibilities for income earning and child care responsibilities that demand greater entitlements to paid leaves. Workers in these industries do not have to bargain for higher wages as they generally have their terms of contracts, and most of them are recruited on a regular basis. As a large number of workers in the RMG sector are hired on casual basis mostly without a terms of contract and hence, they have to bargain for higher wages.

More than 90% of the sample workers, irrespective of gender and type of industry, applied for better terms and conditions with the help of supervisors. They did not involve unions or other influential sources such as employers' agents in making their demands. As RMG industries operate by the private entrepreneurs purely with a profit motive, lack of discipline on the part of workers is not tolerated. Given the heavy competition for wage employment, the workers generally abide by existing rules and regulations of the industry. There is a number of obstacles that make protest against the above problems and poor working conditions relating to wages and leave and other aspects. The management tries to impede in particular the developments of unity and solidarity of the workers. Salary is used as an instrument for this policy. One worker reported how the wages are calculated (Bachmann, 2002, p. 24):

> "It depends on the efficiency: So it is different. It happens that, you have ten workers, same job, but not equal wages. (.....). At first, when you are new, they ask for experiences, that is how many years one has been working in the RMG, the wages are fixed according to that."

Due to the individual negotiation of wages the worker compete each other. This is one strategy management uses to keep the workers isolated to each other since as long as the workers are envious one after another they hardly develop a we-group-identity. Thus they are more unwilling to risk and organise collective actions (Dannecker, 1998). As regards to outcome, excepting their lower wages, women are in a slightly better position in comparison to their male counterparts. For example, paid leaves were sanctioned to 80% of women and 73% of male workers in the RMG industries. The corresponding figures for other manufacturing units are 96% and 87% respectively.

Table 8.8
Proportions and Profiles of Workers who Demanded Better Working Conditions, 1998-99

Respondent's Category	Types of Demand Made		
	Paid Leave (%)	Higher Wages (%)	Change in Night Duty (%)
Garment Industry (N=153)			
Male	63.2	61.8	27.6
Female	50.6	55.8	29.9
Other Manufacturing Industry (N=60)			
Male	76.7	3.3	13.3
Female	90.0	6.7	10.0

Source: Data Set I

Excepting the questions of profit, access to cash income and meeting the demand schedule of the buyers, it is difficult to explain the employer's justification for conceding or rejecting demands of their employees. However, it is not only a question as to whether demands made by workers are approved but whether they can enjoy rights in reality or if they have to bear any cost.

For example, nearly one-third of the respondents experienced salary cut for taking leave of absence mainly due to sickness. The onus in this regard falls more heavily on women (one-third) compared to their male counterparts (one-fifth). Women workers are more susceptible to sickness and fatigue arising of their double burdens of domestic chores, child care and office work and also as a result of systematic deprivation of entitlement of food which they suffer from childhood. In the other survey, it is found that among those who took leave, seven out of ten women, compared to nearly half of their male colleagues, took sick leave and more than four out of every five took 5.1 days sick leave, on an average in the month preceding the survey, for their own sickness. Nearly a fifth of them, as opposed to less than a tenth of their male counterparts also took sick leave for other family members, including children. The results also showed that 42% and 16% of the female and male respondents respectively from the sample RMG industries were sick in the month preceding the survey. It suggests the need for greater entitlement to paid sick leaves to workers of RMG industries, particularly women.

This obviously brings the whole issue of union, management and inspections into part which are beyond the scope of my thesis. Here it is sufficient to say that merits of demands are examined informally and unilaterally by employers and hence, the interest of the workers may not necessarily be protected. Again, the study by Paul-Majumder and Zohir (1994) show that, 68 percent of the firms examined pay the salary in the second week of the month, some even later.

Again the study (Bachmann, 2002, p.21) perceives the following workers name a number of main problems relating to the working conditions in the garment industry:

"The factory, that is like a jail, nothing else, (.....) because of many reasons. First-the door is closed. You can not leave the factory, not even if there is fire (....) so often (.....) the worker burn to death. So you cannot leave the factory , even not if you want to or if you have to, there is no chance to leave it. (...) there is no canteen , we have one hour for lunch, but where can we go? There is no place to go. So mostly we sit on the roof of the factory for lunch: And we have no family life any more, even no children, they have to stay at the parents or with relatives, and the mother seldom sees her children. This is like as a prison, in a jail, no family life. You can also see the health conditions, I mean there is no medical facilities. What can we do ? We need medical facilities. So you see. It is like a jail, really like that."

(Second worker) "When the child of a worker, if there is something happen, let us say an accident, or something, and the child needs some help, so somebody goes to the factory and says, 'There is an accident, can this lady go for helping her child?', but nothing will happen, the worker will not know about this accident, because nobody will tell her, they do not want that she goes so no one tells her about it."

With the above quotation, a whole complex of difficulties is mentioned. The factory door is, according to some authors, always closed in order to protect the workers from masthans,[215] as the workers recognise by themselves and as well to prevent pilferage. The news papers regularly report about factory fires where workers are victims of the lack of fire safety (Dhaka Courier, 1998). For instances, in 1996, 32 women workers burnt to death in two garment factories, since there no fire extinguishers exitsted.

On the other hand, it is encouraging to learn that a large number of women also burgeoned for better working conditions at par with their male counterparts and the outcome also does not differ much along the gender line. Yet, women often suffer greater penalty of salary cut due to greater propensity to take sick leave than men. Nari Uddog Kendra's (NUK), a renowned NGO, working for the well being of women in the country) health insurance scheme, which ensures periodic medical check up for women workers with the help of some employers and immunisation and other productive as well as general

215 Bangla expression for street gangster, often engaged on behalf of the persons or organisations to assert their interest by force.

health related services provided by Unity Through Population Services (UTPS) in 93 garment industries of Dhaka city, are welcome moves in this direction, which should be replicated at a large scale.

8.6 Social Dimension of Female Urban Adaptation

With increasing independent migration by women, who come predominantly to work in RMG industries, new types of families such as branch families, single member families are emerging.[216] It is interesting to observe that, a quarter and a third of male and female garment industry workers respectively live in branch family, including a few live in mess or boarding houses. Given the existing negative attitude on the single women earners and lack of housing or hostel facilities for them, and also highly insecure situation in terms of law and order, branch families appear to be the most sensible arrangement.

8.6.1 Strategies Women Workers Adopt to Cope with Urban Environment

The living conditions of garment workers are appalling. A problem faced by working women (migrants) in urban areas is the lack of proper accommodation and cope with that environment. The workers of the multi-billion dollar industry face problems in getting decent accommodation, transport, and commute security and suffer as migrant workers on a daily basis. Low wages and lack of access to basic needs compel workers on a compromise with the problems of living in urban centres (Absar, 2000). Zohir and Paul-Majumder (1996) show that living in a factory accommodation is the most secured housing system. Unlike the conventional wisdom of urban anonymity, female migrant workers depend largely on family members to earn their livelihood in the city based industries. Living with family members and relatives is still most common among migrant female workers of the garment industry (Table 8.9). Three quarters of them live either in their own nuclear units or as a member of the extended family nexus. The remaining one-quarter of those workers either live in sub-let arrangements (16%) or in mess[217] (9%). Those who live in sub-let arrangements either with siblings and cousins (42%) or co-workers (42%). A few also live with single parents. In total, only 7 female workers of the garment sector live in mess or boarding house with co-workers. They are mainly divorced or separated, though a few are currently unmarried, and almost all migrated between 1991 and 1996. None of the female workers from other manufacturing units live in a mess or boarding house and only 3 out of a total 30 respondents live in sub-let arrange-

[216] Branch family can be defined as a family without a married couple but essentially consists of two or more adult members related by blood such as more than one sister, sisters and brothers, mother and daughter or aunt and niece, in sub-let arrangements.

[217] Mess is a dormitory type group house where people live, not necessarily female garment workers only.

ments. While nearly a quarter of garment industry workers live in with co-workers, be it relatives or friends, this type of living arrangement is almost non-existent among female workers of other manufacturing units. The type of living arrangement usually relates to other socio-demographic characteristics of workers. As opposed to a large number of female workers from the RMG sector, who are young and currently unmarried, their counterparts from other manufacturing industries are predominantly married (two-thirds) and live in family units, either nuclear (60%) or joint and/or extended (40%). It should be recalled that workers of the RMG sector are often the first generation settlers in Dhaka city, whereas women workers from other manufacturing industries are either non-migrant or long-term migrants. Hence, they (the latter) are already entrenched in the existing family set up and do not need to create new ways to sustain themselves in urban society. Family based living arrangements give women workers necessary protection from theft and other untoward incidence and provide some necessary services e.g. child care, education for children etc. Nearly a tenth of female workers of RMG sector, as opposed to one-fifth of their male counterparts experienced theft in their place of residence while out for work. Incidence of theft is even higher in the case of male workers of their manufacturing units than their female counterparts. Zohir and Paul- Majumder (1996) show that living in a factory accommodation is the most secured housing system. According to them, a factory located in Rampura area of Dhaka city provides accommodation to 70 Garo[218] women workers. These workers are charged Tk. 150 (US$ 3) for accommodation and Tk. 300 (US$ 6) for food per month, which is very low even in the context of standard of living in Bangladesh. This means only US$ 9 for accommodation and food per month. This help a worker on a minimum wage[219] of US$ 10-18, to save at least US$ 1 to US$ 9 per month. On the other hand, one worker reported when (Absar, 2000, p.134) asked about their accommodation in Dhaka city is as follows:

> "After we lost everything in the 1988 floods, we came to Dhaka. Since then we are here, in a bostee[220], and everyday is a problem. It is very difficult to live here because of the high cost of living. My village home has gone under water otherwise I would be living there."
>
> Runa, a factory helper

[218] Tribal people and minorities of Bangladesh

[219] I have mentioned minimum wage earlier in this chapter.

[220] A Bostee (slum) is a Bangla word for the Hindi word bastee. In Bangladesh a bostee comprises a group of thatched or tin-roofed one room houses that stand next to each other with inadequate shared sanitation facilities. Those living in bostees are subject to unhealthy living environment. It is also insecure in the sense that sometimes bostees are uprooted by the law enforcing agencies because they are built on others' land without permission and proper papers.

Fatema's accommodation and rent does not provide any kitchen, private bathroom and modern toilet:

"I cook outside, just next to my entrance to the room. There is a shade. I cover my mud stove with a (broken) tin to protect it from the rain water. However, I cannot protect my room from the rain water. See the monsoon make my mud floor muddy. I have to live like this with my children because I cannot afford the rent of rooms with cemented floors."

Table 8.9
Percentage of Distribution of Respondents by Types of Living Arrangement

Respondents	Family Unit		Mess/Boarding House		Sublet		Others		All (No.)	
RMG	Male	Female	Male	Female	Male	Female	Male	Female	Male	Female
Non-migrant	66.7	80.0	33.3	-	-	-	-	20.00	3	5
Long-term Migrant	65.7	75.7	17.1	2.7	8.6	16.2	8.6	5.40	35	37
Recent Migrant	36.8	65.7	44.7	17.1	7.7	17.1	-	-	38	35
All	52.6	70.0	31.6	9.1	7.9	15.6	9.2	2.31	76	77
Others										
Non-Migrant	61.5	75.0	7.7	-	15.4	-	15.4	25.00	13	16
Long Term Migrant	16.7	78.6	25.0	-	8.3	21.4	50.0	-	12	14
Recent Migrant	40.0	-	60.0	-	-	-	-	-	5	-
All	40.0	76.7	23.3	-	10.0	10.0	26.7	13.30	30	30
All (RMG & Others)	49.0	72.0	29.2	6.5	8.5	14.9	13.2	6.50	106	107

Note: Others include employer's land and squatting government/public land.
Source: Own Survey, 2000

Please note that half of men, workers of the RMG sector as opposed to a quarter of their women colleagues had none, or in some cases housemaids, to look after their houses when they go out (Table 8.10). Moreover, one out of every seven female workers of the RMG sector, compared to a fraction (3%) in their male counterparts, received help from their neighbours in this regard. In the absence of responsible family members and relatives, who can look after the house during working hours, a good number of male workers who live in mess are more susceptible to theft than female workers.

Support from family members in terms of child care is also an important factor, which facilitates female workers to work outside home (RMG industry), in the absence of any institutional support. Those female workers from who had children under 5, almost 9 out of 10 got familial support, as opposed to nearly three-fifths of their counterparts in other manufacturing units. A large number of the later group (nearly two-fifths) depend on maid servants to look after their children. Male workers on the contrary, depend overwhelmingly on family members for child care. Lack of child care facilities in many of the emerging mega cities poses a big problem for women's outside work and occupational mobility. Although families still provide necessary support for child care, how long it can continue to playing such role needs to be examined, especially in a situation where a large majority of female garment workers are currently unmarried.

Being the first generation workers in a metropolis and infrastructurally least equipped to meet the basic needs of the poorer people through cost-effective measures, female RMG factory workers adopted group identity and shared mode to cope with intense competition in availing basic amenities.

Table 8.10
Distribution of Respondents by Migration Status and Sources Who Look after The House/Mess When Go Out to Work

Year of Migration	Family Members/ Relatives (%)		Neighbour/ Friend (%)		Maids/ Servants (%)		None (%)		All (No.)	
Garment	Male	Female	Male	Female	Male	Female	Male	Female	Male	Female
Non-Migrant	66.7	80.0	-	-	33.3	-	-	20.0	3.0	5.0
Long Term Migrant	57.1	59.9	2.9	16.2	14.3	8.1	25.7	16.2	35.0	37.0
Recent Migrant	36.8	51.4	10.5	14.3	15.8	7.8	30.3	20.8	76.0	77.0
Others										
Non-Migrant	61.5	56.3	7.7	12.5	-	12.5	30.8	18.8	13.0	16.0
Long Term Migrant	16.7	42.9	-	-	16.7	42.9	66.7	14.3	12.0	14.0
Recent Migrant	40.0	-	-	-	20.0	-	40.0	-	5.0	-
All	40.0	50.0	3.3	6.7	10.0	26.7	46.7	16.7	30.0	30.0
All (Garment & Others	48.0	59.0	6.0	13.0	15.0	14.0	37.0	21.0	106.0	107.0

Source: Own Survey, 2000

The bulk of these workers live in low rental accommodations, where they share latrines, bathrooms and cooking gas burners or heaters with 10-15 families. Excepting a few owners, e.g. Mr. Salam of Karailer Math and an NGO, NUK[221] they do not get lodging facility. Subsequently they wake up earlier than their male colleagues and surmount the heavy odds in the settlement process. In city

[221] "Nari Uddug Kendra (NUK)" is a Bangla word, which means Women's Efforts Centre

proper viz. Karailer Math in Mahakhali and Kalapani area in Mirpur, Dhaka, they live largely in one room accommodation sharing with four/five other family members and relatives with a floor area ranging between 15 and 200 square meters and in a semi-durable type of structure. The amount they pay for house rent constitutes nearly half of their urban income and hence, they cannot afford to live alone. They generally lack cemented bathroom or covered space and running water facilities for bathing. It is learnt from the FGD with respondent's relatives, family members and neighbours at community of residence that there is acute shortage of running water supplied by the Dhaka Water and Sewerage Authority (WASA) in those areas. Not only do they pay for collecting water from a few tubewells that are found in the area but travelling a distance and spending their precious time for this purpose execerbate women's existing workloads. Even after spending almost half of their wage, they have to share two/three latrines and 5/6 gas burners with 10/15 families as cost-saving strategy because houses, equipped with all basic amenities for the private use of a single family, are not within the reach of their budget.

Their group identity on the road works as a protective shield in the otherwise unprotected lonely dark lanes, as they are often engaged in night shift. Like theft, young migrant women are generally protected against violence, physical or sexual assault on their way home to office or vice-versa by their co-workers and family members in the absence of cheap and safe public transportation system facilities. Nine out of every ten female RMG industry workers live in the same ward as the industry or nearby and walk to their workplace. The remaining 10% of these workers travel either by tempo[222] or rickshaw. However, whether they walk or ride on a rickshaw, they are always accompanied by co-workers and or family members. Seldom do they go to office alone, particularly at night. With the help of focus group discussions with male and female industry workers and their relatives, it is observed that incidence of sexual harassment, including kidnapping and rape, largely occurs when a women was found alone on the road.

Women's increased participation in the labour market and entry into formal manufacturing sector gave rise to group culture, including kinship as the way of life, instead of individualism. Unlike the dictates of the conventional wisdom which presumes self motive and individual identity as the way of life of industry workers, female workers of the RMG sector in Bangladesh generally value their family more than their self-interest. Although they became assertive and competitive in course of time, yet they adopt norms of sharing and caring to survive in a highly competitive and grossly mismanaged urban society.

[222] Wide-bodied auto-rickshaw which can accommodate about 10 to 15 persons at a time. Although highly polluting, it is one of the cheapest and fastest mode of intra-city group transportation.

8.7 Concluding Remarks

Rural women are coming to the cities in order to get work. Relative lack of female involvement in the agricultural sector, changes in land tenure and agricultural modernization mean that there are very few wage-earning opportunities for women in rural areas. They are migrating to cities with their husbands or parents or neighbours and in accordance with cultural and religious constraints. But generally speaking, women's labour is generated by a need for income and also by a desire for income to buy consumer goods: cloths, radios, sewing machine etc., and to invest in business and education (Siddiqui, 1999). But the unmarried young female migrants are sent by their families for doing domestic work as maid servants, and in most of the cases in the garment industries. They receive low wages and often have to sent a large proportion of the wages they have to their families. (Brydon and Chant, 1989, Miller and Vivian, 2002) Growth of RMG industries in Bangladesh lead to at least two important socio-economic changes in Bangladesh apart from its recognized role as the major foreign exchange earner. First, it enhanced women's mobility defying all purdah and geographical barriers and thus visualizing women's economic participation and contribution to the family and the society at large. Second, it lead to poverty alleviation to the great extent by creating employment opportunities for the rural poor predominantly from landless families. The study suggest that from no income of their own, more than 80% of the migrant women workers earn above poverty threshold income. Autonomous migration enabled poorer women to avail income earning opportunity outside domestic and personal services sector, like their male counterparts. Migrant female labour of RMG industry largely got recognition of an independent income-earner which would have been almost impossible for poor, unskilled and illiterate or semi-literate women from landless families.

Regular payment of salaries and overtime in the fourth week of every month should be made mandatory by legislation. This would saves the workers from malnutrition and the threat of eviction. Side by side, the government should create a congenial atmosphere to reduce procedural delay in quota distribution, banking and custom clearance as well as other formalities to minimize the risk of uncertainty and compulsion for over time work to meet the delivery of finished goods. The establishment of an international standard fashion design institution is expected to provide "on the job training" to women workers needed for their upward mobility and bridge the gender gap in wage, and help Bangladesh to compete per excellence with other countries, even after the MFA phasing out in the year 2005. Attention in the next chapter, therefore, would cover the in-depth case studies on RMG industries.

CHAPTER NINE
CASE STUDIES ON READYMADE GARMENT INDUSTRIES

9.1 Introduction

Five case studies on export-oriented readymade garment industries have been taken for having insight into the issue from users perspective. As has been stated earlier, export oriented textile industry has two dimensions, one is the Supply Side (spinning, weaving, dyeing, printing, and finishing), on the other represents the Demand Side (e.g. woven and knit RMG). In keeping with this provision, five case studies have been undertaken, 3 from woven and 2 from knit sector. These five RMG industries from the demand side have been selected by random sampling from the BGMEA members list supplied by BGMEA head office in Dhaka from the two categories of sampled RMG industries. These are as follows:

9.1.1 Woven RMG

1) PALMAL Group
2) Azim Group
3) Cambridge Garment

9.1.2 Knit RMG

1) Minar Group
2) Miswar Group

Each of these case studies cover a wide range of issues, namely, type and nature of business, management, employee strength, production, export performance, product range, export market network, sourcing of raw materials, qualitative aspects of raw materials, types of fabric used, problem of local sourcing raw materials, changing pattern of requirements of fabrics over the years, problems and critical issues and impact of trade liberalization.

In order to get access to the RMG industries, I at first contacted different management offcials and their BGMEA staffs in Dhaka. Because, over the city and in the immediate sorroundings more than 80% of garment industries are located. For collecting in-depth about management and the whole issues of RMG industries, I personally met with the management staff, the ECO and other concern officials of these industries. I have made case studies on the above issues in the year 2000. But many changes occured in the mean time on this industry due to the global recession, US TDA-2000, EU's special preferences for Pakistan and Sri Lanka's RMG industry, the accession of China into the WTO, and the economic fall-out from the September 11, 2001 terrorist attack in the United States.

9.2 Findings of the Case Studies

The brief summery of the findings of these case studies are given below: All of five case studies have been presented after the findings.

9.2.1 Salient features

Out of the three case studies on woven RMG two have been selected from large RMG group comprising multiple garment units under one entity (namely, PALMAL Group and Azim Group) and one has been selected from small RMG industries (namely, Cambridge Garment). In the case of Knit RMG, both the two units have multiple units under them. All the five case units were established in the early eighties. All have exhibited steady production and export performance. These units have access to the most prestigious export market leaders of clothing industries in EU, USA and Canada.

9.2.2 Sourcing of Raw Materials

Two of the three woven garment industries (PALMAL group and Azim group) are 100% dependent on imported fabrics while the remaining one (Cambridge Garment) is dependent 100% on local fabrics. But the Azim group and the PALMAL group procure about 10% knit fabrics from local source. Of the two Knit RMG industries, one procures 50% of its total requirement of yarn from local source while other procures only 20% from local market.

9.2.3 Qualitative Aspects of Raw Materials i.e. Fabrics and Yarn

Two of the three woven RMG groups (PALMAL and Azim Group) consider local fabrics are unacceptable to their buyers on the grounds of various qualitative aspects, such as, nature of dyeing, appropriate colours/shades/prints, colour fastness, type of wash, everness and so on. But Cambridge Garments meets its total requirement of fabrics from local source.

In the case of Knit RMG, the basic raw materials is yarn, manufactured mainly by open-end/Rotor Mills. Both the owners consider the local yarn as acceptable to them and to their buyers. The problems relate to timely delivery in appropriate volume.

9.2.4 Changing Pattern of Requirements

The owners of all five units have expressed that the requirement of fabric and yarn are undergoing changes in response to seasonal change, change in fashion/

design, and change in consumer's taste pattern. Some of these chnges in requirements are met in the weaving process (e.g. changing construction, thickness, design in weaving etc), some are met through dyeing, finishing and printing process (e.g. by changing colours, shades, print etc.) while others are met at washing stage (both fabrics washing and garment washing). It was learnt from the owners of two woven garment units that local facilities are inadequate to meet the international standard in meeting these changes while one unit (Cambridge) informed that it is possible for local suppliers to meet these changing requirements. The knit garment owners consider local yarn manufacturers are capable of meeting the changing requirements of yarn.

9.2.5 Problems and Critical Issues

The common problems identified by the RMG units during case studies are as follows:

a) Socio-political instability, frequent hartals (strikes), work closure, extortion (toll collecting by hooligans), hizacking, looting of goods during transportation, insecurity etc.
b) Socio-political instability and social unrest is disappointing the foreign buyers. In the long term this disappointment may lead to stoppage of import from Bangladesh in fabour of some other developing countries like China, Vietnam, India, Sri Lanka, Caribbean countries etc.
c) Fragment strike, work closure etc. are adversely affect the export-oriented RMG sector. Export commitments are often delayed/ defaulted due to country wide strikes at port and due to various other problems.

9.2.6 Case Studies at a Glance:

Matrix: Case Studies

Salient Features	Palmal Group	Azim Group	Cambridge Group	Minar Group	Miswar Group
Introduction	Palmal group is one of the largest export-oriented RMG groups in Bangladesh. With its modest start in 1984 as a small RMG factory, the company has now assumed the stature of a large group consisting of 16 export-oriented RMG industries i.e. woven, knitted and sweater, garment washing and dyeing plant, export oriented packeging unit and transportation unit. Besides these, the group has few other non-apparel industrial units.	Azim Group occupies a prestigious position amongst the selected few industrial houses, who pioneered the export of RMG from Bangladesh. The first unit of the group, Azim Mannan Garments Ltd, was set up in 1980. Since then, as many as 12 (twelve) considerably large RMG industries were established during the last 20 years and thus the company assumed the stature of a large industrial group.	Established in 1984, Cambridge has earned reputation as one of the most successful export-oriented garment units, which depends cent percent on local fabrics. The units is unique on several accounts. First, it is totally dependent on local fabrics for its exports. Secondly, over the last 18 years, it has expanded its production capacity, machinery, export turnover, manpower etc. But instead of proliferating into several units like most others, it maintained its status as a single unit. The choice of this unit for undertaking case study depends to a great extent on this uniqueness.	Minar Group is one of the pioneers of the export-oriented knitting and knit garment industries in Bangladesh. Established in the year 1952, Minar Textiles used to produce various knit products for the local market. It was one of the market leaders of traditional hossiery industry of Narayangonj. Since 1967, Minar Textile started exporting its knit products along with few other local knitting industries to Europe. During the liberation war in 1971, the process of export was stopped for various reasons. Later on, export of knitting and hossiery products by Minar Textile was restarted in 1978 under some favourable policy support.	Miswar group is one of the largest knitting and knit garment manufacturer and exporters in Bangladesh. The first unit of this group, Miswar Hosiery private Ltd. was established in the year 1990. Subsequently, the group saw a very fast growth over the last decade and established a total of 10 units.

Corporate Management	The Group is managed by one Chairman cum Managing Director and six other Directors. The miniscule Corporate Management of the company comprises four divisions, namely, the Top Management, Finance and Administration, Commercial and Banking, Marketing and Production. Each of the units heads reports to the Managing Director directly.	Rapid expansion of its industrial and commercial activities as well as the geographical dispersal of its various units in Dhaka and Chittagong have led the group to develop its corporate management structure. The corporate head quarter looks after the top management deals with production, quality control, shipping and so on.	Though small in size, there is clear division of management functions amongstdifferent layers of its management.The Chairman cum Managing Director takes care of marketing and finance along with top management functions. Other functions such as production management, quality control, labour management etc. are left with the production manager.	The total activities of the group are managed at two levels of management. Marketing and procurement are controlled centrally while production, shipping etc. are done at unit level.	The Group's corporate management office is located at Dhaka while most of the units are located at Narayangonj. Marketing, finance and banking etc. activities are dealt with its Dhaka office.
Employee Strength	Total of 6000 employees engaged in its various units. These employees include managerial personnel, technical and supervisory personnel and skilled and semi-skilled workers.	The Group maintains a total of 7500 employees including managerial and technical personnel and skilled and semi-skilled workers.	The industry has a total of 430 employees, including managerial personnel, supervisory staff and skilled and semi-skilled workers.	The group has a total of 600 employees engeged in its various units.	The group has a total of 1400 manpower engaged in its various units, of which around 600 are engaged in knitting and knit dyeing while the rest are engaged in knit garments.

Group Image	The group has earned high reputation through rapid expansion in appropriate form and direction. In recognition of its remarkable success, the Group was conferred upon Presidential Export Trophy for the year 1992-93 and 1994-95.	The group has established excellent track record of rapid expansion of its export performance over the last two decades.	Cambridge has earned great reputation as one of the successful garment units of the country.	The group is one of the pioneer of the export-oriented knitting garment industries in Bangladesh.	Miswar Group has earned reputation as country's the largest knitting and knit garment manufacturers since 1990.
Production and Export Performance	Diversification of exports has helped the group to attain continued success in the various aspects of its production and export performance. Some of these areas are as follows:	Continued efforts to upgrade its quality and expansion of export market by deversifying its products, the company earned high reputation in the international apparel market. Aspects of its production and export performance are described in the following paras.	The company was established in the financial year 1984-85, when the RMG industry of Bangladesh was undergoing serious crisis due to imposition of quota on few major items. The unit had learnt the technique of crisis management by surviving the catastrophe of mid-eighties. Some aspects of its production and export performance on the unit are as follows:	After establishment in the year 1952, Minar textiles used to produced various knit products for the local market as it was one of the market leaders of traditional hossiery industry which are described below:	Hossiery and knitting are the main products of the group which enjoyed extended market penetration in the EU and US.
Production Capacity	Monthly production capacity of the group may be described as follows: Woven Garments	The annual production capacity as well as export turn over of the group reached 85,00,000 pieces or	The unit has in all 240 sets of sewing machine and other support machinery. The factory produces a total of 5000	Annual production capacity of the group described as follows: Knit Fabrics: 2100 Tons per annum	Annual production capacity of the group may be described as follows: i) Knitted Fabrics: 16,300 Kg.

	30,000 Dozen, Knit Garments 29,000 Dozen, Sweaters 12,000 Dozen, Knit Fabrics 500 MT, Fabrics, Dyeing and Finishing 40 MT, Garments, Dyeing and Finishing 12 MT	70,80,000 dozen pieces.	dozen pices of RMG per month or 60,000 dozen pieces of RMG per annum	Knit Dyeing: 3000 Tons per annum Knit Garments: 6,00,000 dozen per annum	ii) Knit Garment: 2,00,000 Kg. iii) Knit Dyeing: 20,000 Kg.
Product Range	Various kinds of woven garments, knit garments, sweater, knit fabrics, woven shirts, knit shirts, blouse, ladies dresses, polo shirts, pants, trousers, sports, cardigans, pull over, night wear, overalls, tank tops, T-shirts, romper etc.	Woven: Shirts, blouses, nightwear, shorts, trousers, swimwear, Dress skirt, Jogging suit, Warm up suit, Padded jacket, Wind breaker, Show suit, Suede shirts, Suede shirts and Creeper. Knitwear: Flat knit and skirt, jacquard, dress & pullover .	The industry produces a wide range of woven garments, namely, shirts, trousers, shorts, pants, sport wear, ladies dresses and so on.	The Group produces various types of knit fabrics and knit garments namely, T-shirts, Tang tops, Long sleeve, Turtle neck short, Vest for men, boys and ladies, Polo shirts etc.	The group produces and export a large number of knit garments, such as T-shirts, Polo shirts, Rugby shirts, sweater, Sweater jacket, Jogging suit, jacket, Body warmer, Wind breaker, Hunting vees, Denim pants etc.
Export Market Network	The group exports its products to EU, USA, Canada, Hong Kong, Australia and other European countries. The group's exportable items belong to as many as 21 Quota categories of USA and 4 Quota categories of Canada. The group has earned	USA:Wal-Mart, Sears, Buggle Boy, K-Mart, A-thco, Atage, Montgomery, Ward, Skiva International, Amerex, Haddad, Esleep, (Bentley), Capital Mercury, Americo, Pacific Trail (London Fag), Host, BRF, Lollytogs Amtai, Apparel Trading, Just	The company exports its products to Germany, U.K. France, USA and Canada. The principal buyers of the company include, among others Auchean (France), Cash Tex (France), Network Fashion (Germany), CM International (U.K.) and so on.	The group exports its products mainly to France, Germany, Sweden, Denmark, Finland etc. The Group has developed good marketing network in EU countries. Of late it has started exporting to the USA.	The group export its products mainly to the EU countries and the US.

	high reputation as exporters of RMG products to various international apparel marketing chains namely: The GAP Inc. (USA), Sears Roebuck and Co. (USA), Wal-Mart Stores Inc (USA), J.C Penny (USA), Sears Canada Inc., Andre H.K. Buying Office Ltd. (Hong Kong), Miss Erica. Inc. (USA), Hudson's Bay Co. (Canada), Moeller & Co. A/S (Denmark), Moeller & Norge A/S (Norway), By Design (U.K.), CHAT (France) and so on.	Erine. Europe: Hucke, Paddocks (Ospinter), Obermeryer, H &M, Vetura Group, Kappahl, De-Groote, Samino, East West, Liz Claiborne, Fanpel Trading, Miles, Hellenic, Globetex, Twining Fat Manufatura Corona, Dr. Rehfeld, Barrimar and Horst Kruger. Canada: Walmart, K-Mart, Sears, Espirito, Trimark, Himco and Wooddi Sports. Japan: Mizuno, Mugen and Sakuraya.			
Sources of Raw Materials	i) Woven Fabrics: 100% imported from Taiwan, Hong Kong, Indonesia and India ii) Knit Fabrics: 90% imported 10% locally produced iii) Accessories : 70% locally procured 30% imported	i) Woven Fabrics: 100% imported from Hong Kong, Taiwan, Indonesia, India and so on. ii) Knit Fabrics: 90% imported and 10% locally procured. iii) Accessories : 60% locally procured and 40% imported.	Although during the initial years the factory had used imported fabrics, but by now it has reached the level of using 100% local fabrics. The company also uses locally procured accessories (like zipper, button, bokrom elastic carton etc).	i) Yarn: 80% imported from abroad 20% procured from local source. ii) Dyestuff: 100% imported from abroad iii) Accessories and Packeging Materials: 90% procured from local source 10% imported from abroad	i) Yarn: Mainly procured from local source ii) Dyestuff: 100% imported from abroad. iii) Accessories and Packeging materials: 90% procured from local source 10% imported from abroad.

Qualitative Aspects of Raw Materials	Fabrics is the principal raw material for RMG and assume special importance in view of its critical role in value addition. Various aspects of fabrics used in different units under Palmal Group, are described in the following paras:	Fabrics is the basic raw material used by Azim Group in its different units. On analysis, the fabrics used by the group are classified as follows:	Fabrics based on the type of yarn used.	Yarn is the basic raw materials used by the Minar group in its different units which is described below:	The main raw materials are yarn, dyestuffs and accessories.
Types of Fabrics Used	100% Cotton fabrics T/C of various combination of cotton and man- made yarn 100% Polyester ii) Based on construction of fabrics: Twill of difference types namely, Plain Twill, Brassed Twill etc. Denim of different types Canvas Poplin of defferent types, namely solid Poplin, printed Poplin Taffeta Spun dex iii) Based on nature of dyeing/printing	100% Cotton fabrics T/C of various combination of cotton and man made fibre 100% Polyster 100% Acrylic ii) Based on construction of fabrics: Twill of different types, plain twill, based twill etc. Denim of different types Canvas Poplin of different types Taffeta Spun dex iii) Based on nature of dyeing/printing, these fabrics belongs to hundreds of types, colours	100% Cotton fabrics 100% Polyster fabrics 100% Viscose fabrics T/C of various combination of cotton and man-made yarn. ii) Bases on construction of fabrics: Satin, Twill Sheeting, Flannel iii) Based on nature of dyeing/printing the fabrics belong to hundred of types, iv) Based on the nature of washing the fabrics are of various types namely, Caustic wash, Stone wash, Garment dye etc	Most of the yarn used by the group fall within the range of 20-30 count. This type of yarn is produced in open-end yarn mills. Although there are considerable number of textile mills in Bangladesh with open-end facility, the group can use the yarn of few mills because of its requirement for high quality. yarn of Squire textile mills, Padma spinning mills, Shameem textiles etc. are often used by the group.	The principal raw materials of the group are as follows: Yarn: 100% Cotton Yarn (Combed & Carded) Count: 26/1, 30/1 and 32/1 Principal local suppliers: Monno fabrics Ltd.: Shameem spinning mills.

	These fabrics are belongs to hundreds of types iv) Based on nature of washing: The fabrics are belongs to the following types Stone wash Sand wash Pigment wash Chemical wash	and shades. iv) Based on the nature of washing, the fabrics are of various types, namely: Stone wash Sand wash Pigment wash Chemical wash			
Qualitative Requirement of Fabrics/Yarn	Since the RMG units under Palmal Group produces and exports garments to various renowned clothing chains, the units have to procure the basic raw material (i.e.fabrics) from abroad through back to back L/C (Letter of Credit). In order to ascertain the qualitative aspects of these imported fabrics, the government concern authority collected samples from Palmal Group and regularly doing necessary tested.	Since the RMG units under Azim Group produces and exports garments to various renowned clothing chains, the units have to procure the basic raw materials (i.e fabrics) from the abroad through back to back L/C. In order to ascertain the qualitative aspects of these imported fabrics, the government's concern authority collected samples from Palmal Group and regularly doing those tested	Cambridge Garments produces garments using local fabrics. Last 10 years this factory has been using local fabrics in various proportions. Although they faced same problems relating to construction, dyeing, printing etc. at the initial stage, now they have overcome those. Samples of the fabrics were collected and have been tested in TIDC labratory.	Since this group is one of the leading knit garment producers in the country, the units have to procure yarn of few mills because of its high quality. But price competition sometimes creates obstacles to sourcing of raw materials locally. For producing knit garments this group is depends on foreign machinary like Taiwan machinaries for high speed and Indian machinaries for low speed.	Miswar group produces knit garments by using both local and foreign yarn and dyestuffs respectively. But for knit machinary this group is totally depends on abroad like Taiwan and India.

Local Sourcing of Raw Materials	Arguments were put forward in support of using imported fabrics: Quality, design, color etc. of local fabrics are not acceptable and approved by the foreign buyers. Quite often the dictation of buyers play key role. Quantity and timely delivery of local fabrics are not often acceptable to the buyers. Reliability of local suppliers in respect of quality, quantity and time has not yet been established.	Arguments were put forward in support of using imported fabrics: Quality, design, color etc. of local fabrics are not acceptable and approved by the foreign buyers. Sometimes the dictation of buyers play key role. Quantity and timely delivery of local fabrics are not often acceptable to the buyers. Reliability of local suppliers in respect of quality, quantity and time has not yet been established	Since Cambridge Garment is one of the very few garments factories which depends 100% on local fabrics. i) Compatibility of local fabrics 'We consider the local fabrics is qualitatively all right and can be used with buyers full satisfaction', informed the owner. The only thing we require is to explain and motivate the buyer about the quality of local fabrics, and continuously monitor the quality, colour, etc.of the fabrics. Thisundoubtedly involves risk and uncertainty.	For yarn only 20% procured from local sources. On the other hand 90% of accessories and packeging materials procured from local sources.	As I stated earlier, the main raw materials are yarn, dyestuffs and accessories from which only yarn is procured from local sources as well 90% of accessories and and packeging materials are also procured from local source.
Changing Pattern of Requirement for Fabrics over Time	In response to a query about the changes in the nature of fabrics, the management of Palmal Group informed the facts : i)Seasonal Change: Construction of fabrics changes from season to season due to weather	In response to a query about the changes in the nature of fabrics, the management of Azim Group informed the following facts: i)Seasonal Change: Fabrics changes from season tseason due to weather condition of the	The owner of Cambridge Garemnts mentioned the following perceptible changes: Change in the Buyer's Sourcing of RMG Around 7-8 years ago, orders from ladies wear, particularly blouse, were mostly placed with RMG industries in	In response to a query about the changes in the nature of yarn, the management of Minar Group informed the following changes: i)Seasonal Change: Thickness of fabrics and yarn very based on the seasonal change of requirement by	Most common changes in the pattern of demand for yarn occur due to changes in the market demand and market demand changes due to season, fashion, design and so on. But the yarn requirement varies between 26/1 count and 32/1 count.

	condition of the countries where the garments are sold. But there is consistency in the construction of fabrics demanded in the various seasons of year. For instance, fabrics of similar construction is demanded every winter. ii)Nature of Dyeing/ Printing : Nature of dyeing/printing goes on changing very frequently. Innovative color combination and printing are dominating the export market. iii) Nature of Washing: Variation in the design is often brought by changing the pattern of washing. Same type of fabrics with variation in washing look totally different. On the analysis of the above facts, two issues become clear: Any weaving mills with modren weaving ma-	countries where the garments are sold. But there is consistency in the construction of fabrics demanded in the various seasons of year. For instance, fabrics of similar construction is demanded every year. ii) Nature of Dyeing/ Printing : Nature of dyeing/printing goes on changing very frequently. Innovative color combination and printing are dominating the export market. iii)Nature of Washing: Variation in the design is often brought by changing the pattern of washing. Same type of fabrics with variation in washing look totally different. On the analysis of the above facts, two issues become clear:	Bangladesh because of comparative cost advantage over China. Since then preference has been shifted from ladies blouse to men's trousers. As a result of this shifting in buyers' preference, demand for fabrics and yarn used for making trousers has shot up. Such changes are common in international trade. But the modern spinning, weaving and dyeing/finishing units are usually equipped with state-of-the-art technology to sustain such changes. ii) Seasonal Change Seasonal change in the demand for RMG is another aspects of export trade of apparel. iii) The fashion, design etc. of RMG undergo changes consequent upon change in time,	the consumers. But there is consistency in the demand pattern of winter, summer and autunm. ii) Nature of Dyeing/Printing: These are changing contonuously. Nature of dyeing/printing goes on changing very frequently. Innovative color combination and printing are dominating the export market. iii) Nature of Washing/ Finishing: On analysis of these, it was concluded by the owner of Minar Group that, these changes affects the requirement of type of yarn. Based on the seasonal change, the group requires various counts of yarn ranging from 20 to 30 count.	

	chinery (i.e. Looms) may adjust with the changing pattern of requirement of fabrics bases on construction and use of yarn (Cotton, T/C or Polyester).		income level, technological innovation and so on.		
Problems and Critical Issues	The major problems faced by the Group are summed up below: Socio-political instability in the country. Frequent strikes, work closure etc. create serious hurdles in executing export order in time. Political-social unrest, fragment strikes, work closures etc. are adversely affect the export-oriented RMG sector. The socio-political instability and social unrest is disappointing the foreign buyers. In the long term this disappointment may lead to stoppage the import from Bangladesh in fabour of some other developing countries	The major problems faced by the Group are summed up below: Political and social unrest, frequent strikes, work closure etc. are adversely affect the export oriented RMG industry. Export commitments are often delayed/defaulted due to country-wide strikes, strikes at port and due to various other problems. Socio-political instability in the country. Frequent strikes, work closure etc. create serious hurdles in executing export order in time. The country-wide insecurity is disappointing the foreign buyers. In the long term this disappointment may lead	The major problems faced by the Group are summed up below: Socio-political instability in the country as well frequent strikes, work closure etc. create serious hurdles in executing export order in time. Political and social unrest, fragment strikes, work closures etc. are adversely affect the export-oriented RMG sector. Export commitments are often delayed/defaulted due to country wide strikes, strikes also at ports and due to various other problems. Social unrest is disappointing the foreign buyers. In the long term this disappointment may	The major problems faced by the group are as follows: i) Frequent strikes, work closure/strikes etc. pose serious problems in production, transportation and exports activities of this industry. ii) Mastans, criminals, touts etc. are other problems. Hizacking/looting of goods/raw materials during transportation is another problem. iii) In case of use of imported yarn for producing knit garments for exports, duty drawback facility is allowed to the exporters. But the process of getting back the duty drawback is	The major problems faced by the group are as follows: i) Lack of timely delivery and inconsistency in the quality of yarn often create serious problems for maintaining export commitment. ii) Supply of appropriate quantity of yarn is another problem. When bulk order is placed, the suppliers often fails to maintain schedule. iii) Social and political problems, namely strike, work closure, pressures from mastans/toll collectors etc. are some of the problems faced by the group.

	like Vietnam, China, India, Pakistan of Asia and Sub-Saharan and Caribbean countries due to TDA- 2000 of the United States of America.	to stoppage of import from Bangladesh in favour of some other developing countries like Vietnam, China, and Caribbean countries etc.	lead to stoppage the import from Bangladesh in fabour of some other developing countries like Vietnam, China, India, Pakistan of Asia & Sub-Saharan & Caribbean countries due to TDA-2000 of the USA.	very long, time consuming and expensive. This works as a hurdle for the exporters.	iv) Power failure is another problem. To overcome this problem, the group maintains its own generators. But that is quite expensive.
Impact of Trade Liberalization	The management of the company holds the following views in respect of the impact of trade liberalization: The Government should create enabling environemt for investment in backward linkage industries (e.g. spinning, weaving, dyeing/ finishing) by making available credit facilities on easy terms, removal of barrier for collateral security. ii) The Group does not have any specific plan to install backward linkage industries. But if the investment climate environment becomes congenial, the	The management of the company holds the following views in respect of the impact of trade liberalization: The Government should create enabling environment for investment in backward linkage industries (e.g. Spinning, Weaving, Dyeing/ Finishing) by making available credit facilities on easy terms, removal of barrier for collateral security etc. The group does not have any specific plan to install backward linkage industries. But if the investment climate/environment becomes congenial, the	The views of the management of Cambridge Garments about the impact of trade liberalization is as follows: i) The withdrawal of GSP, quota etc. in the wake of implementation of WTO will bring disaster for RMG industries of Bangladesh. No significant steps are being taken up either by govt. or by the trade bodies. The management are very alarmed of disastrous consequences of trade liberalization after 2005 . ii) Backward linkage in textile is possible. Both the government and the private sector must work in close coopera-	The knitting and knit garment sub-sector covers three stages (i.e. knitting, dyeing/printing/finishing and garment making) of textile processing except spinning. If the local spinning sub-sector grows in the same speed as it did during the last decade, it would be able to provide the required amount of yarn. And if backward linkage is established by expanding spinning sub-sector, the knitting and knit garment sector would not face serious problem during post 2005 period. ii)Government should encourage the existing entrepreneurs of RMG and knitting and hosiery sub-	.The withdrawal of GSP, quota etc. in the wake of implementation of WTO will bring disaster for RMG industries of Bangladesh. No significant steps are being taken up either by govt. or by the trade bodies. The management are very alarmed of disastrous consequences of trade liberalization after 2005. ii) Backward linkage in textile is possible. Both the government and the private sector must work in close cooperation to attain that end. Governemnt should frame appropriate policies to encourage the

	company may invest in such industries. iii) The Government and private sector association (e.g. BGMEA, BKMEA, BTMA) should develop appropriate policy package to face the challenge of WTO regime during the post 2005 period.	company may invest in such industries. The government and private sector association (e.g. BGMEA, BKMEA, BTMA) should develop appropriate policy package to face the challenge of WTO regime during the period from 2005 onwards.	tion to attain that end. Government should frame appropriate policies to encourage the entrepreneurs who are using local fabrics. Tensible benefits should be allowed to the users of local inputs. iii) Investment climate should be made congenial. Credit facilities should be allowed to the successful exporters using local fabrics. Dominance of the selected few large defaulters in the capital market should be stopped. iv) Social recognition, like national award, export trophy, CIP etc. are now captered by coterie groups. All the trade bodies are directly or indirectly dominated by those selected few. The users of local fabric are too small to be identified and recognized in this present situation. This should be reversed.	sectors to set up spinning mills by allowing credit facility on easy terms and low percentage of equity (say 25%). Under this arrangement, the RMG/knit garment owner would set up the spinning mill by choosing the equipment, which would produce yarn required by them. This would remove marketing problem of yarn on the one hand and facilitate establishment of backward on the other. iii) Government should put special emphasis on adjustment with the WTO regime during the period from 2005. Appropriate institutional arrangements should be made and the government should adopt policy measures to encourage the entrepreneurs to set up backward linkage industrial units.	entrepreneurs who are using local fabrics. Tensible benefits should be allowed to the users of local inputs. iii) Investment climate should be made congenial. Credit facilities should be allowed to the successful exporters using local fabrics. Dominance of the selected few large defaulters in the capital market should be stopped.

9.3 Concluding Remarks

The in-depth case studies on selected woven and knit RMG industries have revealed the true picture of the export oriented RMG sector. From the above five case studies, it is clear that the Bangladesh textile and RMG industries have so far developed in a haphazard manner with little balancing among spinning, weaving, and dyeing/printing/finishing sub-sectors. All the five owners of case units have indicated their apprehension of impending crisis in their business due to implementation of WTO. They consider this will adversely affect the growth of their business and the country's export will stumble. To offset this, they recommended for immediate government intervension in respect of creating environment for investment, social recognition of users of local inputs, awareness development about trade liberalization and encouraging investment in backward linkage industries.

CHAPTER TEN
MAJOR FINDINGS, CONCLUSION AND RECOMMENDATIONS

10.1 Introduction

This chapter purports to provide findings and conclusions of the study. Suggestions and policy implications for boosting readymade garments exports are also discussed in light of the findings of the study. The major findings of the study are given below:

10.1.1 The Major Economic Findings of the Study

1. Bangladesh readymade garment is the most important sector, contributing 76% of the total export earning of the country. RMG industry plays a vital role in Bangladesh economy. RMG is not only earning lion's share of the total export earning, but also a claimant of employing directly 1.8 million workers and indirectly 10 million workers. It represents about 3500 members.
2. Bangladesh is the 4th largest apparel exporters in the EU market in terms of quantity and value. In the US market it is the 6th largest exporters in terms of value and it is the 10th largest exporter with 3.25 per cent market share of total US import of clothing. The US market and the EU market have some major distinctions both in terms of products as well as in terms of different market competitors. In the EU market 35 per cent of the exports are comprised of knitwear where as only 15 per cent of the US. Exports comprise the same.
3. In EU the main competitors of Bangladesh are China, India and Thailand whereas in the US market Bangladesh competes with Mexico.
4. The European Union instituted its own GSP scheme in July 1971 following an agreement on the matter under GATT. The purpose of GSP was to promote trade and economic growth in developing countries. GSP allows substantial reductions in common customs tariffs on imports into EU from developing countries. As the products of a least developed nation, export from Bangladesh are exempt from tariffs, and importantly, quotas. These exemptions give export products from Bangladesh a substantial competitive advantage vis-a-vis the export of developing countries such as China and India.
5. India, Pakistan and Sri Lanka will lose their GSP privileges when textile trade is fully integrated into the WTO on 1st January 2005 as per agreements of the Uruguay Round. From this date onward exports from Bangla-

desh will attract the full customs duty if the originating status of these exports by the value addition criterion is one of the three countries.

6. There are few RMG producers in Bangladesh who can achieve more than 50 per cent domestic value-addition in woven apparel production. They will not be entitled to duty-free GSP benefit if they use imported fabrics regardless of the source. Regional cumulating gives them the opportunity to reduce EU customs duty by only 1.92 per cent until 2005. This is too small a benefit for too short a time to engage in large-scale changes in souring of inputs. As reported in the recent EU Newsletter, 90 per cent of the woven exports to EU do not receive GSP treatment. The situation is unlikely to change very rapidly in the near future. On the other hand, the growth of clothing exports to the EU market has not been very significant through GSP imposition as Bangladeshi competitors asked for it.
7. Local yarn production constitutes only 25% of the total demand for yarn in Bangladesh. There are only few industries producing export quality yarn and availing the opportunity of indirect export. The market share of the export quality yarn held at present by local yarn suppliers is perhaps no more than 35%, which is likely to decrease in the short term due to the new EU rules of origin for knitwear products. On the other hand the weaving sector is able to supply less than 10% of the woven fabric consumed by garment exporters as reported by BGMEA. The limited success of the local manufacturers in supplying the RMG market is mainly due to a lack of price competitiveness as well as indifferent quality consistency. In the weaving sector, the raw material account for around 60% of the total cost of grey fabrics, which suggests a situation similar to spinning. Because Bangladesh has to import cotton at higher price, the cost of domestic grey fabrics is higher. Though more spinning mills, more weaving mills are needed but they do not get highest priority, as the investment requirement is very high. Financing of these industries should also get high priority.
8. Bangladesh is the highest exporter of T-shirt to the EU with a 20 per cent market share as China and India face quota.
9. Buyers restricted by quotas, are putting the higher value added items to China and India as they are in terms of quantity not valued. So, they are putting the orders to China and India and actually putting the net-value added items to Bangladesh. So the lowest average price does not actually mean that Bangladesh is more competitive than her competitors but actually indicates the technological backwardness.
10. Backward linkages being a supplementing condition is not enough for Bangladesh to keep Bangladesh protected from the post-MFA challenges. There is a problem of supply chain management. A crucial point will be how to put Bangladesh in the total global network of production.
11. The TDA 2000 had two major impacts on the US garment market. The United States awards the Caribbean Basin Initiative (CBI) to 24 countries

of the Caribbean Basin. They have already started export RMG into US market free of duty and quota. Bangladesh faces serious competition from these nations. The same facility has been given to the 48 sub-Saharan African (SSA) countries through an agreement called USTDA-2000. This is so in spite of the beneficiary countries not having the capability to export. The facility went into operation from October 1, 2000 and is expected to continue until September 30, 2008. On the surface this means that the effect of the MFA phase-out will be virtually nil on these countries. In addition during the last few years Mexico has gained increasing access to the U.S. markets through the operation of the NAFTA. The slowly changing trade regime for the garment sector will culminate on December 31, 2004 when the US quota system ends and trade will be determined by comparative advantage.

12. According to the officials of the BGMEA, there is a clear-cut indication of Bangladesh losing her market share to these 72 privileged countries. Amongst SSA and CBI countries, there are 33 least developed countries under the WTO Umbrella, will be benefited out of this TDA-2000 Bill. Due to this decision, another 14 LDC countries including Bangladesh are being deprived from the advantage.
13. For Bangladesh the quota system is very beneficial. It gave time for the industry to develop and to learn the skills in production, logistics, and marketing needed to produce at a competitive price.
14. The garment industry had enjoyed a specific environment to flourish that was created by multi-fibre arrangement. The prime focus behind the whole of this was demand-pool. Here, the hardship of some personalities, government policy framework like back to back L/C, bonded warehouse and the negotiation strategy that Bangladesh took, helped in flourishing the garments sector.
15. The present environment will be different after the year 2005. But, a quite intelligent, talented entrepreneur class has already formed that will make the industry to sustain and will take the sector in the way of flourishment.
16. Existing trade blocs like NAFTA, EC and ASEAN have inter-country trade at liberalized rates, which hurt the non-member countries. Added to this is the latest initiative of the Free Trade Areas of Americas (FTAA), constituting of 34 countries, are likely to go into effects from 2005.
17. Bangladesh is always concentrated only at the lower value items, not in the higher value products. As a policy package there is no attempt to move forward to higher or more expensive items. One of the things, which Bangladesh has ignored, is the marketing and promotional effort. Bangladesh should device strategies to go into the production of high value added products
18. Right now, correctly, a 50-50 ratio in financing is enforced. Bangladeshi entrepreneurs do not have funds with which they can finance these back-

ward linkage industries. Special rate of interest, concessional rate of interest must be introduced in order to promote the backward linkages.

19. Even if Bangladesh had zero-tariff privileges, we may not get market access, if the large importers decide to impose non-tariff barriers in different forms. It should be labour standards, which can be transformed into non-tariff barriers and it could be human right question, which can be transformed into non-tariff barriers.
20. Bangladesh faces a lot of unfair competition abroad, including anti-dumping laws. The government should use diplomacy to solve the problems.
21. Bangladesh has some advantage in the forums of multilateral trade negotiations as all developing countries are together and taking unified position of these non-trade, but LDCs and have some disadvantage in bilateral trade arrangements as measurements should be taken in issue like child labour elimination in the RMG sector, hygiene-standard in the all exportable industries, trade union in the EPZs and the environment hazard and labour-standard in the garment industries.
22. Though the incentives provided for foreign investments in Bangladesh are one of the best, it is not well implemented.
23. Approximately 80% of the garment accessories like cartons, threads, buttons, labels, poly bags, gum tapes, shirt boards, neck boards etc. are now being produced in Bangladesh, contributing to the GDP. But in spite of this most of the high value items suppliers tend to import thread and buttons from China or Sri Lanka because of better quality and competitive pricing.
24. Presently, the total fabric requirement in Bangladesh captive market is for about 3 billion yards, of which about 85-90% is imported from countries like China, Pakistan, India, Hong Kong, Singapore, Thailand, South Korea, Taiwan and Indonesia. Fabric requirement is increasing at 20% per annum. This spells tremendous opportunity for further industrialization of the country.
25. The level of financing that is required to cater to large international buyers is unavailable to most Bangladeshi exporters. It is mostly only when the buyers take an initiative to support the exporters that the exporter can offer better quality products due to higher expenses.
26. Back-to-back L/C was one of the most important factors in the initial and continuing success of the RMG. It considerably eases the financing requirement of garment business for the local entrepreneurs. The entrepreneurs are able to complete the complicated process of manufacturing and export with a very little of their own funds for working capital.
27. The competitive advantage Bangladesh enjoyed in RMG production was due mainly to a very large reservoir of very low wage workers
28. The government of Bangladesh is not inquiring all these key issues of long term competitiveness.

29. Value addition in RMG in the domestic market is very low. The government of Bangladesh currently imposes a restriction that the value of the import L/C cannot exceed 75% of the value of the export L/C. The rule is apparently designed to ensure that the net foreign exchange earning is at least 25% of the value of the export. The abuse of import permits is also reduced.
30. From the five case studies, three case studies relate to woven garments while the remaining two dwell on knit garments industries. Two of the three woven garment industries are 100% depend on local fabrics, while one out of two knit garment industries procures 50% of its total requirement of yarn from local sources, on the other hand, other procures only 20% from local sources.
31. While stating the reasons for not using local fabrics, the two woven garments identified qualitative deficiencies, such as lack of uniformity in dyeing, inappropriate colours, shades and prints, colour fitness, type of wash etc. But other woven garment considers that the quality of local fabrics is compatible and it is not facing any difficulty due to local fabrics. On the other hand, both the knit RMG industries consider that the local yarn is qualitatively fully compatible.
32. The owner of all five units expressed that the requirements of fabrics and yarn is undergoing changes in response to change in seasons, fashion, design, customer's taste pattern etc. These changes in the requirements can be fully satisfied by undertaking necessary adjustment in the weaving process as well dyeing, printing and finishing process.
33. While enumerating the problems and critical issues the owners mentioned socio-political instability, hartals, strikes, work closure, extortion, hijacking are the problems from the one side, on the other procedural bottlenecks in availing the benefits of GSP, alternative cash incentive, duty drawback, bank formalities, load shedding, power failure, delay in gas connection, under developed roads and infrastructure and lack of support from bank and financial institutions etc.
34. All the five owners of case studies have identified their apprehension of impending crisis in their business due to the implementation of WTO. They consider this will adversely affect the growth of their business and the country's export will stumble. To offset this they recommended for immediate government intervention in respect of creating enabling environment for investment, social recognition of users of local inputs and their workers, awareness developments about WTO and encouraging investment in backward linkage industries.

10.1.2 The Major Social Aspect Findings of the Study

1. The RMG industry employs more than 1.8 million workers of whom about 90% are women who have migrated from rural Bangladesh in search of better economic future. The cumulative employment figures show that there are 0.2 million men and 1.6 million are women who have been employed by the sector. This has made women visible in statistics and has brought about a social change in Bangladesh.
2. The primary problem readymade garments industry of Bangladesh is facing is not technology, but low standards of labour. Bangladeshi labour is ill paid, over-worked and suffers from very low quality of life. Labour productivity is the most important element in the competitiveness of the garments industry.
3. European U0nion is increasingly putting pressure on Bangladesh to upgrade her labour standard and the frequent occurrence of fires in the garment industry. The Union also now putting pressure on Bangladesh for her not to extend the work time over 60 hours per week, which the manufacturers usually need to do in order to make up for the lost time from political agitation and other inevitable circumstances.
4. Women are coming to the job market, but they are concentrating in more and more hazardous jobs in spite of some developments in their career.
5. The social study '95 shows that 70 per cent of employees were women while in 2000 the percentage decreases to 60 per cent. Here technology is a key factor. Garments sector in Bangladesh is concentrating in knitwear, where production technology demands more male than female workers.
6. Bangladesh is now producing labour-intensive, low -value-added products. But ultimately she has to shift to skill-intensive products.
7. In the past, women were employed in the garment industries because they did not involve themselves in trade unions. As they are gradually involving themselves in trade unions, they do not get privileges from the owners any more.
8. Garments workers have huge disadvantages because they are women. It is not necessarily true that because they are female labour or migrant labour. That is generally a fact being a women.
9. Growth of RMG industries in Bangladesh lead to at least two important socio-economic changes in Bangladesh apart from its recognized role as the major foreign exchange earner. First, it enchanged women's mobility defying all purdah and geographical barriers, and thus visualizing women's economic participation and contribution to the family and the society at large. Second, it leads to poverty alleviation to a great extent by creating employment opportunities for the rural poor predominantly from landless families. From no income of their own, more than 80% of the migrant women workers earn above poverty threshold income. Autonomous migration enabled

poorer women to avail income earning opportunities outside domestic and personal services sector, like their male counterparts. Migrant female labour of RMG industry largely got recognition of an independent income-earner which would have been almost impossible for poor, unskilled and illiterate or semi-literate women from landless families.

10. There has been a new movement in the village economy, so the industries based on the low labour wage must suffer in the long run.
11. Despite some improvements in income levels generated by employment opportunities, the workers face severe deprivation and exploitation in terms of benefits, poor working conditions, lack of standard safety measures etc. These factors, while securing profit for the owners in the short run, may become major constraints to the long term viability of the sector. So, the working conditions in the garment industry is not of high standard. Though it will raise cost, but the raise in cost should be shadowed by the increase of efficiency.
12. Of the growing size of work force, the majority are new-entrants that should have some effect on the average age of the work force.
13. More educated unmarried than the average women are coming to the big towns to work in garments, and they are sending a more money than the others. It could be a part of a family-strategy of survival, as they are coming mostly from landless families. It has been investigated in many countries like Taiwan and Indonesia that as part of the survival strategy families send their sons and daughter to work in the industries in big towns. Sending sons have always been practice. Sending daughters is rather a new practice and that should bring a change in the society.
14. In the highly patriarchal and paternalistic society like Bangladesh, the control of sexuality of women is always in the hands of the men. Having that reality and coming from very poor background, their first reaction to their profession is how much money they can get per month. That makes them to do long over-time work.
15. Above all the garment sector has not yet developed to a full-fledged industry. From the beginning of entry into this industry workers suffered from mental strain as her service is very temporary. This is a big problem facing the workers in organizing themselves. Because of their temporary nature of work they are very easily retrenched whenever they make an attempt to form a trade union. So it is very difficult to organize workers in this sector. In the absence of workers' organization working conditions can never be improved. Another problem is that the workers are in a floating position. Forming of trade union by floating workers is not possible.
16. Workers' rights to organize themselves into an association is protected in Bangladesh by the Industrial Relations Ordinance. But the workers in the garment sector, are deprived of this right. Trade unionism has not yet developed in the garment industry in spite of the large-scale violation of workers'

rights in this sector. The workers willing to be involved with trade unionism reported that they do not join trade unions because of the fear of retrenchment.

17. The existing labour laws are not very relevant to the garment industries. The existing laws should be changed according to the specific requirements of this industry.
18. Bangladesh does not have the access to the latest technological know-how of the industry due to the sheer amount of investment required which hardly any entrepreneur can fund. This is in terms of both machinery and manpower. Even if the machinery is procured, local workers do not possess the skills to use them and therefore a further financial burden has to be incured by the manufacturers in terms of foreign labour, which is manifold more than the local wages and salaries. According to the unofficial sources, less than 10% of the Bangladeshi RMG units are well equipped with modern technology.

10.2 Hypotheses Reconsidered

From the above findings of the study it has been identified that, there are many impacts of trade liberalization on the RMG industry in Bangladesh. So, considering all evident and all arguments presented in the chapters, I have to clearly reject the two null hypotheses.

10.3 Conclusion and Recommendations

In the context of the above findings, here I suggest two types of policy recommendations and suggestions in order to sustain the smooth growth and developments of the garment industry of Bangladesh.

10.3.1 Economic Considerations

A liberalized trade and investment regime presents opportunities and challenges for the textile and clothing industry of Bangladesh. Elimination of quotas by the year 2005 and reduction of tariffs presents opportunities for exports of increased labour-intensive RMG products from Bangladesh. However, liberalization of trade regimes also implies that competition in RMG exports is likely to be more intense. Furthermore, Bangladesh is located far away from major markets such as the European Union, the United States, and Japan. Existence and possible expansions of free trade blocs such as the EU and NAFTA provide opportunities through increased trade and investment relationships to Central, East European, Mediterranean countries, Mexico, the Caribbean and Central American countries but challenges to a country like Bangladesh. Furthermore, Bangladesh is at a disadvantageous position compared to several other Asian countries like China, India and ASEAN countries. China and India have large domestic markets with a higher degree of integration in the textile and garment sector. The ASEAN countries being close to Japan, South Korea, Taiwan, and Hong Kong, are increasingly becoming an integral part of the regional network of production, trade, and investment in East Asia. However, labour costs in Bangladesh are still lower than in most RMG exporting countries. In the post-Uruguay period, Bangladesh must continuously upgrade its comparative advantage in high value added products. So, considering the above global liberalized trade situation as well the Bangladesh position, we can say this industry has become an overwhelmingly important sector for the Bangladesh economy. It promotes the developments of other key sectors of the economy, including banking, transportation, insurance, tourism and so on. The country needs to be well conscious about its weaknesses, strengths, opportunities and threats in determining strategies of strengthening competitiveness in readymade garments. And Bangladesh will be able to prepare herself to meet the globalization and trade liberalization challenges and other internal challenges in the future. On the context of the above global trade liberalized scenario, the government, policy makers, business, trade, industry, and various other related institutions and organizations will have to come forward and strive hard to face the above mentioned challenges of global competition during the post-2004 era. Based on the findings of the study, a few suggestions and policy implications on the economic and social context are outlined below:

10.3.1.1 Phasing out of MFA

The main challenge which lies ahead is that the Agreement on Textile made under the auspices of the Uruguay Round of the trade agreements stipulates phasing out of MFA by the year 2005. Apparently this sounds good; but all concerned are in tension because of the impending danger of free competition from 2005. It will be difficult for Bangladesh to compete with textile rich countries like China, India etc. in the export market under quota-free situation by importing fabrics from its competitors. At present, there exists a serious gap between the requirement and supply of fabrics and yarn. Very slow growth of backward linkage industry is leading to expand this gap year after year. The garment owners are seriously alarmed about the impending danger. This will also have a differential impact on men and women working in the garment industry. Women from about 68% in the woven garment manufacturing, which enjoys quotas, while their proportions are only 35% in the knitwear, which enjoys preferential access through GSP. Many entrepreneurs and workers are not aware what lies ahead beyond 2005. In view of this, a number of recommendations have been put forward for necessary consideration of the policy makers.

10.3.1.2 Seeking Preferential Access

Elimination of quotas under MFA would not necessarily reduce garment exports, if new measures like preferential access, labour standards and eco-labeling are undertaken. Bangladesh as a Least Developed Country is already trying for duty-free access of its products to the market of developed countries. In the first WTO Ministerial conference held in Singapore in December 1996, this has been incorporated in para 14 of the declaration.

10.3.1.3 Setting up Backward Linkages

A major threat is the phasing out of MFA by the year 2005, when quotas will be eliminated. According to BGMEA, the development of the textile industry is imperative in view of the impending changes of quota free environment. Although Bangladesh offers excellent incentives for foreign investment, still they are not coming in a big way for investment in the textile sector. This may be because as Bangladesh does not produce cotton, it has to ensure yarn supply from cotton producing countries. China and India, which produces mostly of the world cotton production, has embarked on a programmes of a billion dollar investment to re-vump its entire textile industry. At present, India exports high value added RMG products, like China, which are not included in the list of products, mentioned in the ATC. Hence, it is suggested that could exploit regional cooperation like SAARC to get duty free textile from India after 2005 and China as a member of WTO. So it is very important to establish backward linkage between RMG and spinning, weaving, dyeing, printing, and finishing industries. In order to attain thess objectives, two broad categories of policies may be undertaken namely, a) creating "Demand Pull" for having backward linkages and b) creating an enabling environment for investing in backward linkage industries.

10.3.1.4 Creation of Demand Pull for Backward Linkage

Effective pollicies towards the creation of demand pull for backward linkage include, among other allowing incentives for the RMG industries, using local inputs (e.g. fabrics, yarn etc) simplifying the incentive schemes, introducing social recognition (e.g. national export trophy, CIP etc.) for using local inputs. These policy measures will encourage the RMG industries to use local inputs, cheaper (through incentive schemes) as well as by allowing social recognition.

10.3.1.5 Creation of Enabling Investment Climate

Investment in backward linkage industries should be directed both towards the improvement of capacity utilization through BMRE, capital restructuring etc. of the existing mills as well as through creation of new capacity. This can be attained by making available invisible funds for setting up of backward linkage industries on easy terms, lowering down of interest rates on long-term credit to 6% from existing 11% and on working capital from existing 16-25% to 8-9%, facilitating joint ventures and foreign direct investment, and accepting export performance as a substitute for collateral in new investment.

10.3.1.6 Appropriate Tariff Structure

Tariff reforms should be export based. Backward linkage industries should be allowed to import their inputs on easy terms and the burden of tax, VAT, import permit fees etc. should be withdrawn. These industries should be given preferential treatment to grow until the full implementation of GATT/WTO by the end of 2004.

10.3.1.7 Development of Infrastructural Facilities

One of the critical factors underpinning the sustainability of export-oriented RMG industries is the efficiency at world level cost-effectiveness. Government support in terms of improved transportation, easy and hustle free-port handling of the exportable items of clothing and textiles, giving priority on uninterrupted supply of electricity, gas etc. should be ensured for making local export-oriented textile industries more efficient, cost-effective and competitive.

10.3.1.8 Continuous Human Resource Development

There is serious inadequacy of training facilities in the country for the RMG sector, the largest export-oriented of Bangladesh. Whatever training infrastructure available with the Department of Textile (DOT) under the Ministry of Textiles, are grossly inadequate in terms of quality of teachers, course curricula, training equipment and so on. Moreover, since the RMG sector is looked after by the Export Promotion Bureau, and the training institutions are managed by the DOT under the Ministry of Textiles, there is no linkage between the needs of the sector and educational programmes offered in these institutions. In oder to overcome this problem, appropriate training infrastructure should be developed under the Export Promotion Bureau or Ministry of Commerce to cater the specific training needs of the RMG sector. Side by side, human resource development programmes must be implemented so that well trained workers, supervisors, computer operators, managers and other personnel are available as and when necessary. Introduction of the kind of training programmes that prevail in Thailand may be considered.

10.3.1.9 Fashion Technology Institute and Testing Facility

Institutional facilities for developing time-honored designs and testing facilities for garment/fabrics/yarn are *sine qua non* for attaining efficiency and establishing backward linkage. These facilities also contribute to value addition. Inspite of long-left need for such institutional facilities, so far none has come forward in this respect. The Ministry of Commerce and EPB should shoulder the responsibility of developing these facilities within the country at the earliest.

10.3.1.10 Additional Support to RMG Sector

In order to provide appropriate cushion to RMG to face the challenges of WTO, the government should consider some non-financial incentives, such as, providing gas and electricity at concessional rates, quicker handling of goods of RMG industries at sea ports and ICD at Kamalapur Railway Station (Dhaka), simplification of bonded godown system and various other systems and procedures affecting the export-oriented RMG sector.

10.3.1.11 Inter-Ministerial and Inter-Organizational Relationship

Inspite of its crucial role in the export earning, export oriented RMG sector suffers from dual control. All the backward linkage processes (e.g. spinning, weaving, dyeing, printing, finishing etc.) are looked after by the Ministry of Textiles, while RMG sector looked after by EPB and Ministry of Commerce. The responsibility of EPB is limited to the export related activities. As a consequence, neither the Ministry of Commerce nor the Ministry of Textiles could make any tangible contribution so far in respect of backward linkage. The government should remove this dualism and all the activities relating to RMG should be dealt with one single agency.

10.3.1.12 GSP and Quota Administration

For the improvement of GSP and quota administration, the office works involved in these processes should be computerized, and manpower should be trained in computer software for quick and timely delivery of services. Use of secret computer codes may be maintained and there should be periodic checks and monitoring of GSP certificates and documents related to GSP.

10.3.1.13 Creation of Enabling Socio-Political Environment

As the largest export-oriented sector, the RMG industry should be treated as "Essential Sector". The government and political parties should keep the sector free from hartal (strike) and political programmes. The law enforcing agencies should provide preferential treatment to the security of transportation of inputs and finished goods of this sector. Government should adopt appropriate measures to make this sector fully ready to face the post-MFA situation during the period from 2005 onwards.

10.3.1.14 Awareness Development

Government and relevant trade bodies should make efforts to develop awareness about the impact of trade liberalization and its adverse effects amongst the officials of various concerned Ministries, agencies, trade bodies and entrepreneurs. This awareness will motivate them to find ways and means to face the challenges of WTO. Studies to be conducted and seminars and symposia should be arranged on various relevant issues.

10.3.1.15 Market Diversification

Entrepreneurs should try hard in finding the potential international markets, then find strategic implications for the markets that were selected. Particular targets should be Indian, Japanese, Russian, Eastern European, Middle Eastern, Australian and ASEAN markets. The share of Bangladesh garment in the Japanese market is 0.1% although Bangladesh imports 75% of the garment machinery from Japan. There is misunderstanding in Japan that Bangladesh produces garment only for Europe and North America. This wrong idea has to be removed. Entrepreneurs along with foreign missions jointly need to play a pragmatic role in this context.

10.3.1.16 Product Diversification

It is a very important fact that there are many items for the RMG product lines which Bangladeshi entrepreneurs have not yet started production. Leather items, life jackets, gloves, bags, etc. are among few such items. Other items are umbrella, nylon school bags and jackets, ice sport kits and wears, staffed toys, high competitive market fashion garments are examples. The manufacturers must pay attention to quality and design in their products. Move from low to high end products, must increase the capability of undertaking market research for product development and product design. The fashion design Institute needs to be strengthened and tailored to the need. In order to remain competitive after 2005, there is an urgent need to diversity into new and higher value products which are not covered by ATC.

10.3.1.17 Comprehensive Strategic Plan

It is important for Bangladesh to understand the real strength and weakness and the strategies of its competitors. For that it must undertake a detailed study to prepare a comprehensive strategic plan which will provide Bangladesh specific actions plan. There will be counter strategy to face the challenges and win over the competitors during the post MFA era. To prepare this strategic plan, an active collaboration between government and the industry is essential.

10.3.1.18 High Quality Business Diplomacy

For market access, the competitiveness of the industry needs to be supported by high quality business and economic diplomacy. It is the diplomats who initially create the impression about the country's image and ability. If we have not been able to enter the Japanese, CIS, Middle Eastern, Australian, Indian or ASEAN market, it is partly due to the lack of efforts at diplomatic levels.

10.3.2 Social Considerations

The findings of the social dimensions and migrating to work of garments industry in Bangladesh is that employment in the garment industry has definitely empowered women, increased their mobility and expanded their individual choice. But this they have achieved at the cost of their health and increased risk of harassment. Hence the process is complex, and there is decomposition of women's subordination through employment in the garment industry. It is important to emphasize that those who are working in the garment industries in 1990, were the first generation of women wage workers. They did not have a "role model" to follow, as they have not seen an older generation of women working in such jobs. The analysis on various social aspects as well migrating to work suggests that on the whole there has been improvement in worker's well-being over the last decade. Women's access to income-earning opportunities had many implications for their position in intra-household relationships. In 1990, entrepreneurs as well as the workers were the first generation of entrepreneurs and workers respectively. They have now set a "role model" for the next generation.

Rural women are coming to the cities in order to get work. Relative lack of female involvement in the agricultural sector, changes in land tenure and agricultural modernization mean that there are very few wage-earning opportunities for women in rural areas. They are migrating to cities with their husbands or parents or neighbours and in accordance with cultural and religious constraints. But generally speaking, women's labour is generated by a need for income and also by a desire for income to buy consumer goods: cloths, radios, a sewing machine etc. and to invest in business and education. But the unmarried young female migrants are sent by their families for doing domestic work as maid servants, and in most of the cases in the garment industries. They receive low wages and often have to sent a large proportion of the wages they have to their families.

The establishment of an international standard fashion design institution is expected to provide "on the job training" to women workers needed for their upward mobility and bridge the gender gap in wage, and help Bangladesh to compete per excellence with other countries even after the MFA phasing out in the year 2005. The improvement in the worker's well being will be sustained in future if proper policy supports are extended to the garment industry and its workers as discussed below:

10.3.2.1 Implementing Labour Laws

The fact that labour laws are not implemented in the garments industry has been mentioned in several studies. Moreover, in the 1995 survey, most entrepreneurs opined that the laws are outdated and need to be changed. Much of the working conditions of the workers would improve if the Labour Law Reform Report 1994 is approved and enforced. These changes include: appointment letter to be made compulsory; maternity leave to be provided for two surviving children; workers need to give 60 day's notice to leave jobs; working hours for women will be from 6 a. m. to 10 p.m.; provision for one day weekly leave; equal wage to be paid to men and women for equal work; fine for not paying the minimum wage; group of establishments at the same location can form one union; unions can not be affiliated with political parties; and trade unions to provide training on labour laws. These provisions will certainly help improve the wage and working conditions of the RMG sector if they are properly enforced. Moreover, NGOs and trade unions need to create more awareness about labour laws and monitor implementations. Unless efforts are made to improve these aspects, trade related employment will continue these aspects: to provide dead-end, low-skill jobs with poor conditions, intensifying traditional segregation.

Moreover, providing maternity leave may be linked with trade in future. Although laws for providing such leave exists, but the ILO convention on maternity leave has not been signed by Bangladesh yet. Maternity leave can be provided in a way that does not penalise enterprises, which employ a lot of women and does not make it more expensive to employ women, if it is funded by the state. Bangladesh will create a unique example if the tax-at-source from the exporters could be used for paying maternity leave to the garment workers.

10.3.2.2 Providing Housing Facilities For Garment Workers

A large proportion of female workers are still rural migrants. There is a need for safe and secured housing, as more women are now living in mess than before. An NGO initiative by NUK has already been mentioned earlier. More importantly, BGMEA with assistance from ILO, UNICEF and UNDP are starting three housing projects for the garment workers in Dhaka. This initiative if undertaken fully, will solve the housing need to a large extent.

10.3.2.3 Providing Transport Facilities

Although attention has given to housing, a stream of women walk to work everyday. This facility is costly and hence, entrepreneurs are hesitant to provide transport facilities. Hence, government with assistance from the donors needs to have a special scheme under the Dhaka City transport project. This will also provide safe and secure travelling to and from industry. Some private sector, more preferably NGOs can start city shuttle services for female workers of garment and other manufacturing industries in the peak hours in the morning, evening and night to enable women perform their normal and overtime work.

10.3.2.4 Improving Access to Health and Education Facilities

Many NGOs have already started to provide health facilities at the factory site. The initiative needs to be expanded. BGMEA could also arrange doctors to visit each industry at least once a week. Measures aimed at improving women's position in the trade related sector have to fit into and be part of a programme addressing women's position in the labour market as a whole, and integrating it with health and education policy. Reducing gender gap in malnutrition should be priority in health policy. Female scholarship for secondary education needs to be expanded for reducing gender gap in secondary education.

10.3.2.5 Providing Banking Facilities at the Industry Site

Although rural women have access to banking through micro credit, the workers in the garment industry do not have access to this facility. The study suggests that in the EPZ saving as well as the proportion of workers having bank accounts are higher than non-EPZ. Hence, it is important to provide banking facilities at the factory site at least once a week. This will also make workers feel secure on their pay day, when mugging usually takes place.

10.3.2.6 Regular Wage Payment

Regular payment of salaries, wages and over-time in the fourth week of every month should be mandatory by legislation. This would save the workers from malnutrition and the threat of eviction.

10.3.2.7 Congenial Social Atmosphere

A congenial social atmosphere in the work place will reduce some stress, especially stress arising out of the supervisors constant pressure to increase production and management's bad behavior. The management and supervisors should be friendly with the workers.

10.3.2.8 Allow Trade Unions at the EPZ

Healthy unionization is very important for the development of working and safety conditions of the garment industries. It is now an established fact that women workers do not unionize. Several studies have shown that there are few women members of the trade union. Workers at the EPZ must have their fundamental rights to collective bargaining.

10.3.2.9 Social Recognition

Considering women's important role in poverty alleviation and in the country's export earning, there is urgent need for policy makers to recognize that women who migrate to towns come not only as dependent but also as earners. This earning women play an integral role in the family economy. At the national level, this recognition could lead to a number of useful gender responsive policies that could ensure a fair deal to the women workers and eliminate exploitation and gender discrimination.

10.3.2.10 Provide Rest and Recreational Facilities

Factory Rules 1979 that provides for recreation rooms for the workers should be implemented. Lunch break should be for one hour. Factory Act 1965, which provides that no worker are to be compelled to work for 6 hours at a stretch without a one hour break or two half hour breaks, should be strictly followed in every industry to relieve the workers' stress.

10.3.2.11 Work Place Safety Programmes for Workers

BGMEA has been implementing a number of programmes to ensure work place safety for workers as well as management personnel of its member organizations. The BGMEA Safety Measures Cell organizes the awareness and training programmes, enforce and monitor safety regulations by the factory management. This type of facilities should be extended to Chittagong and Narangonj garments village areas also.

10.3.2.12 Provide Safety Net for Affected Workers

Bangladesh has set an unique example by developing a safety net programme for child labour. A similar programme could be developed for those workers who are producing the products listed in the ATC.

10.3.2.13 Compliance with SA 8000

One recent challenge is that beyond 2005, the industries will also have to comply with Social Accountability (SA) 8000. The standard and its verification system are based on established business strategies for ensuring quality, such as those used by international standards organization for ISO 9000. BGMEA will shortly undertake a programme for SA compliance by all its members.

10.3.2.14 Institutional Framework

In the process of entering into new markets, one vital aspect is the availability of required institutional facilities. The institutional framework as is exists today, comprises the Export Promotion Council, the Export Promotion Bureau, the State Trading Corporation, the Bangladesh Garments Manufacturers and Exporters Association, the Bangladesh Textile Mills Association, the Ministry of Commerce, the Ministry of Finance, the Ministry of Textiles, the European Commission Office in Dhaka, the International Labour Organization Dhaka Office, the UNICEF, the UNDP Dhaka Office, Non-government Organizations, the Dhaka City Corporation, the Chamber of Commerce and Industry and other service support organizations like, the Institute of Foreign Trade, the Trade Development Authority, etc. It is suggested that Commodity Boards, a Trade Fair Authority, and an Institute of Foreign Trade and Labour Welfare Directorate should be set up for looking after the export expansion of readymade garments as well as social well being of the garment workers. It may be a joint effort of all such institutions which can boost our garments export and thereby effectively respond to the market challenges and global competition.

Many of the suggestions and policy implications made above have been long overdue. Therefore, it is essential on the part of exporters, policy makers, non-government organizations, government agencies and international organizations to go for these reforms and policy changes to rectify the weaknesses as well potential challenges by the existing problems facing this sector. The suggestions and policy reforms, if implemented properly can lead Bangladesh to go a long way in achieving a much better economic development in the future.

10.4 Directions for Further Research

Based on the research work undertaken during the study period the research hinted that certain areas of the global trade liberalization and Bangladesh readymade garments industry need extensive research. It is in the fitness of the things that certain guidelines be proposed for the further research:

1. There is need of a comprehensive and continuous study of trade liberalization in the context of Bangladesh readymade garment industry after the phasing out of MFA in 2005.
2. A comprehensive study on backward linkages to readymade garments should be conducted covering yarn, spinning, weaving and knitting sectors.

3. To penetrate into new markets as well export expansion a detailed market wise intensive study of exportable readymade garments may be undertaken.
4. It is evident from the present study that the country's export base has remained very narrow. Successful export diversification in product coverage is the prime factor in attaining the overall objectives. Hence a full fledge study in the area of product design and product development is desirable.
5 For promoting Bangladeshi readymade garments in foreign markets, Bangladesh has been participating in trade fairs and exhibitions abroad. The impact of this participation in promoting Bangladeshi export image should be studied.
6 China is now a very influential member of the WTO in the context of RMG products. After China's inclusion into WTO, a few of Bangladeshi RMG items exports to the EU and US have declined. A comparative study of RMG exports from Bangladesh and China may be conducted which will help in understanding the differences in the two countries.
7 From the present study it is also evident that the RMG sector has made the working women a matured, disciplined and regimented workforce. Change in women's social status and their firm participation in household decision-making is the contribution of the garment industry. A comprehensive study may be conducted on how this industry helps the women workforce in creating savings and empowerment.
8 The major player for the development of RMG industry in Bangladesh is women work force migrated from rural to urban areas. A detailed study may be undertaken to systematically evaluate the impact of the garment industry on the lives and livelihood of female garment workers in Dhaka city.
9 Properly implementation of labour laws in the garments sector is very important for the smoothly growth of this industry. A comprehensive study, if these laws are properly implemented in the RMG industries, may be undertaken.
10 Working conditions is also a serious issue in Bangladesh RMG industry. A detailed study on the nature and extent of working conditions as well as this impact on RMG workers may be undertaken.
11 Many organizations and institutions have been established by the government and entrepreneurs for promotion and growth of the RMG industry. They are engaged in providing assistance to the exporters in many respects. A through study on the role and function of these organizations such as the Export Promotion Bureau, the Bangladesh Garments Manufacturers and Exporters Association, the Bangladesh Textile Mills Association, the Bangladesh Knitwear Manufacturers and Exporters Association, the Chamber of Commerce and Industry, and the Export Promotion Council should be undertaken to know their strengths and weaknesses.
12 Given the extreme degree of competition in the world textile and apparel market trade, it is necessary to continuously study the international market conditions, new developments, innovations and fashion changes in order to prepare the industry for any emerging external challenge.

Appendix

1. Global Trade Liberalization and Bangladesh Readymade Garments Industry: Definitional Issues and Some Technical Terms

In order for grasping the substances in the subsequent chapters trouble free I thought it logical to incorporate some key aspects and terminologies in the sphere of textiles and clothing, mostly being pertinent to this study. This attempt made in this chapter is attributed to this objective merely.

Carding Machine: A devise which has a "card covered with slips of wire placed round a cylinder". Richard Arkwright upgraded the machine which comprised "a cylinder carding engine, incorporating a crank and comb mechanism. The comb up and down, removing the carded fibres from the doffing cylinder in a continuous filmy fleece."[223]

Comber Machine, Rovings, Yarn: When carding is completed, the fibres need to undergo further processing in a machine, called comber machine, in order to generate combed yarn where the short stands are taken out. Then it is processed into silver. The silver is then supplied to the draw frame, and speed/roving frames. Here silver is twisted to shape what is called roving.[224] Finally, the roving is placed in spinning frame in order to exert further twisting and drafting to produce yarn, which is again spun around a bobbin or cone with the help of autoconers or cone winding/reeling machines. The yarn is then packed and marketed.

Spinning: The spinning of wool, cotton, or flax [225]was, initially, carried out by the spindle[226] and distaff. "The distaff, a stick about 3 ft long, was held under the left arm, and the fibres of wool drawn from it were twisted spirally by the forefinger and thumb of the right hand. As the thread was spun, it was wound on the spindle".[227] Spinning refers to the process in which fibres are drawn out into yarn and a twist is initiated. Later this yarn is used in weaving as either wrap (longitudinal threads) or weft (interlacing the wrap threads) to produce cloth.

---

223 "The Textile Industry". The Spartacus Internet Encyclopedia homepage. The British History 1700-1950 (http://www.spartacus.schoolnet.co.uk/Textiles.htm, downloaded on 11 October, 2000

224 "The Textile Industry of Bangladesh" by Azizur Chowdhury http://www.ais-dhaka.net/SENIORS/textileazizur downloaded on 12 December, 2001.

225 The thread got from the stem of the flax plant, used in making linen (Oxford Dictionary, 1997)

226 A thin rod on which thread is twisted or wound during spinning (Oxford Dictionary, 1997)

227 The Spartacus Internet Encyclopaedia homepage, Op.Cit.

Spinning Jenny: Spinning Jenny refers to a machine that "used eight spindles onto which the thread was spun from a corresponding set of rovings.[228] Later developments on the machine enabled the number to be raised to eighty. This yarn was "suitable only for the filling of weft" (the cross-thread of wrap) as the same was coarse and lacked strength.

Roller Spinning: This is a machine, which has two sets of rollers which travelled at different speeds. This draw out a silver of wool to the right thickness before spinning it. By 1741 this machine, powered by donkeys, was being used in a mill in Birmingham.[229]

Flax Spinning Machine: Two men from Darlington, John Kendrew and Thomas Porthhouse, registered a patent for a new flax spinning machine in June 1787 which was made up of drawing frames with drums large enough to roll out long flax fibres and a spinning – frame with four spindles .[230]

Handloom Weaving: This method involves interlacing one set of threads of yarn with another. The wrap threads are spread out lengthwise in the weaving loom while the weft, the cross-threads, are woven into the wrap to make the cloth.

Backward Linkage: Backward linkage refers to the value added portion of a finished product, e.g. supplying fabric is a backward linkage to the cutting and sewing of the garment.

Clean Cloth Campaign (CCC): This is a Dutch group formed in 1998, and finalised a code of conduct based on International Labour Organization (ILO) conventions including provision of freedom of association, hours of work, and a living wage. The initiative created a foundation model for monitoring compliance with its code of conduct called the Fair Wear Charter Foundation. The foundation, comprised of unions, NGOs, retailers and manufacturers, hires external monitors to evaluate and certify apparel companies and their supplier factories.

Greige, Mercerising: Woven cloth which has not been processed further is called Greige. But when cotton fabric is treated with cold concentrated sodium

---

228 'A Guide for the Planning , Design and Implementation, of Wastewater Treatment Plants in the Textile Industry' Water Research Commission, Pretoria, Republic of South Africa. http://www.und.ac.za/und/prg/publications/textguide/guide1 downloaded on 27 December, 2001.

229 Ibidem

230 The Spartacus Internet Encyclopedia Homepage, Op.Cit.

hydroxide to attach sheen and to improve the water absorption, it is called Mercerising.[231]

Size and sizing: Size refers to a coating applied to wrap yarn to improve its weaving efficiency while sizing is the application of size to the wrap yarn. Again, sizing is applied only in the woven sector of the industry.[232]

Grey: The initial stage of fabric produced by using looms or knitting machines is called grey.[233] The term "grey" indicates that the fabric has no colour at this stage.

Knitting: As an alternate to looms, circular knitting machines are used for knitting for making fabrics. These machines employ needles fed with yarn that run in an up and down motion and knit interlocking arrangements of yarn.[234] This knitted fabric is much softer and more flexible than that produced on looms.

Dyeing, Printing, Finishing: Grey fabric pass through a process called the batch method[235] (scouring, bleaching, and dyeing). Scouring involves the treatment of grey in chemical solutions to take out the size, natural fats, waxes, proteins and other impurities, as well as, to bring about the fabric hydrophilic, i.e. it no longer repels water. The next process is bleaching which is vital to turn the cloth a clean white. Bleaching could be accomplished either 'with dilute hypochloride solution at room temperature, or by using hydrogen peroxide solution at elevated temperatures, usually 80 to 90 degrees celsius. The latter method usually results in better and longer lasting whiteness, however it is the more expensive of the two methods".[236]

Dying and shrinking: After bleaching, the scoured cloth is dyed, and then printed on. Printing is carried out "using perforated rollers that allows certain chemicals and colours to diffuse through the holes". Then fabric is "washed, soaked in chemicals under elevated temperatures for colour fixation, and then washed again". In case of knitted fabrics[237], scouring, bleaching, or dying processes are ended by a jigger machine when the fabrics are loaded on it. Now, the fabric placed on de-watering or de-twisting machine which removes water from the fabric. Again the fabric passes through a shrinkage tensionless drier for drying, shrinking, and relaxing the knitted fabrics. Compacting is the final process

---

[231] "Water Research Commission, Pretoria", Republic of South Africa, Op.Cit
[232] Ibidem
[233] Azizur Chowdhury, Op.Cit.
[234] Ibidem
[235] Ibidem
[236] Ibidem
[237] Ibidem

before the fabric is prepared for use. Here, the fabric is "steamed and ironed between a roller assembly" after which it is folded for marketing and for RMG industry utilization.

Silk: Silk filament[238] is a fine, tough, elastic fibre produced by caterpillars called bombyx mori, its scientific name. The entire process of producing silk thread has been enumerated plainly in the Spartacus Internet Encyclopedia homepage as below:

"For thirty-five days after it has hatched from the eggs laid by its parent moth, the caterpillar, normally referred to as a silkworm, spends its time eating the leaves of a mulberry tree. It then, in the course of two or three days' spinning, surround itself in a cocoon which consists of a continuous and very fine filament of silk. The silkworm then turns itself into a moth, which escapes by making a hole through the cocoon. First the cocoons were placed into very hot water to soften the sticky gum, sericin that holds the filament together. The ends of the filament are found and are then unwound. This process is called reeling. The silk filament, which can be as much as a mile long, is then put on to large reels, known as swifts. Unlike cotton or wool, silk is not spun but twisted. Hence the term throwing rather then spinning. Throwing involves the revolving of two sets of bobbins[239] at different, carefully adjusted, speeds."

Automated and Computer Aided Design (CAD): CAD is relevant to the industry specific design system where computer is used as a tool. In today's world, CAD is used to design anything from an artificial to knitwear and it was launched in textile and apparel industry in the 1970s[240]. Computer only expedites the cloth making process, for example, repeat making, colour changing, motif manipulation etc. Thus, automation refers to such labour saving process with the aid of CAD. Automation is also attributed to improved quality with lesser time.

Textiles fibre: Textile fibres include (a) natural fibres such as cotton (b) cellulosic such as rayon, acetate and triacetate, and (c) synthetic or non-cellulosic fibres such petrochemical derivatives as nylon, polyester, and acrylic.

Developed and Developing Countries: Developed countries include the European Union, Iceland, Norway, Switzerland, the USA, Canada, Japan, Australia

---

238 A very thin strand, like a thread (Oxford Dictionary, 1997)

239 Bobbin refers to A small cylinder round which thread, wire, etc. is wound for use in a machine (Oxford Dictionary, 1997).

240 The Lemelson Centre for the Study of Invention and Innovation, National Museum of American History, Smithsonian Institution, Op. Cit (http://www.si.edu/lemelson/centerpieces/whole_cloth/u7materials/sfPac5.html) downloaded on 11 October 2000.

and New Zealand. Developing countries include all other countries including East European countries in transition.

The Generalised System of Preferences (GSP): The Generalized System of Preference (GSP) is a system whereby preferential treatment by way of a reduced or duty-free tariff rate is granted by developed countries. Under this scheme manufactured, semi-manufactured or a few primary and agricultural products will be admitted duty free or at concessional rates by the developed countries. This preferential treatment is granted without any reciprocal obligation on the part of the developing countries.

Bangladesh Garment Manufacturers and Exporters Association (BGMEA): A sectoral trade body which is non-government in nature and free from traditional bureaucracy to assist the RMG sub-sector to boost up the country's foreign exchange earnings. It was founded in 1977. Since its commencement with only nineteen garment manufacturers and exporters, BGMEA has grown in time into strong and dynamic body comprising about 3500 garment manufacturers and exporters as its members. The basic objective of BGMEA is to establish a healthy business environment with sound relationship between the manufacturers, exporters and importers to ensure a steady growth in the foreign exchange earnings of the country.

Multi-Fibre Arrangement (MFA): The MFA, adopted by GATT in 1994, allowed discriminatory quantitative/quota restrictions in textile and clothing exports of developing countries on bilateral or unilateral basis. It was extended six times, upto 1994, in most cases further intensifying restrictions on imports and enlarging product coverage, specially affecting the developing country exporters of the textile and clothing products.

Trade Liberalization: Trade liberalization is the process of facilitating and increasing trade between two or more States, extending to trade in products as well as transfer of technology, ideas and knowledge. Trade liberalization is based on the theory of comparative advantage. Under this theory, a State has a comparative advantage in the production of a particular good or service in that State is low compared to the cost of other States. The rationale is that if each State focuses production on the particular goods and services on which it has a comparative advantage, the global output of goods and services will increase. With trade between States, consumer can access more goods and services and thus increase their standard of living. Efficiency improvements are also likely to result from the increased competition that domestic producer face from foreign goods and services (Bullock & Trombley, 1988).

World Trade Organization: It's an international organization of 146 member countries which is both a forum for negotiating international trade agreements and the monitoring and regulating body for enforcing the agreements. The WTO was created in 1995, by the passage of the provisions of "Uruguay Round" of the General Agreement on Tariffs and Trade (GATT). Prior to the Uruguay Round, GATT focused on promoting world trade by pressuring countries to reduce tariffs. But with the creation of the WTO, this corporate inspired agenda was significantly catched up by targeting so-called "non-tariff barriers to trade" essentially any national or local protective legislation which might be construed as impacting trade.

References

Abdullah, A.Y.M. [1997]: "International Trade Implication and Future of Readymade Garments Sector of Bangladesh", Dhaka University Journal of Business Administration, Vol.23, No. 2 & 3.

Abdullah, T.A. and Sondra A. Zeidenstein [1982]: "Village Women of Bangladesh: Prospects for Change", Oxford University Press, London.

Absar, Syeda Sharmin [2000]: "Why Women Work in Garment Factories in Bangladesh? Voice of their Own", National Centre for Development Studies (NCDS), Australian National University, Canberra, Australia.

Absar, Syeda Sharmin [2001]: "Living Conditions of Women Workers in the RMG Sector in Bangladesh", National Centre for Development Studies (NCDS), Australian National University, Canberra, Australia.

Afroz, Mahfuza [2001]: "Industry Report on the Readymade Garments Sector of Bangladehs", Indian Institute of Foreign Trade, New Delhi, July 1.

Afsar, Rita [1990]: "Women's Employment and Occupational Diversification in Bangladesh", New Delhi; ILO/ARTEP Working Paper.

Afsar, Rita [1995]: "Causes, Consequences and Challenges of Rural-Urban Migration in Bangladesh", Ph.D. Thesis, University of Adelaide, Australia

Afsar, Rita [1996]: "Application of Demographip Analysis in Assessing Gender Based Urban Poverty in Bangladesh", A paper presented at the 8th National Conference of the Australian Population Association, Adelaide, Australia.

Afsar, Rita [1998]: "A Case Study of the Gender Dimensions of Labour Migration in the Formal Manufacturing Sector in Dhaka City", Paper presented for Centre for Policy Dialogue and UNRISD project on Women's Employment in Bangladesh.

Afsar, Rita [2000]: "Gender, Labour Market and Demographic Change: A Case Study of Women's Entry to Formal Manufacturing Sector of Bangladesh", Oxford University Press, London

Aggarwal, Vinod K. [1985]: "Liberal Protectionism: The International Politics of Organized Textile Trade", Los Angeles.

Ahmed, Faruquddin & Khan, Syed Ahmed [1996]: "Review of Exports from Bangladesh", Paper Presented at the Seminar on Development and Finance of Exports of Bangladesh, Bangladesh Bank on April 15-16.

Ahmed, Helal & Warr Peter G. [1994]:"Bangladesh and the Uruguay Round. A General Equilibrium Analysis", The Bangladesh Development Studies, Vol. XXII, No. 4, December.

Ahmed, Jasim Uddin & Giasuddin, Kazi Md. [1996]: "Export of Readymade Garments", Trade Information Centre, Export Promotion Bureau, Dhaka, April. 15-16.

Ahmed, Khandkar Habib [2002]: "Backward Linkage to Readymade Garments: Bangladesh Perspective", Academic Press and Publishers Ltd, Dhaka, January; p.iv.

Ahmed, Kutubuddin. [2002]: "Capacity Building for 2005", A Paper Presented in the BATEXPO Seminar at the Pan Pacific Sonargaon Hotel, Dhaka, March.

Anderson, Kym [1989]: "China and Multi-fibre Arrangement", Australia University of Adelaide, Centre for International Economic Studies.

Anderson, Kym [1992]: "New Silk Roads: East Asia and World and World Textile Markets", Cambridge, New York, Cambridge University Press.

Aspand, R. J. and Edward A. Vaughn [1997]: "75 Years of Change in American Textile Manufacturing Industry", Clemson University, Clemson, S.C. Raleigh.

Bachmann, Suse [2002]: "Women in the Industrial Labour Force in Bangladesh", Sociology of Developemnt Research Centre, University of Bielefeld, Bielefeld.

Baden, S. and S. Joekes [1993]: "Gender Issues in the Developing of the Special Economic Zones and Open Areas in the People's Republic of China", IDS, Sussex University, Brighton (mimeo).

Balassa, B. [1979]: "A Stage Approach to Comparative Advantage" , Economic Growth and Resources, Vol. 4, Macmillian, London.

Banerjee, Nirmala (ed.) [1990]: "Indian Women in a Changing Industrial Scenario", Indo-Dutch Studies on Development Alternatives, New Delhi, Newbury Park, London.

Bangladesh Bureau of Statistics (BBS) [1995] : "Report on the Household Expenditure Survey 1991-92", Ministry of Planning, Dhaka.

Bangladesh Bureau of Statistics (BBS) [1996]: "Statistical Pocket Book", Ministry of Planning, Dhaka.

Bangladesh Bureau of Statistics (BBS) [1998]: "Household Expenditure Survey 1995-96, Statistical Division, Ministry of Planning, Government of Bangladesh, Dhaka.

BIGUF [1999]: (Bangladesh Independent Garments Workers Union Federation) "Country Report, Informatiuon on the Current Situation of Garments Factory Unions in Bangladesh", Unpublished.

BATEXPO [2000]: "Duty Free Access To Developed Countries: From the Perspective of the Economics in Transition", 11th Year of Bangladesh Apparel and Textile Exposition, Pan Pacific Sonargaon Hotel, Dhaka.

Baysan, Tercan and Sattar, Zaidi [2000]: "Trade Liberalization in Bangladesh, Who Gained, Who Didn't , and Why", The Daily Star, Feature page, Volume 3, Number 209, March 29.

Bhattacharya, Debapriya [2001]: "Development of Backward Linkage Industry in the Bangladesh Textile Sector: Promises and Achievements", Tex-Bangla Seminar, Centre for Policy Dialogue, Dhaka, May 28.

Bhattacharya, Debapriya and Rahman Mustifizur [1999]: "Female Employment under Export- Propelled Industrialization: Prospects for Internalizing Global Opportunities in Bangladesh's Apparel Sector", UNRISD, Geneva.

Bhattacharya, D and Rahman Mustafizur [2000]: "USA Trade and Development Act 2000: A Response from Bangladesh Perspective", Centre for Policy Dialogue, Dhaka, July

Bhattacharya, Debapriya and Rahman Mustifizur [2000]: "Dialogue on Implementation of WTO ATC: Current Status and Implication for Bangladesh", Centre for Policy Dialogue, Dhaka, September.

Bhattacharya, D. and Rahman M. [2002]: "Experience with Implementation of WTO-ATC and Implication for Bangladesh", Centre for Policy Dialogue, Dhaka.

Bhuiyan, Azizur Rahman. et al. [1997]: "Bangladesh's Cotton Textile Industry, Constraints and Policy Options", Bangladesh Development Studies, Dhaka.

Bhuiyan, M. Zakir Hossain [1998]: "Export Marketing of Non-traditional items in Bangladesh: Problems and Prospects", Ph.D Dissertation, Aligar Muslim University, Aligar, India, November.

Bhuiyan, M.M. and Harvey Shaw [1994]: "Profile of the Textile and Clothing Industry in Bangladesh", Textile Outlook International, May.

Blackhurst, R. et. al. [1995]: "The Uruguay Round and the Market Access: Opportunities and Challenges for Developing Countries", Paper presented at World Bank Conference on the Uruguay Round and the Developing Economics, Jan.1995, Washington D.C.

Blokker, N. [1989]: "International Regulation on World Trade in Textiles, Lesson for Practice: A Contribution to Theory", Boston, Martius Nijhoff; Norwell, Kluwer Academic publishers, p.4.

Borowice, Mieczyslaw [1992]: "Bangladesh Export Development and Promotion, Report on Two Phase Mission", (Phase I, January 20 -February 21; 1992 and Phase II, May 15May 30 & June 2 – June 11), International Trade Centre, UNCTAD/GATT, Sept, 21.

Bow, Josephine [2000]: "Bangladesh Export Apparel Industry: Into the 21st Century: The Next Challenges", The Asia Foundation, Gulshan, Dhaka, October.

Brook, Stuart [1992]: "Bangladesh Production Considerations Related to Export Product Development for Bangladesh Knitwear", Report on Two Missions (February 20 March 20 & May 3May 23, 1992), International Trade Centre, UNCTAD/GATT, Sept. 9, pp.5,11,& 14.

Brydon, Lynne and Chant, Sylvia [1989]: "Women in the Third World: Gender Issues in Rural and Urban Areas", Edward Elger Publishing Ltd, England.

Bullock, Alan and Trombley, S. (eds.) [1988]: "The Fontana Dictionary of Modern Thought", (Rev. Edn.) p.686.

Cable, V. [1987]: "Textiles and Clothing in a New Round of Trade Negotiations", World Bank Economic Review, p.625.

Cain, et.al [1979]: "Class Patriarchy and the Structure of Women's Work in Rural Bangladesh". A paper presented at the ADC-ICRISAT Conference on Adjustment Mechanisms of Rural Labour Markets in Developing Areas, Hyderabad, India.

Chaudhury, R. H [1978]: "Determinants and Consequences of Rural Out-Migration: Evidence from Some Villages in Bangladesh", Oriental Geographer, 221 (1-2), pp. 1-20.

Chaudhury, R. H and Curlin, G.C. [1975]: "Dynamics of Migration in a Rural Areas of Bangladesh", Bangladesh Development Studies, 3(2) pp. 181-230.

Chowdhury, Naimuddin [1989]: "The Handloom Economy in Transition", The Quarterly Journal of Bangladesh Institute of Development Studies, Vol.XVIII, No. 1 & 2.

Chowdhury, Shahriar Rahman [1994]: "A Study Report on Knit Garment Industry in Bangladesh", Research and Economic Development, Bangladesh Shilpa Bank, Dhaka, Sept. pp. 5-10.

Cookson, Forrest E [2000]: "Trade and Development Act 2000 and the Bangladesh Garments Industry", A Paper Presented in the Seminar of Tex-Bangla, Dhaka, November.

Cornell, J. B. Dasgupta, B.L. and Lipton, M. [1982]: "Migration from Rural Areas: The Evidence from Village Studies", Oxford University Press, Delhi.

CPD [1999]: "The Textile and Clothing Industry of Bangladesh: In A Changing World Economy", Centre for Policy Dialogue, Report No. 18, Dhaka.

CPD [2001]: "Phasing out of Multi-fibre Arrangement: Impact on the Livelihood Conditions in the RMG Sector of Bangladesh", A Concept Paper for a Global Campaign, Centre for Policy Dialogue, Dhaka, October 10.

Dannecker, Petra [1998]: "Between Confirmaty and Resistance: Women Garments Workers in Bangladesh", Sociology of Development Research Centre, University of Bielefeld, Bielefeld.

Dhaka Courier [1998]: "Fire Broken out in Garments Industry", Feature Page, August, 28.

Dickerson, K., G [1999]: "Textile and Apparel in the Global Economy", Upper Saddle River (New Jersey): Prantice Hall.

Dixit, Avinash K. and Grossman, Gene M [1982] "Trade and Protection with Multistage Production", Review of Economic Studies, Vol. 49, No. 4, October

Dowlah, C.A.F. [1998]: "The Consequences of GATT Uruguay Round for the Textile and Garments Sector in Bangladesh", Bangladesh Institute of International Strategie Institute, Dhaka.

Dowlah, C.A.F. [2000]: "The Agreement on Textiles and Clothing under the Uruguay Round: A Mixed Bag for the Developing Countries", Bangladesh Journal of International Institute of Strategic Studies, Vol. 19, No. 2, p. 157.

Ellison, Thomas [1968]: "The Cotton Trade of Great Britain", Frank Cass and Company Limited. London.

Elson, D. and R. Pearson [1981a]: "The Subordination of Women and the Internationalization of Factory Production", in K. Young, C. Wolkowitz and R. McCullagh (eds) Of Marriage and The Market: Women's Subordination in International Perspective, London, CSE Books.

Elson, D., and R. Pearson [1981b]: "Nimble Fingers Make Cheap Workers: An analysis of Women's Employment in Third World Export Manufacturing", Feminist Review, 87-107.

Export Promotion Bureau (EPB) [1990]: "Prospects of Knitwear Product Export from Bangladesh: A General Study", Export Promotion Bureau, Dhaka.

Export Promotion Bureau (EPB) [1999]: "Study of the Situation on the Production of Local Yarn and Fabrics for Use in RMG Sub-Sector of Bangladesh", Bangladesh Project Management Institute, Lalmatia, Dhaka.

Findley, Sally E. and Linda Williams [1991]: "Women Who Go and Women Who Stay Reflections and Family Migration Process in a Changing World", Population and Labour Policies Programme, Working Paper No. 176, International Labour Office, Geneva.

Financial Express (FE) [1999]: "Garment Workers Pass Hard Days", FE Report, August.

GATT (1973): "Arrangement Regarding International Trade in Textiles", 25 U.S.T. 1001, T.I.A.S. No. 7840, art, 1, para 2.

GATT [1984]: "Textiles and Clothing in the World Economy", A GATT Analysis of Textiles Trade Policies, Geneva.

Greenaway, David and Chris Milner [1993]: "Trade and Industrial Policy in Developing Countries", Ann Arbor: University of Michigan Press.

Graves, Nancy B. [1994]: "Adaption of Polynesian Female Migrants in New Zealand", in James T. Fawcett, Siew-Ean Khoo, Peter C. Smith (ed.) Women in the Cities of Asia, Migration and Urban Adaptation, Westview Press, Boulder, Colorado.

Graves, Nancy B. and Graves, Theodora D. [1987]: "Preferred Adaptive Strategies: An Approach and Understanding of New Zealand's Multi-Cultural Work Force", New Zealand Journal of Industrial Relations, Wellington.

Haggblade, S., Hazel, P. and Reardon, T [2002]: "Strategies for Stimulating Poverty –Alleviating Growth in the Rural Non-Farm Economy in Developing Countries", New York: Barnes and Nobles.

Hamilton, Carl [1990]: "Textile Trade and the Developing Countries: Eliminating the Multi-Fiber Arrangement in the 1990s", World Bank. Washington DC.

Hammond, M.B. [1897]: "The Cotton Industry: An Essay in the American Economic History", Macmillan Company, New York.

Hasan, Faruque [2002]: "Impact of US TDA-2000 and the Terrorist Attacks of 11 September 2001 on Readymade Garment Exports viz a viz on Bangladesh Economy", A Paper Presented in the BATEXPO Seminar at the Pan Pacific Sonargaon Hotel, Dhaka, March.

Hasan, Feroz M. [2000]: "The Readymade Garments Sector of Bangladesh: How to Make the Industry More Value Added?" BATEXPO, 2000, 11th Year of Bangladesh Apparel and Textile Exposition, Pan Pacific Sonargaon Hotel, Dhaka, November.

Haque, S. [1994]: "The Garment Industry of Bangladesh: The Impact of Regional Economic and Trade Agreement", Key Note Speech in thc Seminar on Garments Industry, Dhaka.

Haque, Wahidul [2001]: "Globalization and South Asia", A Public Lecture Jointly Organized by Bangladesh Institute of Development Studies and Chittagong University, June.

Hertel, Thomas W. (ed.) [1997]: "Global Trade Analysis: Modelling and Applications", Cambridge University Press, New York.

Hossain, H., R. Jahan and S. Sobhan (ed.) [1990]: "No Better Option: Industrial Women Workers in Bangladesh", University Press Ltd, Dhaka.

Hossain, Mahmud [1989]: "Export Incentive Advantages and its Impact on Exportable RMG and Leather Goods: An Evaluation", Dhaka University Journal of Business Administration, Vol.14 &15, No.5.

Hossain, Md. Afzal [1990]: "Export Marketing of Garments from Bangladesh: Patterns, Problems and Prospects", The Dhaka University Studies, Part C, vol. 11(2), p.167-180.

Hossain, M. Afsar, R. and Bose, M.L. [1999]: "Growth and Distribution of Income and Incidence of Poverty in Dhaka City", in Hossain Zillur Rahman (ed.) Bangladesh: Dynamics of Development in the 90s, University Press Ltd. Dhaka.

Hossain, M., I. Bose, M.L., Chaudhury, A. and Dick, R.M [2000]: "Changes in Agrarian Relations and Livelihood in Rural Bangladesh", In: Ramchandran, V.K. and Swaminathan, M. (eds.) Agrarian Studies: Essays on Agrarian Relations in Less-Developed Countries, Preceedings of the international conference 'Agrarian Relations and Rural Development in Less Developed Countries', January 3-6, Tulika Books, Kolkata, New Delhi.

Hossain, M., I. Bose, M.L., Chaudhury, A. [2003]: "Changes in Agriculture and Livelihood in Unfavourable Ecosystems: Implications for the Rice Research Strategy", Bangladesh Agricultural Research Council, Dhaka.

Hossain, M., I Khan, I.A. and Seeley, J. [2003]: "Surviving on Their Feet: Changing the Mobile Livelihoods of the Poor in Bangladesh", Paper presented for the Conference 'Styling poor: Chronic Poverty and Development Policy', University of Manchester, April 7-9.

Hossain, Najmul and Brar, Jagjit, S. [1988]: "The Garment Workers of Bangladesh-Earnings and Perceptions towards Unionisms", Dhaka University Journal of Business Administration, Vol. 14, No. 4.

Hugo, Graeme J. [1978]: "Population Mobility in West Java", Gadjah Mada University Press, Yogyakarta, Indonesia.

Hugo, Graeme J. [1991]: "Rural-Urban Migration, Economic Development and Social Change: Some Important Issues", Paper presented at the Workshop "Urbanization and Urban Poor", BIDS, Dhaka.

Hyvarien, Antero and Lipman, Abbey [1992]: "Bangladesh Supply Study on the Garments Industry", (Project No. BGD/85/164). International Trade Centre, UNCTAD/GATT, July.

IBC and UIL [2000]: "Report on Impact of SAARC Cumulation Agreement on Bangladesh RMG and Textile Sectors and Overall Economy of Bangladesh", Sena Kalayan Bhavan (7th Floor), 195, Motijheel Commercial Area, Dhaka, December.

International Finance Corporation (IFC) [1999]: "Bangladesh: Textile Study", Washington, D.C.

International Labour Office (ILO/UNCTC) [1985]: "Women Workers In Multinational Enterprises in Developing Countries", Geneva.

International Labour Office [1996]: "Bulletin of Labour Statistics", ILO, Geneva

International Trade Commission (US) [1999]: "Industry Trade Summary: Apparel", USITC; Publication 3169, Washington D.C.

Islam, A.F.M. Mofizul [1996]: "Origin and Growth of Cotton Textile Industry in Bangladesh", Dhaka University Journal of Business Administration, Vol. 22, No. 3 & 4, June, p.21.

Islam, Mir. Shamsul [1992]: "Product Group: Knitwear and Hosiery, Regulatory/Procedural Constraints", Export Development Project, No. BGD/85/164, UNDP/ITC, July 25, pp. 2-8.

Islam, N. and Begum, J. [1983]: "Internal Migration in Bangladesh: A Review of Literature", Monograph No. 9. Centre for Urban Studies, University of Dhaka.

Islam, S. M. Emdadul [2002]: "Requirement of Technical Competence and Improving Productivity in RMG Industry to Compete in the Open Market", BATEXPO Seminar, Dhaka, March 24.

Islam, Sadequl [2001]: "The Textile and Clothing Industry of Bangladesh in a Changing World Economy", Centre for Policy Dialogue & The University Press Ltd, February.

Jabbar, Sk. Jenefa Khanam [2002]: "Compliance of the Code of Conduct at the Work Place in the Main Essence for Survival of the RMG Sector after 2004", A paper presented at the 12th BATEXPO Seminar at Dhaka, March 24.

Jared, L. Landaw [1989] : "Textiles and Apparel Trade Liberalization: The Need for a Strategic Change in free Trade Arguments", Colum Bus Library Rev. 205, 205 n.l.

Joekes, S. [1987]: "Women in the World Economy", New York: INSTRAW and Oxford University Press, Oxford.

Joekes, S. and R, Moayadi [1987]: "Women and Export Manufacturing: A Review of Issues and AID Policy", Report prepared for the Office and Development, USAID, and International Research Centre for Research on Women, Washington.

John F. Cobau and Arther Watson [1998] : "Legal Issues in International Trade in Textiles and Clothing: A Post Uruguay Round Perspective", in The Commerce Dept. Speaks on Int'l Trade and Investment, 239, 243 (PLI Corp. Law and Practice Course, Handbook Series No. 1075).

Jong, Gordon F. de and Richter, Kerry [1996]: "Gender, Values and Intention to More in Rural Thailand", International Migration Review, Fall 30 (3).

Jurgen, W. [1983]: "Selective Protectionism and Structural Adjustment", Berlin, pp.47-48.

Kabeer, N. [1991]: "Cultural Dopes or Rational Fools? Women and Labour Supply in the Bangladesh Garment Industry", European Journal of Development Research, 3(1): 133-160

Kabeer, N. [1995]: "Necessary, Sufficient or Irrevalent? Women, Wage and Intra-Household Power Relations in Urban Bangladesh", Working Paper No. 25, Institute of Development Studies, Sessex, U.K.

Kabeer, N. [1997]: "Women, Wages and Intra-Household Power Relations in Urban Bangladesh", Development and Change, Vol.28. No.2:261-302.

Kamal, M. R [2002]: "It Is A Vital for Us Revamping Readymade Garments Sector?", The Independent (Internet Edition), Dhaka, May.

Khundker, Nasreen (ed.) [2001]: "Globalization and Gender: Changes Patterns of Women's Employment in Bangladesh", Centre for Policy Dialogue and University Press Ltd, Dhaka.

Kibria, N. [1995]: "Cultural, Social and Income in the Lives of Women Garment Workers in Bangladesh". Gender and Society, 9 (3): 289-309.

Kirmani, N., Molanjani, P. and Mayer, T. [1984]: "Effects of Increased Market Access on Exports of Developing Countries", IMF Staff Paper, Washington.

Kitty, G. Dickerson [1996]: "Textile Trade: The GATT Exception", 11 ST. JOHN'S J. Legal Comment, 393,n.1.

Lachenmann, G. [1998a]: "Strukturanpassung aus Frauensicht: Entwicklungskonzepte und Transformationsprozesse", In: Klingenbiel/ Randeria 1998, pp. 294-319.

Lachenmann, G. [1998b]: "Frauen und Globalisierung. Aktuelle Entwicklungen und kritische Diskurse", Working Paper No. 284 of the Sociology of Development Research Centre, University of Bielefeld, Bielefeld.

Lim, L [1990]: "Women's Work in Export Factories: The Politics of a Cause", in I. Tinker (ed.) Persistent Inequalities: Women and World Development, Oxford University Press, Oxford.

Maddison, Angus [1969]: "Economic Growth in Japan and the USSR", New York, pp 24-25.

Markovic, M. and Manderson, L. [2000]: "European Immigration and the Australian Labour Market: A Case Study of Women from former Yogoslavia", Journal of Ethnic and Migration Studies, Vol. 26, No.1: 127-136, January, Taylor and Francis Ltd, Hants, U.K.

Martin, Will and Alam, Winters [1996]: "The Uruguay Round and the Developing Countries", Cambridge University Press, New York.

Mellor, J., W. [1976]: "The New Economics of Growth: A Strategy for India and the Developing World", New York: Cornell University Press.

Menezes, Antonio de Souza [2000]: "Improving Workers' Productivity in the RMG Sector of Bangladesh", Paper Presented at the BATEXPO 2000 Seminar, Dhaka, November, p.2.

Miller, Carol and Vivian Jessica (eds.)[2002]: "Women's Employment in the Textile Manufacturing Sectors of Bangladesh and Morocco", UNRISD, Geneva.

Ministry of Commerce [1996]: "The Impact and Implications of the Agreement on Textiles and Clothing", carried out by TSMU, Ministry of Textiles under Uruguay Round study project, Ministry of Commerce, GOB, Dhaka.

Ministry of Commerce [2001]: "Report on Impact of SAARC Cumulation Agreement on Bangladesh RMG and Textiles Sectors on the Overall Economy of Bangladesh", GOB, Dhaka.

Mitchell, Andrew D. [2001]: "Broadening the Vision of Trade Liberalization: International Competition Law and the WTO", World Competition, Law and Economics Review, Vol. 24, No. 3 September.

Mitra, S. N. et al. [1994]: "Bangladesh Demographic and Health Survey 1993-94", Calverton, Maryland: National Institute of Population Research and Training, Mitra and Associates and Macro International Inc.

Nath, N. C [1993]: "Multi-fibre Agreement, Uruguay Round and Interest of the Developing Countries in garments Trade", Paper presented at the Seminar on GATT and the Uruguay Round, 17-21 January, Dhaka, Organized by the International Tariff Commission and and the GATT Secretariat.

Nath, N. C. [2001]: "External Competitiveness of RMG Industry of Bangladesh: Analysis of Status and Strategies", BIDS, Dhaka.

Noman, Herbert E. [1940]: "Japan's Emergence as a Modern State", New York.

Paul-Majumder, P. [1995]: "Health and Status of Garments Workers in Bangladesh: Findings from a Survey of Employers and Employees", BIDS, Dhaka.

Prakash, V. [1988]: "Financing Urban Services in Developing Countries", In D.A. Rondineli and G.S. Cheema (ed.), Decentralization and Development: Policy Implications in Developing Countries, Beverly Hills, California: Sage.

Porter, M. [1990]: "The Competitive Advantage of Nations", New York, Free Press.

Quddus, Munir and Rashid, Salim [1998]: "Entrepreneurs and Economic Development: The Remarkable Story of Garment Exports from Bangladesh", The University Press Ltd, Dhaka.

Rahman, Mustafizur [1994]: "Implication of GATT Multilateral Accord for Bangladesh: Emerging Challenges, Upholding Opportunities", Dhaka University Journal of Business Studies, Vol. 15 (2). P. 111-140.

Rahman, Mustafizur [1995]: "GSP and Export Competitiveness of Bangladesh, Some Emerging Issues of Post-GATT Phase", Dhaka University Journal of Business Studies, Vol.16 (2). P. 103-123.

Rahman, Shamsur & Rahman, A.K.M. Atiqur [2001]: "Development of Backward Linkage Industry in the Textile Sector: Promises and Achievements", TexBangla Seminar, Dhaka, May 28.

Rothschild, C.S. and Mahmud, S. [1989]: "Women's Role in Agriculture: Present Trends and Potential for Growth", UNDP and UNIFEM, Dhaka.

Rozario, S. [1998]: "Disjunctions and Continuties: Dowry and the Position of Single Women in Bangladesh", In: Carla, Risseuw and Karmala, Ganesh (ed.) Negotiation and Social Space; New Delhi.

Scot, G. L. and Marilyn. Carr [1985]: "The Impact of Technology Choice on Rural Women in Bangladesh: Problems and Opportunities", Washington D.C.

Siddiqi, Hafiz. G.A. [1996]: "Product Diversification in the Readymade Garment Sector of Bangladesh: Why and How?", A Key Note Paper Presented at the BATEXPO 1996, International Seminar sponsored by BGMEA, Dhaka, October 3-5.

Siddiqi, Hafiz, G.A. [1998]: "Globalization vs. Regional Trade in the Concept of MFA, Tariff and Non-Tariff Barriers as well as Possibility of Zero-tariff for LDC's", A Paper Presented at the BATEXPO Seminar, Dhaka.

Siddiqi, Hafiz G. A. [2000]: "Beyond 2004: Impact of MFA Phase - out on the Apparel Industry of Bangladesh", A Key Note Paper Presented at BATEXPO-2000, Organized by BGMEA, Pan-Pacific Sonargaon Hotel, Dhaka, November.

Siddiqui, Khaleda Akter [1999]: "Urban Working Women in the Formal Sector in Bangladesh", Peter Lang, Europäischer Verlag der Wissenschaften, Frankfurt am Main.

Skeldon, R. [1997]: "Migration and Development: A Global Perspective", Belhaven Press, London.

Spinanger, Dean [2000]: "The WTO ATC and Textiles and Clothing in a Global Perspective: What`s in it for Bangladesh?", Centre for Policy Dialogue, Dhaka, September.

Standing, Guy [1989]: "Global Feminisation Through Fexible Labour", World Development, Vol. 17, No. 7, pp. 1077-1095.

Stark, Oded [1976]: "Rural to Urban Migration and Some Economic Issues: A Review Utilization Findings of Surveys and Empirical Studies Covering the 1965-1975 Period", Working paper No. 38 for the World Employment Programme, International Labour Office, Geneva.

Taylor, E.J. [1999]: "The Economics of Labour Migration and the Role of Remittances in the Migration Process", International Migration Quaterly Review, (37) 1.

Thwin. et. al.[1996]: "Health and Demographic Profile of the Urban Population of Bangladesh: An Analysis of Selected Indicators", Special Research Report No. 47. MCH-FP Extension Project (Urban), Health and Population Extension Division, ICDDR'B, Dhaka.

Toufiqe, K. A. and Turton, C. (eds) [2002]: "Hands Not Land: How Livelihoods are Changing in Rural Bangladesh", Dhaka and London, Bangladesh Institute of Development Studies and DFID.

Trela, I. and Whalley, J. [1990]: "Global Effects of Developed Country Trade Restrictions on Textile and Apparel", Economic Journal, December.

Uchatius, Wolfgang [2003]: "Im Takt von tausend Nähmaschinen", Die Zeit, Hamburg, January 2. p.16

UNCTAD [1986]: "Protectionism and Structural Adjustment", Geneva.

UNCTAD [1998]: "The Least Developed Countries 1998 Report", Geneva.

United Nations [2002]: "World Urbanisation Prospects: The 2001 Revision", Population Division, Department of Economic and Social Affairs, UN Secretariat, New York.

UPTS [1999]: "Poverty, Work, Health and Sexual Behaviour of Women and Men in Garment Factories in Dhaka", BIDS, Dhaka.

Wichterich, Christa [1998]: "Die globalisierte Frau. Berichte aus der Zukunft der Ungleichheit". Reinbek.

Williamson, John [1999]: "Evaluating the Success of Trade Liberalization in Bangladesh", Dhaka, September.

Wohn, Alice J.H. [2001]: "Toward GATT Integration: Curcumving Quantitative Restrictions on Textiles and Apparel Trade under the Multifibre Arrangement", Journal of International Economic Law, Volume 22, No. 2.

World Bank [1993]: "Study of Export Prospects of Garments Industry", Dhaka (mimeo).

World Bank [1994]: "World Bank Country Report", Washington D.C. p. 81.

World.Bank [1996]: "Bangladesh: Labour Market Policies for Higher Employment", University Press Ltd, Dhaka.

World Bank [1999]: "The State in a Changing World", World Development Report 1999 Oxford University Press, Inc. New York.

WTO [1998a]: "WTO Agreement on Textile and Clothing: An Explanatory Rate", Paper presented at the International Seminar on Implementation of the Agreement on Textiles and Clothing, under the auspices of BGMEA and WTO/ITC, Dhaka.

WTO [1998b]: Trade Policy Review of European Union, Geneva.

Yang, Y., Martin, W. and Yanagishima, Y. [1997]: "Evaluating the Benefits of Abolishing the MFA in Uruguay Round Package", in Hertel, T. (ed.) Global Trade Analysis: Using the GATP Model, Cambridge University Press, New York.

Youssef, N. Buvine, M. and Kudat, A. [1979]: "Women in Migration: A Third Focus", A Case Study by the International Centre for Research on Women, United States Agency for International Developemnt, Washington, D.C.

Zohir, Salma Chowdhuri [2000]: "Beyond 2004: Strategy for RMG Sector in Bangladesh", A Paper Presented in the Seminar of Bangladesh Readymade Garment Industry, Dhaka.

Zohir, S. and Majumdar, P.P [1994]: "Socio-Economic Conditions of the Female Workers Engaged in the Garment Industry of Bangladesh", BIDS, Dhaka.

Zohir, S. and Majumdar, P.P. [1995]: "Empowering Women, Wage Employment in the Garment Industry", Empowerment 1995; Vol. 2, pp. 83-112, Dhaka.

Zohir, S. and Majumdar, P.P. [1996]: "Garment Workers in Bangladesh: Economic, Social and Health Condition", Research Monograph, 18, BIDS, Dhaka.

WORK – TECHNOLOGY – ORGANIZATION – SOCIETY
ARBEIT – TECHNIK – ORGANISATION – SOZIALES

Edited by Wiking Ehlert, György Széll and Heinz Sünker
Herausgegeben von Wiking Ehlert, György Széll und Heinz Sünker

Band 1 György Széll/Wiking Ehlert (eds.): New Democracies and Old Societies in Europe. 2001.

Band 2 Norbert H. Pieper: Arbeitsmarktpolitik in Deutschland und Japan im Vergleich. 1996.

Band 3 Volker Telljohann: Globaler Wettbewerb – lokale Entwicklung. Gewerkschaftliche Konzepte innovativer Industriepolitik zur Nutzung endogener regionaler Entwicklungspotentiale am Beispiel der Erfahrungen im Bereich der Maschinenbauindustrie Bolognas. 1997.

Band 4 Roderick Martin/Akihiro Ishikawa/Csaba Makó/Francesco Consoli (eds.): Workers, Firms and Unions, Part 1. Industrial Relations in Transition. 1998.

Band 5 Martin Schwanholz: Informationstechnologien im Wandel. Marktstrukturen – Aufholprozesse – Wettbewerbschancen. 1998.

Band 6 Klaus Tischler: Betriebliches Umweltmanagement als Lernprozess. Theorie und Praxis organisationsorientierter Umweltbildung als Beitrag zur Steigerung der Fortschrittsfähigkeit der Unternehmung. 1998.

Band 7 Maria Deuling: Qualifikationsanforderungen in den kaufmännischen Berufen. Regionale Arbeitskräftebedarfsanalyse. 1999.

Band 8 Kotaro Oshige: Konvergenz der Interessenvertretungen durch Globalisierung? Ein Vergleich der Funktionsmechanismen der Arbeitnehmerinteressenvertretungssysteme in Deutschland und Japan am Beispiel der Elektroindustrie. 1999.

Band 9 Khaleda Akter Siddiqui: Urban Working Women in the Formal Sector in Bangladesh. 2000.

Band 10 Akihiro Ishikawa/Roderick Martin/Witold Morawski/Veljko Rus (eds.): Workers, Firms and Unions, Part 2. The Development of Dual Commitment. 2000.

Band 11 Karl Bruckmeier/Wiking Ehlert (eds.): The Agri-Environmental Policy of the European Union. The Implementation of the Agri-environmental Measures within the Common Agricultural Policy in France, Germany, and Portugal. 2002.

Band 12 Désirée M. Nana: L'éducation environnementale des enfants et jeunes au Sahel. L'exemple du Burkina Faso. 2001.

Band 13 Wiking Ehlert: Unternehmen und betriebliche Umweltschutzverbände. 2002.

Band 14 György Széll, Dasarath Chetty, Alain Chouraqui (eds.): Participation, Globalisation & Culture. International and South African Perspectives. 2002.

Band 15 Olaf Winkelmann: Entwicklung in der Mitbestimmung - Industrial Relations, Industrial Districts und Netzwerke. Das Beispiel *Betriebsräte-Netzwerk* im Industrial District Ostwestfalen-Lippe. 2002.

Band 16 Thomas Volkening: Ansätze zu organisatorischen Reformstrategien in einem Krankenhaus in kommunaler Trägerschaft. Eine Bestandsaufnahme. 2004.

Band 17 György Széll / Gian Primo Cella (eds.): The Injustice at Work. An International View on the World of Labour and Society. 2002.

Band 18 Lydia Kocar: Globale Ökonomie und nationale Politik. Die Forschungs- und Technologiepolitik der EU. 2003.

Band 19 Heinz Sünker: Politik, Bildung und soziale Gerechtigkeit. Perspektiven für eine demokratische Gesellschaft. 2003.

Band 20 Nicola Bücker: Historische Aspekte und Entwicklungstendenzen des japanischen Beschäftigungssystems. 2003.

Band 21 Faping He: Struktur und Funktionsweise des chinesischen Arbeitsmarktes. Der Gestaltungsprozess des Arbeitsmarktes unter dem wirtschaftlich-sozialen Strukturwandel in der VR China seit 1978. 2003.

Band 22 Thomas Swiderek: Kinderpolitik und Partizipation von Kindern. Im Spannungsfeld von Vergesellschaftung und der Möglichkeit größerer Selbstbestimmtheit, Mündigkeit und dem Erlernen von Demokratie. 2003.

Band 23 Heinz Sünker / Russell Farnen / György Széll (eds.): Political Socialisation, Participation and Education. Change of Epoch – Processes of Democratisation. 2003.

Band 24 Birgit Riße: Mündigkeit in der Postmoderne. Ansatzpunkte und Zielperspektiven von Erwachsenenbildung als Identitätsbildung im Rahmen der gegenwärtigen gesellschaftlichen Wandlungsprozesse. 2004.

Band 25 Francesco Garibaldo / Volker Telljohann (eds.): Globalisation, Company Strategies and Quality of Working Life in Europe. 2004.

Band 26 Serajul Hoque: Global Trade Liberalization. Impact on the Readymade Garments Industry in Bangladesh. 2004.

www.peterlang.de

FSC
www.fsc.org
MIX
Papier | Fördert
gute Waldnutzung
FSC® C083411

Kolibri 360 GmbH
Ferdinand-Jühlke-Straße 7
99095 Erfurt, Deutschland
produktsicherheit@kolibri360.de

Druck:
CPI Druckdienstleistungen GmbH
im Auftrag der
Kolibri 360 GmbH
Ferdinand-Jühlke-Str. 7
99095 Erfurt